Cross-national studies of the quality of education: planning their design and managing their impact

Cross-national studies of the quality of education: planning their design and managing their impact

Edited by

Kenneth N. Ross

and

Ilona Jürgens Genevois

United Nations
Educational, Scientific and
Cultural Organization

International Institute
for Educational Planning

Internationale Weiterbildung
und Entwicklung gGmbH

The designations employed and the presentation of material throughout this review do not imply the expression of any opinion whatsoever on the part of UNESCO or the IIEP concerning the legal status of any country, territory, city or area or its authorities, or concerning its frontiers or boundaries.

The publication costs of this report were covered by a contribution from the Internationale Weiterbildung und Entwicklung, Capacity Building International, Germany (InWEnt), a grant-in-aid offered by UNESCO, and by voluntary contributions made by several Member States of UNESCO, the list of which will be found at the end of the volume.

Published by:
International Institute for Educational Planning
7-9 rue Eugène Delacroix, 75116 Paris
e-mail: info@iiep.unesco.org
IIEP web site: www.unesco.org/iiep

Cover design: Sabine Lebeau
Composition: Linéale Production

ISBN: 92-803-1289-8

Contents

About the authors

Carola Donner-Reichle (Germany) is Director of the Social Development Division for Internationale Weiterbildung und Entwicklung gGmbH, Capacity Building International, Germany (InWEnt). She is also responsible for overall policy for InWEnt with respect to the Millennium Development Goals. Formerly she was Deputy Head in the Minister's Office at the Ministry of Economic Co-operation and Development, before which she was responsible for the Ministry of Economic Co-operation's negotiations concerning follow-up for the UN World Social Summit. She was a Research Fellow at the Institute of Development Studies in Dar Es Salaam, in Tanzania and an ILO expert in the Regional Office for Asia and the Pacific in Bangkok, Thailand. She holds a Doctoral degree in Political Science from the Free University of Berlin.

Pierre Foy (Canada) is a Senior Researcher at the IEA Data Processing Center in Hamburg. He has a Master's degree in statistics and extensive experience in the field of survey sampling and international comparative studies in education. He worked for many years at Statistics Canada on the development of survey and sampling methods for a variety of national surveys. Over the past 12 years he has been involved as a sampling expert for the Third International Mathematics and Science Study (TIMSS) and the Progress in International Reading Literacy Study (PIRLS). He is also a sampling consultant for other IEA studies and UNESCO projects.

Patrick Griffin (Australia) is Professor of Education at the University of Melbourne, and Director of the Australian Assessment Research Centre. He holds a doctoral degree in Educational Measurement from Florida State University, and he has published many research reports and articles in the fields of educational evaluation and the assessment of learning. His current research interests include language proficiency assessment, industrial literacy, school literacy and numeracy, profile development, and portfolio assessment. He has conducted a number of international educational research projects in the Pacific, Asia, and Europe.

Aletta Grisay (Belgium) graduated in philosophy and letters, and spent most of her career at the *Service de Pédagogie Expérimentale* of Liège University. As a member of the research team in charge of the IEA data collections in the French community in Belgium, she was involved in a number of IEA surveys (Reading Comprehension Study, Literature

Study, English as Foreign Language Study, Reading Literacy Study, and Second Civic Education Study). She has also directed the design and implementation of a number of national assessments in Belgium, France, and developing countries. She is currently serving as a member of the Technical Advisory Group for the OECD's PISA research programme.

Ingrid Jung (Germany) is Head of the Education Division at the Internationale Weiterbildung und Entwicklung gGmbH, Capacity Building International, Germany (InWEnt). She holds a doctoral degree in linguistics from the University Osnabrück. She worked for several years as education advisor, project officer, and consultant in Latin America. Her research activities have concentrated on educational provision for multilingual societies in Latin America and Africa. She has published a series of articles and books on bilingual education, literacy, and teacher training.

Ilona Jürgens Genevois (Germany) is an Assistant Programme Specialist at the International Institute for Educational Planning (IIEP-UNESCO). Prior to this she worked for a number of international organizations on projects related to the development of evaluation measures for political and economic actions. She holds a *Diplôme d'Etude Approfondie* in economic sciences from the *Institut d'études politiques* in Paris and a *Diplom-Volkswirtin* degree from Germany. She has published studies on an approach to measuring well-being and its contribution to the socioeconomic debate. Her current research interests include educational finance and measuring the transfer of educational assistance from North to South.

Thomas Kellaghan (Ireland) is Director of the Educational Research Centre in Dublin. He holds a doctoral degree in education from Queen's University, Belfast, and he is a Fellow of the International Academy of Education. His areas of research include assessment, programme evaluation, and educational disadvantage and he has worked in a number of countries in Africa, Asia, and Latin America. He is co-editor of the *International Handbook of Educational Evaluation.*

Rainer Lehmann (Germany) is Professor of Educational Measurement and Research at the Humboldt University, Berlin. He holds a doctoral degree in theology and a doctoral degree in education from Hamburg University, Germany, and he has published research reports and articles on educational evaluation and the assessment of educational achievement in a number of different domains (written composition, history, reading comprehension, civic education, among others). His research activities have included large-scale assessments at national and regional levels that were designed to monitor and improve education systems. Some of these studies have followed true longitudinal designs aimed at establishing causal relationships.

Pirjo Linnakylä (Finland) is Professor of Educational Assessment and Evaluation at the University of Jyväskylä, Finland, and also Vice Director of the Institute for Educational Research. She holds a doctoral degree in educational sciences from the University of Turku, Finland. Her fields of expertise are large-scale international assessments and educational system evaluation as well as comparative educational research. She was the Finnish National Co-ordinator for the IEA Reading Literacy Study and the International Adult Literacy Survey, and she has been responsible for the Finnish part of reading literacy assessment in PISA. She has also more than 30 years' experience as a mother tongue teacher, teacher educator, researcher, and university professor.

Demus Makuwa (Namibia) is a Senior Educational Planner in the Monitoring and Evaluation Division of Namibia's Ministry of Basic Education, Sport, and Culture. He completed a Master's degree in social sciences at the Karl Marx University and is a graduate of the Harvard Programme in Educational Policy and Planning. He has been Namibia's SACMEQ National Research Co-ordinator for the past four years, and his very successful implementation of the SACMEQ II data collection resulted in Namibia being one of the first countries whose data were prepared for analysis.

Katharina Michaelowa (Germany) is Head of the Program on Development and Integration at the Hamburg Institute for International Economics. She holds a doctoral degree in eonomics from Hamburg University and her research interests cover development, economics of education, and the economics of aid. Before joining the Hamburg Institute, she worked at the OECD in the areas of development and education. She is member of the Scientific Board of the *Programme d'analyse des systèmes éducatifs de la CONFEMEN (PASEC)*, a programme carrying out regular surveys on educational achievement in francophone sub-Saharan Africa.

Saul Murimba (Zimbabwe) is the Director of the Southern and Eastern Africa Consortium for Monitoring Educational Quality (SACMEQ). He holds a Master's degree in education management from the University of Zimbabwe, and has worked in Zimbabwe's Ministry of Education as a researcher and evaluator in its Policy and Planning Section. He has a special interest in large-scale survey research for policy development, and has participated in collaborative policy research with other educational planners in Eastern and Central Africa.

Juliana Nzomo (Kenya) is Regional Programme Co-ordinator (Educational Evaluation) for the Aga Khan Foundation, previous to which she was Principal Economist in the Planning Department of Kenya's Ministry of Education, Science, and Technology. She completed a Master's degree in educational administration at the University of Nairobi, and is a graduate of the IIEP's Advanced Training Programme in Educational Planning and Management. She was Kenya's SACMEQ National Research Co-ordinator for five years, and she has been a member of Kenyan research teams for the preparation of national education sector analyses.

Laura Paviot (Argentina) is a Resident Fellow at the International Institute for Educational Planning (IIEP-UNESCO). She started her career as a teacher in primary and secondary schools in Argentina. She has a Master's degree in international development with a specialization in programme design and monitoring from *La Sorbonne* University in France. She has worked at the IIEP in the area of education for emergencies and post-conflict reconstruction. Prior to joining the IIEP, she worked for a non-profit organization as Co-ordinator of Educational Projects in association with the Inter-American Development Bank. Her current research interests include the coverage and growth of private tuition in developing countries.

Mary Joy Pigozzi (United Kingdom) is the Director of the Division for the Promotion of Quality Education at UNESCO, where she oversees work in the fields of: education for sustainable development, education for peace and human rights, education in response to the HIV/AIDS pandemic, and health education. She has a doctoral degree in education from Michigan State University. Before joining UNESCO she was responsible for the development of both the UN system-wide Girls' Education Initiative and UNICEF's Global Girls' Education Programme. Her other professional contributions have been the development of strategic approaches to education in emergencies and policy development on the linkages between education and child labour.

T. Neville Postlethwaite (United Kingdom) is Professor (Emeritus) of Comparative Education at the University of Hamburg, and he is a Fellow of the International Academy of Education. He holds a doctoral degree in comparative education from Stockholm University, and is the author of many research reports and articles in the area of international comparative studies of the quality of education. He was senior co-editor of the first and second editions of the 12-volume *International Encyclopedia of Education*. He has been presented with a number of awards by universities and governments to honour his lifelong contributions to the advancement of educational research. He is currently working for UNESCO and the World Bank as an educational consultant in Africa and Asia.

Kenneth Ross (Australia) is Co-ordinator of Technical Project Management at the International Institute for Educational Planning (IIEP-UNESCO). He completed a doctoral degree at the Centre for the Study of Higher Education, University of Melbourne, and he is a Fellow of the International Academy of Education. He worked as an educational researcher in the Survey Section of the Australian Council for Educational Research, and later held the position of Reader in Education at Deakin University, Australia. His research interests cover two main fields: quantitative research methods for educational policy research and the use of formula-funding approaches in school finance models.

Jeanne Rubner (Germany) is a Senior Editor at the Süddeutsche Zeitung in Munich, Germany's largest national daily newspaper. She received her high school education in France, studied physics in France, Germany and the US and completed a doctoral degree in physics at the Technical University of Munich. At the Süddeutsche Zeitung she works in the domestic policy section covering mostly educational and scientific topics. She is member of several advisory boards and committees, among them the board of the University of Regensburg as well as the Transatlantic Science and Humanities Program of the Humboldt Foundation.

Andreas Schleicher (Germany) is Head of the Indicators and Analysis Division of the OECD Directorate for Education. In this role he is responsible for the development and analysis of benchmarks on the performance of education systems. This includes the management of the OECD Programme for International Student Assessment (PISA), the OECD Education Indicators Programme (INES), and the OECD/UNESCO World Education Indicators Programme. Before joining the OECD he was Director for Data Analysis at the International Association for the Evaluation of Educational Achievement (IEA). He studied physics at the University of Hamburg and received a Master's degree in mathematics from Deakin University.

Maria Teresa Siniscalco (Italy) is a Research Consultant in Education. She holds a doctoral degree in education from the University of Rome (*La Sapienza*). She was the National Project Manager for the OECD's PISA project at the *Istituto Nazionale per la Valutazione del Sistema dell'Istruzione (INValSI)* in Frascati. Her research interests cover the fields of text comprehension, television literacy, and international education indicators. She has worked as consultant for a range of national and international organizations.

Ulrike Wiegelmann (Germany) is Senior Project Manager at Internationale Weiterbildung und Entwicklung gGmbH, Capacity Building International, Germany (InWEnt). She holds a doctoral degree in philosophy from the University of Münster, Germany, and she has conducted research on the educational achievement of students attending Arabic and Francophone primary schools in Senegal. At InWEnt, she is responsible for the design and implementation of dialogue and training programmes in the field of educational quality and HIV/AIDS and education.

List of abbreviations and acronyms

ABC	Assessing Basic Competencies
BETD	Basic Education Teachers' Diploma
BRR	Balanced Repeated Replication
CONFEMEN	*Conférence des ministres de l'Éducation des pays francophones*
DIF	Differential Item Functioning
EFA	Education for All
ELTDP	English Language Teacher Development Programme
ETS	Educational Testing Services
FIMS	First International Mathematics Study
FISS	First International Science Study
IAEP	International Assessment of Educational Progress
IALS	International Adult Literacy Study
IC	Intraclass Correlation
ICT	Information and communication technology
IEA	International Association for the Evaluation of Educational Achievement
IIEP	International Institute for Educational Planning
INES	International Indicators of Education Systems
INRA	French National Initiative of Agronomy Research
IRT	Item Response Theory
ISCED	International Standard Classification of Education
JRR	Jack-knife Repeated Replication
KIE	Kenya Institute of Education
LLECE	Latin American Laboratory for Assessment of the Quality of Education
MBESC	Ministry of Basic Education, Sport and Culture
MCS	Minimum Cluster Size
MDG	Millennium Development Goals
MLA	Monitoring Learning Achievement

MOS	Measure of Size
MPCC	Management Policy Co-ordinating Committee
NAEP	National Assessment of Educational Progress
NALS	National Adults Literacy Study
NGO	Non-governmental organization
NPM	National Project Manager
NRC	National Research Co-ordinator
OECD	Organisation for Economic Co-operation and Development
OREALC	*Oficina Regional de Educación para América Latina y el Caribe*
PASEC	*Programme d'analyse des systèmes éducatifs de la CONFEMEN*
PIRLS	Progress in International Reading Literacy Study
PISA	Programme for International Student Assessment
PPS	Probability proportional to size
PRSP	Poverty Reduction Strategy Paper
RCS	Reading Comprehension Study
RLS	Reading Literacy Study
SACMEQ	Southern and Eastern Africa Consortium for Monitoring Educational Quality
SIMS	Second International Mathematics Study
SISS	Second International Science Study
STATCAN	Statistics Canada
TCMA	Test-curriculum Matching Analysis
TIMSS	Third International Mathematics and Science Study
UNDP	United Nations Development Programme
UNESCO	United Nations Educational, Scientific and Cultural Organization
UNICEF	United Nations Children's Fund

List of tables, figures and boxes

Preface

The worldwide awareness of the need to achieve Education for All has been accompanied by a challenge to ensure that increased participation in education is delivered in association with improved conditions of schooling and student achievement. This intense focus on the quality of education has been encouraged by the belief that education systems can act as pathways to national economic development in an increasingly globalized and competitive world.

These patterns, when taken together with the enormous government expenditures on education, have precipitated demands for more information and accountability concerning the quality of education. One response by governments in industrialized countries has been the establishment of systems for monitoring and evaluating quality based on cross-national studies organized by the International Association for the Evaluation of Educational Achievement (IEA) and the Organisation for Economic Co-operation and Development (OECD).

Governments in less developed countries have shown interest in establishing similar monitoring and evaluation mechanisms. In some cases they have done so with a regional approach in which groups of neighbouring countries with similar levels of social and economic development have worked together to implement cross-national studies. The most prominent of these have been the projects organized by the Southern and Eastern Africa Consortium for Monitoring Educational Quality (SACMEQ), the Latin American Laboratory for the Assessment of the Quality of Education (LLECE) organized by UNESCO's Regional Office for Latin America and the Caribbean (OREALC), and the Programme on the Analysis of Education Systems (PASEC) organized by the Conference of Francophone Ministers of Education.

In early 2004, several staff members from UNESCO's International Institute for Educational Planning (IIEP) and Germany's Internationale Weiterbildung und Entwicklung gGmbH – Capacity Building International (InWEnt) met in Paris to discuss the implications of the worldwide growth of interest among governments and international agencies in cross-national studies of the quality of education. At this meeting it was agreed that ministries of education – particularly those in less developed countries – should only become involved in these studies if they had been actively engaged in all steps related to *planning the design* and *managing the impact* of the research.

The IIEP and InWEnt therefore decided to join forces to hold an International Policy Forum that would facilitate the sharing of knowledge and national experiences concerning the topic of: 'Cross-national studies of the quality of education: planning their design and managing their impact'. The Policy Forum was held at IIEP Headquarters in Paris on 17 and 18 June 2004, and was attended by around 50 participants from Argentina, Australia, Canada, Finland, France, Germany, Guinea, India, Ireland, Italy, Japan, Kenya, Malawi, Mozambique, Namibia, Norway, Peru, South Africa, Sweden, Uganda, United Kingdom, Yemen, Zambia, and Zimbabwe. The participants included ministers of education, senior ministry officials, educational planners and researchers, university professors, donor agency specialists, and the senior staff of international organizations.

This book is based on the invited papers presented at the Policy Forum and the intensive discussion about these papers that occurred during the 'Open space sessions' that concluded the forum.

The Policy Forum papers cover three main themes:

- *Background issues.* These papers commence with an overview of terminology, concepts, and definitions related to cross-national studies of the quality of education, and then consider what has been achieved and how this has been judged by researchers and senior decision-makers.
- *Planning the design.* These papers examine the three key educational policy research design questions that must be satisfactorily answered in order to proceed with the design and implementation of scientific cross-national studies of the quality of education: 'What will be measured?', 'Who will be measured?', and 'What are the financial and logistical costs?'.
- *Managing the impact.* These papers present case studies that illustrate how ministries of education and international organizations have managed the dissemination of the results of cross-national studies of the quality of education.

The Policy Forum's Open space sessions consisted of small and flexible discussion groups within which the participants could reflect upon, critique, and synthesize the key issues that had emerged. These sessions covered many topics and a diversity of national experiences. They also gave rise to many important *Policy Forum messages* and *recommendations*, which have been documented in the final chapter of this book, concerning the guidance that should be given to ministries of education so as to ensure that they derive maximal benefits from cross-national studies of the quality of education.

The Policy Forum messages and recommendations are a rich resource for further productive discussion and debate – both within ministries of education and among ministries and various external partners. The IIEP and InWEnt are therefore delighted to offer this book as a contribution towards expanding and strengthening opportunities for national and international exchanges that serve to build the capacities of countries to plan and manage the quality of education that is offered by their school systems.

Mark Bray
Director, International Institute for Educational Planning (IIEP)
United Nations Educational, Scientific and Cultural Organization
(UNESCO)
Paris, France

Carola Donner-Reichle
Director, Social Development Division
Internationale Weiterbildung und Entwicklung
Capacity Building International, Germany (InWEnt)
Bonn, Germany

Chapter 1

Introduction: the origins and content of the Policy Forum

Kenneth N. Ross, Laura Paviot, and Ilona Jürgens Genevois

Introduction

In 1958 a group of educators (including Bill Wall, National Foundation for Educational Research in England and Wales; Arnold Anderson and Benjamin Bloom, University of Chicago; Robert Thorndike, Columbia University; and Torsten Husén, University of Stockholm) held a series of meetings at UNESCO's Institute of Education in Hamburg, Germany. The aim of these meetings was to explore how research might be used to make more valid comparisons of the quality of education that was being delivered by the world's school systems.

These educators believed that research on the quality of education required an international focus because variations among countries in terms of educational policies, practices, and traditions provided a natural laboratory for the study of those aspects of the educational environment that were likely to have a substantial and consistent impact upon improved student learning. They also argued that cross-national studies of the quality of education offered much more than national studies because "custom and law define what is educationally allowable within a nation, [whereas] the educational systems beyond one's national borders suggest what is educationally possible" (Foshay *et al.*, 1962: 2).

From these modest beginnings, Wall and his colleagues launched the International Association for the Evaluation of Educational Achievement (IEA) – which subsequently developed into an independent non-governmental organization with some 60 member countries. The IEA's first research initiative during 1959-1961 was a small-scale pilot study of the quality of education in 12 countries. This was the first occasion on which systematic data had been collected about school systems by giving the same tests (translated into different languages) to students in a number of different countries. Over the following 45 years the IEA conducted many other cross-national studies of the quality of education (see Postlethwaite, 2004).

An increased interest in the quality of education

Until the late 1980s the results of much of the IEA's research programmes were shared mainly among researchers and educators with an interest in comparative education, curriculum, and quantitative research methodologies. The international research reports written for IEA studies were often based on complex statistical analyses, and written in a formal academic style that 'ordinary people' found to be somewhat inaccessible. Governments were therefore only occasionally involved in sharing or discussing the use of IEA research results for policy purposes – except in countries like the United States where commentators often whipped up anxieties about a 'national education crisis' based on league tables of student achievement scores.

Things began to change in the 1990s as governments – and not just the academic community – became interested in monitoring and evaluating the quality of education. This increased governmental interest had its origins in: (a) the emergence of a widely held belief that the relative cross-national performance of education systems was a key element in strategies designed to achieve improvements in national economic development, and (b) public concerns that the enormous government expenditures devoted to education needed to be accompanied by higher levels of scrutiny and accountability concerning the quality of education.

Major forums organized by international agencies also turned their attention towards issues related to the quality of education. The declarations of the 1990 Jomtien World Conference on Education and the 2000 Dakar World Education Forum both called upon the nations of the world to broaden their view of Education for All (EFA) beyond a concentration on increased access to education. These declarations emphasized that to achieve EFA by 2015 would require, in addition to increased participation in education, all nations "to improve all aspects of the quality of education and ensure excellence so that recognized and measurable learning outcomes are achieved by all".

The widespread growth of interest in the quality of education and the associated general acceptance of education's critical role in the context of a globalized and competitive world have also been reflected in influential reports emerging from international agencies. For example, the 2004 report of results from the Programme for International Student Assessment (PISA) conducted by the Organization for Economic Cooperation and Development (OECD) began with the statement that: "the prosperity of countries now derives to a large extent from their human capital, and to succeed in a rapidly changing world, individuals need to advance their knowledge and skills throughout their lives." (OECD, 2004: 3). Similarly, UNESCO's *EFA Global Monitoring Report: 2005* stated that "there is good evidence to suggest that the quality of education – as measured by test scores – has an influence upon the speed with which societies can become richer and the extent to which individuals can improve their own productivity and incomes." (UNESCO, 2004: 43).

The emergence of networks for monitoring the quality of education

Towards the end of the 1990s and into the new millennium, the increased levels of national and international dialogue about the importance of the 'quality of education' resulted in decisions by many countries to participate in networks that conducted large-scale cross-national educational research studies. These studies were aimed at collecting, analysing, interpreting, and comparing data about the quality of education systems in terms of the general conditions of schooling, the educational achievements of students, and equity in educational provision and outcomes.

The most prominent of these research programmes have been: the Third International Mathematics and Science Study and its repeated versions (TIMSS and TIMSS-R) organized by the International Association for the Evaluation of Educational Achievement (IEA) – covering around 60 developed and five developing countries; the Programme for International Student Assessment (PISA) organized by the Organisation for Economic Co-operation and Development (OECD) – covering around 30 OECD countries and 10 non-OECD countries; the SACMEQ Projects organized by the Southern and Eastern Africa Consortium for Monitoring Educational Quality (SACMEQ) – covering 14 developing countries; the Latin American Laboratory for the Assessment of the Quality of Education (LLECE) organized by UNESCO's Regional Office for Latin America and the Caribbean (OREALC) – covering 13 developing countries; and the Programme on the Analysis of Education Systems Project (PASEC) organized by the Conference of Francophone Education Ministers (CONFEMEN) – covering 15 developing countries (Postlethwaite, 2004).

These research programmes have increasingly employed advanced research methodologies in the fields of (a) educational measurement – using new approaches related to Modern Item Response Theory; (b) sampling – using computer-based design and selection of complex multi-stage probability samples; and (c) data analysis – using multi-level modelling to examine linkages between educational environment variables and student educational achievement (National Research Council, 2002).

The sources of research-policy connections

Before committing substantial resources to involvement in an expensive large-scale cross-national study of the quality of education, ministries of education need to justify participation with respect to the potential policy benefits for education systems. These benefits can be grouped under three broad areas – depending on whether they are derived from descriptive research results, inferential research results, or whether they flow from indirect sources arising from participation in the research.

Policy benefits may arise from sources based on **descriptive research results** that systematically portray the common and distinctive features, structures, and operations of different education systems. For example:

(a) Comparing the salient features of education systems across countries can magnify particular aspects of a national education system that are problematic or unusually excellent because they differ from other 'similar' countries;

(b) Benchmarking aspects of the educational environment can allow decision-makers to judge their education systems against examples of best practice and/or high performance that prevail in other countries; and

(c) Monitoring trends in the educational environment and outcomes of schooling over a period of time can provide information about improvements or declines in one country or many countries – thereby providing information for accountability purposes and/or for making sound comparative and evaluative judgements.

Policy benefits may also be obtained from sources based on **inferential research results** that require a deeper understanding of the patterns of relationships among factors which describe student characteristics, educational contexts, and measures of student achievement. For example:

(a) Understanding differences in the conditions of schooling and student educational achievement for socially-defined groups can provide systematic assessments related to equity in educational provision and outcomes; and

(b) Interpreting relationships among factors related to the conditions of schooling and student educational achievement can be used to identify more effective approaches to school organization and resource allocation.

Finally, policy benefits may arise from sources that are **indirect** such as the encouragement of productive debates and the enhancement of opportunities for various forms of professional interactions. For example:

(a) Participating in informed debate about research results within and across education systems can help decision-makers to clarify issues and highlight successful practices used elsewhere, and from this gradually encourage policy reform based on information rather than anecdote and speculation; and

(b) Integrating previously isolated national education systems into regional and global networks can draw governments into international exchanges that encourage them to reform unproductive policies and practices, and can also provide technicians with opportunities to develop advanced conceptual and technical skills through working with more experienced colleagues.

The processes behind research-policy connections

The above discussion concerning three research-based 'sources' of policy guidance provides only a limited view of the 'processes' by which research and policy become connected in a manner that is likely to lead to action. Over the past 50 years there have been dramatic changes in theories that seek to explain these processes.

Earlier 'linear' conceptions of the connections between research and policy focused mostly on the mechanical aspects of delivering information from researchers to decision-makers. This assumed a direct sequence of events that started with the identification of the problem and the knowledge gap, and then moved to research that would deliver findings and recommendations, and finally resulted in the review and revision of existing policies and/or the formulation of new policies.

However, many scholars now accept Weiss' (1982) conclusions about the diffuse nature of the connections between research and policy – whereby ideas that emerge from research gradually connect with decision-making by providing organizing frameworks within which policy-makers are able to make sense of experience and interpret problems and priorities. This 'enlightenment model' of the processes by which research connects with policy suggests that research enhances the environment in which policy reform takes place through several processes: generating clarifications of new concepts, giving hints about possible alternatives, stimulating innovative perspectives, and incrementally altering the language and issues discussed in policy-making circles.

That is, research provides a background of data, empirical generalizations, and ideas that 'enlighten' the way policy makers think about problems. It influences their conceptualization of the issues with which they deal, affects those facets of the issue that they consider inevitable and unchangeable and those that they perceive as amenable to policy action, widens the range of options that they consider, and challenges some taken-for-granted assumptions about appropriate goals and activities.

'Essential pre-conditions' for successful research-policy connections

In 1989 the IIEP held an international seminar (Ross and Mahlk, 1990) that examined questions concerning the processes by which ministries of education could collect, analyse, and use research-based information to enhance the policy reform environment related to planning the quality of education. The seminar report was subsequently employed by the IIEP and a group of ministries of education to guide the design and management of training and research programmes for a series of cross-national studies of the quality of education (Ross *et al.*, 2004).

The conclusions of this seminar examined fundamental research and training needs that needed to be addressed by ministries of education in order to assist educational planners and researchers to provide the kind of information that decision-makers would find accessible and relevant. A number of these conclusions were associated with the content and structure of educational management information systems. However, many of the suggestions also implied that there were **two essential pre-conditions** for undertaking the kind of research that Weiss' enlightenment model would recognize as likely to enhance the environment in which productive policy reform takes place.

The first pre-condition was that educational policy research studies aimed at generating beneficial policy related to the quality of education required ministries of education to be closely involved in planning the design of the research according to the highest possible technical standards – so that only valid and useful data are entered into decision-making processes.

The second pre-condition added that these studies also required ministries of education to be closely involved in managing the impact of the research through an open and meaningful dialogue – so that information providers and users are able to work together to reflect upon the meaning behind the research results and thereby optimize the chances that they will be used for productive policy purposes.

The Policy Forum

In early 2004 several staff members from UNESCO's International Institute for Educational Planning (IIEP) and Germany's Internationale Weiterbildung und Entwicklung gGmbH – Capacity Building International (InWEnt) met in Paris in order to discuss the worldwide growth of interest among governments and international agencies in cross-national studies of the quality of education. They noted that this trend was evident in both developed and developing countries, and that it had been expressed in concrete terms by a major expansion in networks established specifically for undertaking these studies.

Both the IIEP and InWEnt emphasized that ministries of education should do everything possible to ensure that their participation in such studies provided valid information that could be used for beneficial educational policy development and reform. They agreed with the important conclusions of the 1998 IIEP International Seminar described above - which warned that 'passive' participation by countries in cross-national studies of the quality of education carried the dangers that a country might participate in a costly and time-consuming initiative that failed to (a) employ research designs that delivered policy-relevant data, and (b) apply results management methods that engaged stakeholders in exchanges aimed at enlightened policy reform. That is, they agreed that ministries of education should only become involved in cross-national educational research studies if they had been 'actively' involved in all steps related to planning the design and managing the impact of the research.

Given the scope and growth of the many initiatives for monitoring, evaluating, and comparing the quality of education delivered by school systems, it was decided that the IIEP and InWEnt should join forces to hold an International Policy Forum that would facilitate the sharing of knowledge and national experiences in this area. The Policy Forum (entitled 'Cross-national studies of the quality of education: planning their design and managing their impact') was held at the IIEP headquarters in Paris during 17-18 June 2004, and was attended by 50 participants from developed and developing countries: Argentina, Australia, Canada, Finland, France, Germany, Guinea, India, Ireland, Italy, Japan, Kenya, Malawi, Mozambique, Namibia, Norway, Peru, South Africa, Sweden, Uganda, United Kingdom, Yemen, Zambia, and Zimbabwe. The participants included ministers of education, senior ministry of education officials, educational planners and researchers, university professors, donor agency specialists, and the senior staff of international organizations.

The Policy Forum papers

The Policy Forum was structured around a series of invited papers and small discussion groups that allowed the participants to reflect upon, critique, and synthesize the issues that had emerged during the formal forum presentations.

For this book, the Policy Forum's papers have been grouped together so as to follow the three themes that were used to sequence the Policy Forum sessions: 'Background issues', 'Planning the design', and 'Managing the impact'.

(a)   Theme 1: Background issues for cross-national studies (5 papers)

The first two papers for Theme 1 'mapped the terrain' by examining definitions and concepts – and they illustrated how many debates in this area arise through misunderstandings in fundamental terminology. **Pigozzi** examined the rich diversity of interpretations associated with the concept of the 'quality of education' and provided some interpretive frameworks that have been accepted for use within UNESCO's education programmes. **Kellaghan** disentangled the three main approaches to quality assessment (national assessments, cross-national assessments, and examinations) by listing the frequently-asked questions of policy makers and then showing which approach provided the best answers to these questions.

The third paper by **Grisay** and **Griffin** provided a comprehensive 'history' of the origins of cross-national studies of the quality of education, and then explored and classified what had been accomplished by the most important of these studies.

The final two papers for Theme 1 explored the viewpoints of 'forgotten actors' in most educational policy research initiatives: ministers of education and senior decision-makers in ministries of education. First, **Murimba** provided some insights into 'what ministers really think' about cross-national studies – including some very interesting observations concerning their anxieties about final research results and how these should be handled by researchers. **Postlethwaite** then presented an overview of the different criteria by which senior decision-makers and researchers judge whether a cross-national study is 'a good study' – with the mission of facilitating discussion between these two groups so that they better understand both the political and the scientific benchmarks for judgement.

(b)   Theme 2: Planning the design of cross-national studies
(3 papers)

The three papers for Theme 2 covered the 'big questions' that must be addressed in the initial design of all cross-national studies of the quality of education: 'What will be measured?', 'Who will be measured?', and 'What are the financial and logistical costs?'.

Lehmann examined the issue of what will be measured by initially listing the main categories of comparison that cross-national studies seek to examine (mean achievement, productivity, literacy distributions, multi-criterion, and equity) in association with the assumptions that are applied concerning relevant explanatory variables. He then explored the two main groups of variables: input and output (including higher order thinking skills and affective measures). Within these two groups he identified issues and challenges to governments with respect to what decisions were required to optimize beneficial policy impacts from the research.

Foy's paper showed that small differences in decisions about who should be measured made major changes in the scope, comparability, and validity of cross-national studies of the quality of education. His systematic step-by-step analysis of the main decision points in sample design provided a road map for scientific sampling that has the potential for application across the whole field of educational survey research.

The final paper for Theme 2, by **Siniscalco**, looked at financial and logistical costs from the perspective of a research office in a country that took part in a large-scale cross-national study of the quality of education. The great strength of this paper was that it described 'what actually happened' – rather than what should have happened – in each phase of the project. Her final section on 'lessons learned' should be required reading in all educational research and planning offices.

(c)   Theme 3: Managing the impact of cross-national studies (5 papers)

The papers presented for Theme 3 each took a case study approach from one of two vantage points. The first three papers were concerned with case studies of managing the impact of cross-national studies of the quality of education from a national perspective, while the final two papers focussed on a cross-national perspective.

The national perspective was explored in papers concerned with both developing countries (Kenya and Namibia), and developed countries (Germany and Finland).

Nzomo and **Makuwa's** coverage of Kenya and Namibia commenced with an interesting overview of 'Which research results did ministries of education find important and/or controversial?' The paper then moved to a description of the different research dissemination strategies that had been adopted in each country, and followed this with a discussion of the policy and practice reforms that were based on the research results.

The papers on Germany and Finland provided quite contrasting accounts of the reactions of governments to the experience of either 'national success' or 'national failure' in cross-national studies of the quality of education.

In the case of Germany, **Rubner** described how *unexpected poor performance* in student achievement in the IEA and PISA projects caused a major shockwave among the general public, the teachers, school principals, state and national ministries of education, and heads of government. The result was the implementation of many reviews of the structure and content of the German education system, and the launching of an extensive list of state and national educational reforms.

In contrast, the paper by **Linnakylä** described official reactions in Finland to *unexpected excellent performance* in student achievement in the IEA and PISA projects. The Finnish government initially responded with rejection and disbelief and then gradually, due to the intense pressure of international interest in Finland's 'secret formula for educational success', moved towards acceptance and pride.

The cross-national perspective for Theme 3 was examined in two papers that covered different contexts (developing countries and an international agency) and different target groups (governments and the media).

Bernard and **Michaelowa** looked at the management of PASEC research results in Senegal, Togo, and Guinea – with the aim of examining some of the common cross-national research results that were used by governments for policy. The authors concluded that the potential for research results to influence educational policy was strongly influenced by the degree of stability of both the research teams and the surrounding political environment – combined with the capacity to mobilize adequate funds to finance educational reforms.

Schleicher provided viewpoints from an international agency through examining the way in which the PISA Project was able to move journalists away from crude 'league table' descriptions of national mean test scores towards a more enlightened debate in which newspapers and television began to seek the more important policy messages that could be extracted from the research results.

Conclusion: the main 'messages' arising from the Policy Forum

On the final afternoon of the Policy Forum – after all invited papers had been presented and discussed – there were two **'Open space sessions'** during which issues could be explored more intensively in small and flexible interest groups. Any single topic being discussed in a group was informed by a floating audience of participants, and the topics selected for discussion within any single group tended to ebb and flow in accordance with who was present.

The Policy Forum's Open space sessions covered many different topics and a diversity of national experiences. In some cases the Policy Forum participants shared a common vision about the suggestions that should made to ministries of education concerning the decisions, actions, and methodologies that were required in order to derive maximal policy benefits from participating in cross-national studies of the quality of education. In other cases the Policy Forum participants identified particular problems and/or complexities related to such studies – and these were used to develop suggestions about research management, dissemination approaches, and training strategies. All of these suggestions have been presented and discussed in the final chapter of this book in the form of **'Policy Forum messages'** and associated **'Recommendations'** that covered five areas: planning measurement designs, planning sample designs, planning logistical designs, managing the impact of research results, and capacity building needs.

References

Postlethwaite, T.N. 2004. *Monitoring educational achievement.* Fundamentals of Educational Planning No. 81). Paris: IIEP-UNESCO.

National Research Council (Board on International Comparative Studies in Education). 2002. *Methodological advances in cross-national surveys of educational achievement.* Washington, DC: National Academy Press.

OECD. 2003. *Education at a glance.* Paris: OECD.

OECD. 2004. *Learning for tomorrow's world: first results from PISA 2003.* Paris: OECD.

UNESCO. 2004. *Education for All: the quality imperative.* Paris: UNESCO.

Part I
Background issues for cross-national studies of the quality of education

Chapter 2
What is the 'quality of education'? (A UNESCO perspective)

Mary Joy Pigozzi

Introduction

There is a need for a new approach to understand the concept of the 'quality of education' because its traditional meaning is no longer adequate for the emerging educational needs of the new millennium. In addition, in many instances, the kind of education that is being offered in many school systems is no longer pertinent to the societies in which we live. These two challenges suggest that the time has come to re-think this concept more comprehensively, particularly in regard to the understanding of the need to focus on 'learning' in the twenty-first century.

What drives the goals of education today?

In most countries of the world, judgements about the quality of education have been an internal affair placed under the responsibility of educational authorities at governmental and institutional levels. Today, however, issues related to the quality of education are no longer the exclusive preserve of educational authorities. Ministries other than the Ministry of Education have begun to take an interest in education. The same is true for NGOs, businesses and the general public, which have all placed different pressures on education systems. The ramifications of these trends extend far beyond the walls of individual ministries or educational institutions. To explain why this is occurring, and why the quality of education has become such a high profile issue, it is necessary to consider several key factors.

First, viewpoints about the importance of the quality of education cannot be divorced from the heightened salience of education policy and education reform within the whole range of public policy, mainly because of widely acknowledged linkages between education and national economic performance. Much government concern about the quality of education derives from the widespread belief that poor quality will frustrate efforts to use education as an effective lever of economic growth and development at a time in world history that is experiencing an acceleration of globalization.

Second, the nature of the problem has been redefined. Traditional approaches to the quality of education have often relied upon proxy measures – such as increases in financing and other inputs in the level of educational provision. While clearly not irrelevant or unhelpful, such outlays may not prove decisive when another criterion for defining and measuring the quality of education is used – namely, measurable educational outcomes (knowledge, competencies, skills, and behaviours). Governments and citizens are increasingly concerned about the discrepancy between outlays and what is learned, and this necessarily raises further questions about 'What works?' in the teaching and learning process.

Third, such questions are fuelling a growing trend towards greater government interest in, and use of, evidence through which student learning achievement may be monitored both nationally and cross-nationally. This interest has two important dimensions. The first is whether students are learning the right things to lead a decent life in a fast-changing world. The second, which is closely related, concerns monitoring student performance over time, and in a cross-national comparative perspective, in order to provide information for assessing how well, or how badly, education systems are preparing young people for future adult roles as creative, thinking citizens who can sustain themselves and contribute to the well-being of their families, communities and societies.

Fourth, such information is becoming more politically sensitive as it points to the unevenness of quality, both within and between education systems. Quality levels vary widely from one education system to another and, within a single education system, there may be sharp variations in quality (for example, between public and private schools, between urban and rural schools, and between education for the majority and education for minorities). Even in the same classrooms, boys and girls can have significantly different learning experiences. The unevenness of quality is therefore a critical issue facing education systems, and is particularly important as regards the widening economic gap between countries and its impact upon the challenges of development, and the effects of internal disparities on national social cohesion.

Fifth, the growing diversification of societies (as a result of migration, urbanization and cultural change) and increased sensitivity to individual and group identities (based on national, regional, gender, cultural, ethnic and religious classifications) are together placing fresh demands upon education systems, and thereby challenging assumptions about the purposes and functions of education. Issues concerning the quality of education cannot be separated from these trends because they can result in problems of discrimination, racism and violence – and these have a major impact on the learning environment provided by schools and other learning spaces.

Sixth (and directly related to all of the issues raised above), are questions that point to the fundamental purposes of education. Disparities in educational quality often mirror other inequalities, which many view as directly tied to the fulfilment of human and other rights. Thus, education is being asked to become one tool, of many, that can build societies based on peace, equality and democratic practice.

'Quality of education' as a dynamic concept

These different pressures have resulted in the concept of the 'quality of education' coming to the fore as learners, parents and communities, educators, leaders, and nations acknowledge that what is learned (and how learning occurs) is as important as access to education. One difficulty is that while most people understand intuitively what they personally mean when they refer to the quality of education, there may not be a common understanding of the term. This is especially true now at the beginning of the twenty-first century when education is increasingly being understood to be 'more than the three Rs' (reading, writing and arithmetic), and extends to an expanded vision of education as articulated by the Jomtien Conference on Education for All in 1990 (UNESCO, 1990), and later reaffirmed by the Dakar World Education Forum in 2000 (UNESCO, 2000).

The understanding of what constitutes the quality of education is therefore evolving. Conventional definitions have included literacy, numeracy and life skills, and these have been linked directly to such critical components as teachers, content, methodologies, curriculum, examination systems, policy, management and administration. However, there is also a demand to reflect upon education's relevance to the modern world. While in the past much of the emphasis on education related to cognitive understanding and development, there is now a need also to address the social and other dimensions of learning. Education is expected to make a contribution to sustainable human development, peace and security, universal values, informed decision-making, and the quality of life at individual, family, societal and global levels.

Rights-based education as the conceptual underpinning of the quality of education

UNESCO promotes a high quality of education as a human right, and supports a rights-based approach to the implementation of all educational activities. There are three important aspects of education as a human right: (a) participation in a high quality of education as an important end in itself; (b) the practice of human rights in education; and (c) education as a right that facilitates the fulfilment of other rights.

UNESCO's work in this area is based on a number of international instruments – including the first Human Rights Convention (United Nations, 1948) – that identify education as a human right. Several of these international instruments have indicated the desired nature, or quality of this type of education. When we look at these instruments together and interpret them, we go far beyond single issues to a web of commitments that speak to the depth and breadth of how we must begin to understand the concept of the quality of education.

The interpretation of these instruments must also be embedded within current local and world contexts and expectations of education. That is, education must be placed and understood in terms of a larger context that reflects learning in relation to the learner as an individual, a family and community member, a citizen and as part of a world society.

The quality of education must recognize the past, be relevant to the present, and have a view to the future. It must also relate to knowledge building and the skilful application of all forms of knowledge by unique individuals who function both independently and in relation to others. A high quality of education will always reflect the dynamic nature of culture and languages, the value of the individual in relation to the larger context and the importance of living in a way that promotes equality in the present and fosters a sustainable future.

The concept of the 'quality of education' in relation to the modern world

Our primary concern is learning; therefore, the relationship between the learner and the teacher is critical. However, the inputs, processes, environments and outputs that surround and foster (or hamper) learning are important as well. These can be seen as affecting the quality of education at two levels: (a) at the level of the learner in his or her learning environment; and (b) at the level of the education system that creates and supports the learning experience. Each of these two levels can be divided to form ten dimensions related to the quality of education – as has been illustrated in *Figure 2.1*. Learning is at the centre, and is surrounded by the 'inner learner level' and the 'outer system level'. Both of these levels operate within a specific context, which can vary considerably from location to location.

Elements within the learner level

■ Seeks out learners

Education must be available without discrimination. This underscores the UNESCO commitment to reach out to those who have been traditionally neglected – including the poor, girls, working children, children in emergencies, those with disabilities, and those with nomadic lifestyles. However, it is not merely a concern with quantity. Learners have a right to an education that will serve as the basis for lifelong education.

A high-quality education, therefore, implies an environment that actively seeks out learners and assists them to learn – using a wide range of modalities, recognizing that learning is linked to experience, language and cultural practices, gifts, traits and interests. Such an approach recognizes that people learn in different ways, each emphasizing different senses and abilities.

A high-quality education also welcomes the learner adapting to meet learning needs. It is inclusive and it strives to ensure that all learners, regardless of sex, age, language, religion and ethnicity are reached, and that they have the possibility of participating in, and learning from, organized learning activities.

■ What the learner brings

What the learner brings to his or her own learning, and to that of a group, is extremely important. It can vary from work skills, to traumatic experiences, to excellent early childhood development opportunities, to illness, or to hunger. A high-quality education has to consider the learner as an active participant and a central part of educational efforts. Learners bring to their learning, and to that of the group in which they participate, a large diversity of experiences, characteristics, skills and conditions, reflecting both their prior and current situation and presenting obstacles as well as opportunities for the way in which they learn.

All of these characteristics determine how a learner learns, behaves in class, interacts with the group and teacher and how she or he interprets the knowledge presented. Therefore, a high-quality education has to recognize, actively respond to, and take advantage of the diversity of learners.

■ Content

The content of education needs to be re-examined in light of the changes that have occurred in the world. Much of what is now taught worldwide may be less relevant to future generations of learners. In many countries, there is a need for modern and relevant curricula and materials covering areas such as literacy, numeracy and 'facts and skills for life' (which includes education on rights, gender equality, respect for the earth and other life forms, health, nutrition, HIV/AIDS, peace, and respect for and appreciation of diversity).

Learners have a right to a quality education that will serve as the basis for lifelong learning.

Access to sufficient educational materials has long been recognized as essential for learning. Low-cost teaching and learning materials can facilitate learning as well as expensive materials. However, the materials themselves need to be reviewed in light of what they convey about rights, obligations and responsibilities – with respect to gender, stereotyping and religion.

■ Processes

The processes of education are a frequently overlooked aspect of the quality of education. How learners are enabled to frame and solve problems, how different learners in the same group are treated, how teachers and administrators are treated and behave, and how families and communities are engaged in education are all processes that affect the quality of education. Differential treatment of children at an early age puts forward the notion that some people do not have the same rights as others, which can foster intolerance towards minority groups.

Figure 2.1   A framework for the quality of education

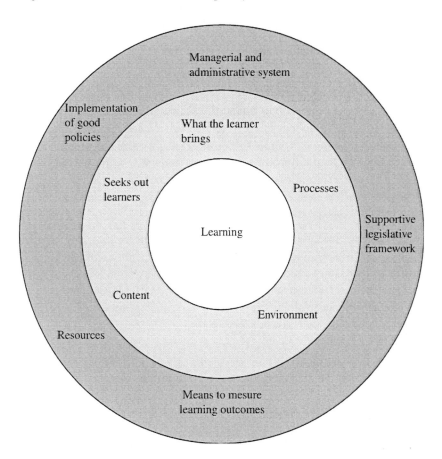

High-quality educational processes require well-trained teachers who are able to use learner-centred teaching and learning methods and life-skills approaches. As a result, even the term 'learner-centred' must be reconstructed to address issues of disparity and discrimination with regard to, for example, culture, language and gender.

How knowledge, skills, and values are transmitted is as important a part of the curriculum as what is learned – because, in fact, the process is part of 'what' is learned. Within the learning environment learners must be able to express their views, thoughts, and ideas – to participate fully, associate freely, and feel comfortable about who they are, where they come from, their sex, and what they believe in. They need to be given dignity.

45

With these facilitating processes in place, learners can develop the self-esteem that is essential for decision-making throughout life, and a sense of self-discipline that will help them pursue their personal goals.

◾ Environment

Evidence is mounting that a suitable learning environment can also be considered as contributing towards the quality of education. There must be adequate hygiene and sanitation facilities accessible to all and, if possible, health and nutrition services in the vicinity. School policies and their implementation must promote safety, and both physical and mental health. While the physical environment is better understood, the psycho-social one, which is at least as important, deserves serious attention – so that practices such as gender discrimination, bullying, corporal punishment, and forced work are eliminated.

Lack of safety and security may be obvious in terms of physical dangers, such as beatings or rape. However, more insidious are the invisible forms of harassment and violence that are often exerted. Recent research has put the spotlight on violence in education, particularly gender-based violence. Violence in all its forms, any action causing emotional or physical harm to a person, will clearly affect learning. The perpetrators may often be other students, but can also include teachers and school administrators. The particular vulnerability of girls with regard to the range of violence they may experience must continue to be highlighted.

Elements within the education system level

◾ Managerial and administrative system

The structure and organization of an education system usually serves as the philosophical underpinning for what occurs throughout the system – whether in the university, the school, or the curriculum development unit of a ministry of education. Because of this, education systems often exhibit a culture that reflects (perhaps necessarily) the dominant culture of a nation.

An education system must be structured and organized so that it is learner-centred. The system must be fair and transparent to all those in it. Rules and regulations need to be clear, with responsibilities and related procedures well articulated and implemented. Teachers need to be facilitated in their work by a managerial and administrative system that is designed to foster improved learning outcomes. Timetables must also be flexible enough to be able to keep children at risk from dropping out, or otherwise losing their right to education.

Well run schools include a space for bringing difficult issues into the open, a key first step to addressing them. Education must be 'approachable' by parents and communities. They must feel positive and comfortable about their roles in the educational process. This will not occur without an enabling structure and organization of the education system at all levels.

It is clear that the structure, organization and management of education play an important role in providing the checks and balances that are necessary in any system. This means that involved institutions (such as teacher training colleges and research institutes) must also play a key role in educational activities.

■ Implementation of 'good policies'

Typically, ministries of education set policies that may not be widely known and understood by all, particularly at the classroom level. Therefore, a helpful starting point is to raise awareness among administrators, teachers and students about these policies. The next step is to ensure that there are mechanisms to implement and enforce the policies, since it is pointless to have rules and procedures if they are not observed.

Some of the more successful efforts to promote, implement and enforce good policies are those that have been built upon the broad involvement of teachers and students in setting and respecting them. All school policies need to be consistent with national laws and legislation, which should be regularly reviewed and updated to ensure relevancy.

Education is not independent of the rest of society, nor of policies that are developed and implemented elsewhere in the country. For example, a high quality of education would require coherent and supportive policies in areas such as a 'responsible' media, health education, youth, early childhood development programmes, and lifelong learning opportunities.

■ Supportive legislative framework

Legislation is essential for ensuring that agreed principles contained within the concept of the right to education can, in fact, be put into action on a daily basis in a sustained way. As with policies, both education legislation and other related legislation must be in place, understood by the general public as well as by experts, and implemented.

47

There must be an enabling legislative framework that does more than pay lip service to the right to education, defined broadly. It must facilitate necessary changes in the education system, both at the macro and micro levels. Clearly, a high quality of education must be accessible to all children. This means that it must be expanded in certain countries to ensure that there are sufficient places. Legislation needs to address the obligations of the provision of education (defined broadly to include both access and quality), resource allocations (human, time and financial), and the overall expectations of the system.

It is important to obligate 'the state', the trustee of the nation, to provide education for all. Too often, compulsory education is seen as a legal framework that places parents and children, especially female, in the negative role of criminal or victim. Other legislation is critical as well. For example, the Convention on the Rights of the Child (United Nations, 1989) indicates that children under 15 years of age must not have their learning diverted due to involvement in hostilities. Similarly, international law also states the minimum age for full-time work, and both labour and education law must be consistent with these agreements.

In many instances, there is a need for compensatory action to ensure equality of educational opportunity. Current data and practice, in an increasing number of countries, suggests that there might be a very strong case for affirmative action, initiated legally, for ensuring educational opportunities for those negatively affected by discrimination

■ Resources

A high quality of education requires resources, recognizing the full range of human and material resources that can be brought to bear in support of education. It is clear that while some countries have been able to reorient budgets to emphasize education as a key engine for national development and a means to build democratic societies, others are not in circumstances where this is possible. Allocating resources to support high-quality education requires a long-term view. For example, international law calls for free compulsory education. It is recognized that this might not be possible immediately, especially as universality is not yet a reality in many countries, but plans must be put in place and action initiated toward this end. In the short-run, it is essential that the costs of education be distributed equitably.

■ Means to measure learning outcomes

This article began by stressing the importance of learning. Thus, it is only appropriate that the last of the ten dimensions of quality come full circle and address learning outcomes. In this regard, the quest for a better understanding of what is wanted from a high quality of education has expanded significantly the desired learning outcomes. The following simple classification of the main types of learning outcomes to be pursued may be helpful: (a) knowledge – the essential cognitive achievement levels that all learners should reach (including literacy, numeracy and core subject knowledge); (b) values – solidarity, gender equality, tolerance, mutual understanding, respect for human rights, non-violence, and respect for human life and dignity; (c) skills or competencies – a secure command of how to solve problems, to experiment, to work in teams, to live together and interact with those who are different, and to learn how to learn; and (d) behaviours – the capacity to put into practice what has been learned.

Our ability to measure learning achievement varies considerably in relation to the kinds of outcomes that are being measured. There are many indicators of learning achievement (or their proxies) already in use, and there are a number of systems in place to measure learning achievement and use the results for the implementation and assessment of educational policies, programmes and practices.

However, more effort has gone into the measurement of knowledge and competencies, than into values and behaviours. A number of mechanisms exist to measure learning outcomes: for example, the UNESCO MLA Project, which attempted to measure life skills as well as numeracy and literacy, and MLL in India and ABC in Bangladesh. The MLL and ABC studies focus on cognitive achievement, although they have also made efforts to measure values, skills and behaviours.

This points to the need for additional work. The evolving understanding of the various dimensions of quality suggests that some of the commonly used indicators might need to be reconsidered as well. It also suggests that while cross-national comparisons are important, they are not the only ones on which countries need to focus. In fact, in some instances, both within-country and cross-country comparisons may be required for policy purposes.

Conclusion

Education systems and their processes cannot be expected to change overnight. To think so is unrealistic. A vision of quality that takes into account its various dimensions sets the standard. While there are common objectives and underlying principles, there is no single approach, no 'one size fits all'. Different contexts, circumstances, systems, and resources mean that there are many different possible entry points. These may be teacher education, curriculum development, additional learning materials, or introducing different assessment systems. Teachers, schools, communities, systems and nations are the ones responsible for determining how this vision should be interpreted and, incrementally, put in place. What is important is that they understand what they expect from education and articulate those expectations in ways that can be measured.

References

Delors, J. 1996. *Learning: the treasure within.* Paris: UNESCO.

UNESCO. 1990. *World Declaration on Education for All: meeting basic learning needs.* New York: UNESCO.

UNESCO. 2000. *The Dakar Framework for Action: Education for All – Meeting our collective commitments.* World Education Forum, Dakar, Senegal, 26-28 April. Paris: UNESCO.

United Nations. 1948. *Universal Declaration of Human Rights.* Retrieved 3 February 2005, from http://www.un.org/Overview/rights.html

UNESCO. 1989. *Convention on the Rights of the Child.* Retrieved 3 February 2005, from http://www.unicef.org/crc/crc.htm

Chapter 3

What monitoring mechanisms can be used for cross-national (and national) studies?

Thomas Kellaghan

Introduction

An interesting and significant development in the area of policy in education in recent years has been a growth in concern with what students learn as a result of their educational experiences. While until fairly recently the main focus in assessing quality in education was on inputs (for example, physical facilities, curriculum materials, textbooks, and teacher training), this is no longer the case. Today, the question posed by many commentators and policy-makers is: 'Are students, as a result of their exposure to schooling, acquiring appropriate knowledge, skills, behaviours and attitudes?'

The strongest, and probably the most influential, statement of concern about student learning is to be found in the document adopted by the World Conference on Education for All, in Jomtien (Thailand) in March 1990, which stated that the provision of basic education for all was meaningful only if students actually acquired useful knowledge, reasoning ability, skills and values. Consequently, Article 4 of the World Declaration on Education for All stated that the focus of basic education should be "... on actual learning acquisition and outcomes, rather than exclusively upon enrolment, continued participation in organized programmes, and completion of certification requirements" (UNESCO, 1990: 5). The 2000 Dakar Framework for Action recommitted national governments, organizations and donor agencies to ensuring" ... that recognized and measurable learning outcomes are achieved by all, especially in literacy, numeracy and essential life skills" (UNESCO, 2002: 13).

In this article, I shall outline a number of reasons for the growth in concern about student learning. I shall then briefly describe three procedures that provide information about what students have learned: (a) public (external) examinations; (b) national assessments; and (c) cross-national assessments (or international comparative studies of achievement).

A superficial examination of the ways in which the procedures are similar might suggest that each can serve a variety of functions equally well. For example, all three are concerned with the outcomes of education or, more precisely, the achievements of students. Furthermore, in all three, students respond to assessment tasks using formalized procedures administered under controlled conditions. Indeed, somebody looking at students at work might not be able to say in which type of exercise they were participating. However, consideration of the specific characteristics of each procedure will indicate that its design and functions limit the extent to which it can provide answers to six questions (listed below) that policy-makers might pose about the quality of students' learning.

Concern about what students are learning

A range of diverse issues can be identified as giving rise to concern about student learning. First, it cannot be assumed that because a child has been in school for six, seven, or eight years that he or she has, in the words of the World Declaration on Education for All, actually acquired "useful knowledge, reasoning ability, skills and values" (UNESCO, 1990: 9, Article 4). Indeed, the available evidence indicates that many students (particularly ones with short educational careers) seem to benefit little from their educational experience.

Second, there is concern that even the competencies acquired by students who stay in the education system for a long time may not be adequate to meet the needs of the information-based global competitive economy of the new millennium. Since economic and technological changes, together with increasing free trade and competitiveness between nations in economic activity, are demanding higher levels of knowledge and skills among school leavers, a country that does not have an effective education system will not have the competent, productive and competitive workforce necessary to maintain and improve economic performance (Guthrie, 1991). However, governments cannot know if their education systems are adequate to meet their economic goals unless outcomes are systematically monitored.

Third, information on student achievements is required to monitor the efficiency of education systems. This need arises from the fact that, in many countries, governments have had to deal with expanding enrolments while implementing structural adjustment programmes that do not allow for additional government spending on education. As a result, the learning achievements of students have often been perceived to be deteriorating. In this situation, the quality of education is unlikely to improve unless efficiency is increased. To obtain evidence on whether or not this is happening, information is required on outcomes as well as on inputs.

Fourth, interest in obtaining information on the achievements of students has been fuelled by the development of corporate and managerial approaches to government administration. Heavily influenced by ideas from the business world, these approaches involve strategic and operational planning, the setting of targets, the use of performance indicators, and a focus on 'deliverables', or results, all of which require information on outcomes.

A final reason for growth in interest in assessing student learning is that, again in many countries, public services are being reorganized to allow for the use of decentralized and relatively autonomous service providers. This has given rise to a need for new contractual arrangements, regulations and compliance monitoring, which in turn require procedures to check that organizations (schools or local education authorities) are delivering flexible cost-effective services to users. Linked to the reorganization of services, though not entirely dependent on it, is a growth in accountability demands, which in recent years have achieved increasing prominence in government administration in many countries. However, given the complex and poorly understood environments in which schools operate, it is difficult to specify responsibilities and to agree to criteria that will be acceptable as indicating that they have been met. One approach that to some extent avoids these issues is to use information on student outcomes (achievements) to bring pressure to bear for change and adjustment on the person or institution considered accountable.

What kind of information about quality might policy-makers find useful in addressing these issues? Answers to at least six questions would seem relevant:

- First, how well are students learning in the education system (with reference, for example, to general expectations, Education for All goals, the aims of the curriculum, or preparation for life)?
- Second, is there evidence of particular strengths or weaknesses in the knowledge and skills students have acquired?
- Third, do the achievements of subgroups in the population differ? Are there, for example, disparities between the achievements of boys and girls, of students in urban and rural locations, of students

from different language or ethnic groups, of students in different regions of the country, or students who drop out early or are repeating grades?

- Fourth, to what extent is achievement associated with the characteristics of the learning environment (for example, school resources, teacher preparation and competence, and type of school) or with students' home and community circumstances?

- Fifth, do the achievements of students change over time? This can be particularly important at a time of major change in the system (for example, when participation rates are increasing, or when new subjects or curricula are being implemented).

- Sixth, how do students' achievements relate to students' achievements in other education systems? (Kellaghan and Greaney, 2001*b*).

There are three major procedures, which exist in many (though not in all) countries, which might provide data that would answer these questions: public (external) examinations, national assessments and cross-national assessments.

Public (external) examinations

In many countries in Africa, Asia, Latin America and Europe, public or external examinations have long occupied a central role in the assessment of individual students, usually at the end of primary schooling, after two or three years of secondary schooling, and at the end of secondary schooling. They serve a number of important functions. First, they help control the disparate elements of the education system by specifying goals and standards for instruction. Second, they are used to certify the achievements of students, providing evidence that students may need in the market place. Third, and this is probably their most obvious function, examinations are used to select students for further education in what is considered an objective and unbiased way in situations in which the number of student places diminishes at each successive level. Fourth, examinations, especially when the results are published, may serve an accountability function for teachers and schools. Finally, examinations at the end of secondary schooling legitimate membership in the international global society, and facilitate international mobility (Keeves, 1994; Kellaghan and Greaney, 1992; Kellaghan and Madaus, 2003).

Countries that do not have a public examination system will have in place other procedures to serve these functions (for example, high-school diplomas based on internal school assessment), though in this context it is worth noting that many countries (for example, the United States and countries in Eastern Europe) are moving away from this form of assessment towards external examinations in the belief that this will lead to an improvement in standards of achievement and greater equity and accountability.

Many studies and official reports have pointed to the limitations of public examinations. These include the fact that a heavy reliance on pencil and paper tests limits the knowledge and skills that can be assessed; that items in examinations measure achievement at a low taxonomic level (involving the recall or recognition of factual knowledge); and that examinations contain very little reference to the everyday life of students outside the school. These deficiencies have important consequences for the quality of teaching and learning in schools, since teachers and students will tend to focus their efforts on what is contained in examinations to the neglect of important curriculum areas and forms of learning. Together with other factors considered below, they also limit the value of examinations to describe student learning in the context of curriculum aims or preparation for future life.

National assessments

While public examinations are a long-standing feature of education systems, national assessments are relatively new. There were a number of reasons why national assessments were introduced to education systems. First was the realization that the data on inputs to education that had typically been collected in the past were often of little value to policy-makers and educational planners, and that the assumption that increased resources are invariably associated with an improvement in the quality of student learning was not tenable (Kudjoh and Mingat, 1993). Second, countries that did not have a public examination system (for example, the United States) had no reliable data on student achievements at the national level. Thirdly, even in countries which had public examinations, the data that they provided were, for a number of reasons that I will consider below, not considered to meet policy-makers' needs.

It was in this context that national assessments were designed to provide information on the 'products' or 'outcomes' of schooling (for example, student learning and inequalities in the system), which, it was hoped, could be used in conjunction with input data to provide a sounder basis for policy-development and decision-making. Thus, the purpose of a national assessment can be said to be to provide decision-makers with relevant and reliable information, which is amenable to analysis and interpretation, about the state of the education system, its achievements, and its problems (Greaney and Kellaghan, 1996; Kellaghan and Greaney, 2001*b*).

While information is obtained in a national assessment by having individual students complete assessment tasks (as they do in public examinations), the primary interest is not in the performance of individuals but in what an aggregation of their performances tells us about the whole education system or a clearly defined part of it. To obtain this information, not all students need to participate. Inferences about the performance of the 'system' can be made based on the performance of a sample of students. Some national and state-wide assessments, however, are designed to provide evidence of the achievements of individual schools, teachers, and even students (for example, in Chile, France and the United Kingdom), in which case all (or most) students at a particular grade or age level will take part in the assessment.

While most industrialized countries have had systems of national assessment, some going back more than 30 years, some established on a statutory basis (as in France and the United Kingdom), it was only following the Jomtien Conference that efforts were made in the 1990s to develop the capacity to administer national assessments in developing countries. By the end of the decade, aided by international projects, most countries in Africa and Latin America had carried out at least one national assessment (Kellaghan and Greaney, 2001*a*). The UNESCO/UNICEF Monitoring Learning Achievement projects assessed basic learning competencies in literacy, numeracy and life skills (awareness and knowledge of health, nutrition, sanitation and hygiene) after four years of schooling and science achievements at Grade 8 in more than 70 countries (Chinapah, 1997; Chinapah *et al.*, 2000; UNESCO, 2000; UNESCO, 2003*a*).

The International Institute for Educational Planning (IIEP) facilitated the establishment of the Southern Africa Consortium for Monitoring Educational Quality (SACMEQ), which was set up in 1995 as a network of ministries of education in Southern Africa and has since been extended to East Africa (Ross *et al.*, 2000; UNESCO, 2003*b*). The first major study was carried out in 1995 in seven countries in which data were collected on educational inputs, general conditions of schooling, and the literacy levels of Grade 6 students. Fourteen countries participated in a study of reading literacy and numeracy between 1999 and 2002.

In the Programme d'Analyse des Systèmes Educatifs des Pays de la CONFEMEN (PASEC), assessment projects focused on achievement in French and mathematics, in grades 2 and 5, in 18 francophone Sub-Saharan countries. In addition to data on achievement, information on a variety of school and background factors was collected from students and teachers (Kulpoo and Coustère, 1999).

There has also been rapid development in the establishment of national assessments during the 1990s in Latin American and Caribbean countries, where practically all ministries of education have now incorporated national assessments into their agenda. The assessments were often associated with the provision of baseline data for educational reforms and were supported by the World Bank, UNESCO, and the United States Agency for International Development.

In Asia, national assessment activity is to be found in many countries, including Cambodia, India, Nepal, Sri Lanka, Thailand and Viet Nam. Some have been carried out with the support of the World Bank, sometimes in the context of ongoing reform programmes.

Cross-national assessments

Cross-national assessments, or international comparative studies of achievement, share many procedural features with national assessments and often address similar questions. They differ from them in a number of ways, however, most obviously in that they involve measurement of the outcomes of several education systems, usually simultaneously, providing data that allow countries to compare the achievements of their students with the achievements of students in other countries (Beaton *et al.*, 1999; Greaney and Kellaghan, 1996; Kellaghan and Greaney, 2001*b*).

Since the 1960s, over 60 countries have participated in cross-national studies in which the achievements of students have been compared in a variety of scholastic areas (for example, reading, mathematics, science, writing and foreign languages). Studies were organized by the International Association for the Evaluation of Educational Achievement (IEA) and, more recently, by the Organisation for Economic Co-operation and Development (OECD). Most participating countries were industrialized; few were from the developing world. Over the years, as the number of participants increased, the proportion of European countries (Eastern and Western) increased, while the proportion of less developed ones decreased. The lack of participation by developing countries is hardly surprising given that the studies were designed with the conditions and standards of countries in the industrialized world in mind.

Sensitivity to the issue that conditions in countries with which comparisons will be made are relevant to a decision to participate in a cross-national study led in the 1990s to a number of countries in a geographical region deciding to carry out a comparative study. In one such study organized by the Oficina Regional de Educación para América Latina y el Caribe (OREALC), basic competencies in language and mathematics were assessed in ten Latin American and Caribbean countries in 1997. Two projects in Africa mentioned above (PASEC and SACMEQ) were also confined, if not to regions, at least to countries at more or less the same stage of economic development. Though initially conceived as national assessments, based on international co-operation, results have been reported in a way that permits comparisons between the performance of students in different education systems.

Answering the policy-makers' questions

How can the information derived from examinations, national assessments, and cross-national assessments contribute to policy-makers' knowledge of the quality of education, and provide a basis for decisions that improve teaching and learning? This question can be addressed by assessing the ability of examinations and assessments (national and cross-national) to provide answers to each of the questions that policy-makers are interested in that I have already posed.

Since examinations and assessments are based on the performance of individual students, we might ask if an aggregation of performances on examinations would provide the same kind of information as a national or cross-national assessment. The fact that many of the countries that have carried out national and cross-national assessments already have public examination systems would suggest that the answer is no, that examinations and assessments provide different kinds of information (Kellaghan, 1996). This issue is explored with reference to the questions posed above.

How well are students learning in the education system?

Two factors are relevant to a consideration of how well examinations and assessments provide information on how well students are learning in the education system: the population taking the examinations and assessments, and the achievements that are assessed.

Examinations provide data only on voluntary and selective populations at predetermined points in the education system. Assessments, on the other hand, provide information on the total population of students (or more usually, a representative sample of them) at other points, allowing inferences to be drawn about the education system in general, not a select section of it. Further, there is a consensus among national assessments throughout the world that information is required before the age at which students normally sit for a public examination. There are two reasons for this. First, an assessment can identify problems and point to the need for intervention early in the primary school years. Second, many students do not get to the point of taking a public examination, but their achievements are of concern to policy-makers.

In considering the achievements that are assessed, it should be borne in mind that any test will contain only a sample of the content and knowledge that are being measured. Of crucial significance in comparing examinations, national assessments, and cross-national assessments is how content is selected in the different exercises.

In the case of examinations, extensive content coverage is not required to discriminate between candidates who are likely to perform well in the next stage of education and those who are likely to perform less well. Indeed, in attempting to achieve maximum discrimination, questions or items that most or very few students are likely to respond to correctly will not be included in the examination. Rather the emphasis will be on selecting questions or items that focus on the level of competence of students who are likely to be selected. Clearly, tests comprised of such items or questions will not cover the whole range of knowledge and skills that a curriculum is designed to foster.

A national assessment, on the other hand, is designed to find out what *all* students know and do not know. Thus, it will have to provide adequate coverage of what students are expected to learn, with reference either to the aims of the curriculum or general expectations. In this context, policy-makers are as likely to be as interested in what students do not know as in what they know.

A further issue can arise relating to the inferences that can be made about student achievements based on their performance in public examinations if high stakes are attached to performance, which will be the case when important decisions are based on results. If, in this situation, teaching and learning in schools is directed more towards meeting the requirements of the examination than to attaining curriculum objectives, it will not be possible to interpret examination performance as evidence of achievement in the broader domain of achievement envisaged in the curriculum (Linn, 1983). A similar problem, of course, could arise if high stakes are attached to performance in a national assessment. In both cases, statements about students' learning in relation to curriculum objectives will be problematic.

Is there evidence of strengths and weaknesses in students' knowledge and skills?

Reports on examinations in many countries provide information on the strengths and weaknesses of a candidature in a chief examiner's report, or in a newsletter to schools. However, such analysis can only provide information based on the content of the examinations, which as we saw, tends to be limited, and the information will also be limited to students who took the examination. In contrast, a national assessment can provide diagnostic data on the curriculum as a whole and for the total population of students.

Do the achievements of subgroups of students differ?

Some contextual information (for example, relating to gender, school location, and type of school) is available for public examinations, and analyses of student performance may consider this. Again, any such analyses will be limited by the restricted range of knowledge and skills assessed and the selective nature of the populations that take the examinations, and so will not necessarily reveal problems in the education system in general (for example, in schools in which early drop-out is common and in which a very low proportion of students sit for an examination).

To what extent is achievement associated with the characteristics of the learning environment, or with students' home and community circumstances?

While the primary purpose in an examination is to make judgements and decisions about individual students, a national assessment is likely to be interested in identifying determinants of achievement – particularly ones that might be alterable through changes in educational policy. Thus, several kinds of information are usually collected. First, what students bring to school from their family and community backgrounds that may contribute to their success or poor performance at school is of interest. A second kind of contextual information, and one that is more relevant to decisions about the distribution of educational resources, relates to provision in schools, that is, to what extent schools provide opportunities to acquire various kinds of knowledge and skills. In concrete terms, we can ask about the physical facilities in schools, the range of curricula offered, the availability of learning-support materials such as textbooks, libraries, and laboratories and their use, as well as the less material aspects of schools, in particular, the quality of instructional leadership and the institutional pressure that the school exerts to get students to learn. Third, as teachers are the key component in any educational system, information is required on their characteristics and the conditions in a school that may enhance or constrain their ability to implement instructional programmes.

To maximize understanding of the factors that affect student achievement, more information than is available in a public examination is collected in national and cross-national assessments in questionnaires administered to, for example, students, teachers, head teachers and parents.

Do students' achievements change over time?

It is important to be able to say if student achievements are improving over time (perhaps as a result of education reforms) or are deteriorating (perhaps because of an increase in the number of students in the education system). To do this, it is necessary to obtain information at different points in time, and to be confident that it provides a valid basis for comparison.

We sometimes hear, because of inferences from a perusal of grade distributions on public examinations over a number of years, that standards of achievement are improving, deteriorating, or static. Are such inferences warranted? The answer would seem to be no. There are a number of reasons for saying that examinations do not provide data that can be interpreted as indicating change over time. The first relates to the standardization of test procedures. In all testing, some standardization has to be imposed on the student behaviour sample that is used, and on how it is interpreted, if performances are to have a comparable meaning for different students, in different places, and at different times. However, public examinations often appear relatively unstructured (at a superficial level at any rate), and their scoring procedures often lack clear specification, relying heavily on the judgements of individual markers. Another obvious deviation from standardization in public examinations is found when students are free to choose the questions they answer. Second, it is impossible to say that examination papers measure the same knowledge and skills, or are equivalent in difficulty level, from year to year. Third, the scoring in many examinations is, explicitly or implicitly, norm-referenced and the proportions of students who are awarded various grades remain constant from year to year. This procedure obviously will mask changes that may be occurring in the actual achievements of students, so that it is not possible to say if a pass (or a particular grade) in one year represents an equivalent level of achievement in another year. Fourth, the procedure will also mask any change in achievement that is brought about by changes in the characteristics of candidatures. Thus, if expanding numbers are associated with a decline in the overall scholastic ability of students, and this is not reflected in grading, we have to conclude that grades are being awarded more leniently (Willmott, 1977).

The situation with national and cross-national assessments is quite different since instruments and methods of scoring are more highly structured, and the same instrument (or one of demonstrated equivalence) is used over time. This is not to say that problems cannot arise. Even minor changes in an instrument (such as a change in the order in which items are presented or in the context in which they are embedded) can affect student performance (Beaton and Zwick, 1990). Furthermore, a change in school curricula, in popular language, or in general social conditions might mean that the appropriateness of an instrument changes over time (Kellaghan and Madaus, 1982).

How do students' achievements relate to students' achievements in other countries?

Examination systems are concerned that the performance of their candidates will be accepted internationally. With an eye to international standards, some systems work in a co-operative cross-national fashion (for example, the West African Examinations Council), others maintain a variety of contacts with examination boards in Europe, while others exchange item writers, markers and other technical personnel.

The design of national assessments also has an international dimension in that it is influenced by practice elsewhere. Furthermore, in some assessments, items from international assessments have been included to provide cross-national comparative data.

However, only specially designed cross-national studies will allow accurate comparisons to be made between the achievements of students in different education systems. Problems, even in the most carefully designed assessments, may still arise, relating to the appropriateness of tests when used in a number of education systems, the translation of instruments, and the equivalence of the populations (and samples) that are assessed.

Conclusion

While performance on examinations is amenable to analysis that will throw some light on the quality of students' learning, the information will be limited by the nature and content of the examinations, the selective nature of examination candidatures, and the fact that high stakes are usually attached to examination performance. Furthermore, examinations can provide only limited information about the factors associated with achievement, and even less about how students' achievements change over time, or about how achievements compare with those of students in other countries. By contrast, national assessments can be designed to address all these issues, apart from comparisons with other countries, which cross-national assessments are designed to address.

While national and cross-national assessments go a long way in describing aspects of the quality of education, with a firm focus on student learning, there is still some way to go in devising and implementing approaches in which the information they provide can be used to improve the quality of teaching and learning in schools. For the most part, the information derived from national and cross-national assessments has been used in policy debate and formulation rather than to affect school practice directly, though many efforts have been made to communicate the research findings to schools and teachers. If the information obtained in an assessment, however, is based on a sample of schools, the problems of individual schools cannot be identified. It is perhaps for this reason that some national assessments are administered in all schools, and the results are used to intervene at the school level. While such a census-based assessment provides a better basis than a sample-based assessment for action at the school level, if high stakes are attached to performance, it may (as in the case of public examinations) provide a distorted picture of student achievement, as well as having undesirable (if unintended) effects on teaching and learning in schools.

References

Beaton, A.E.; Postlethwaite, T.N.; Ross, K.N.; Spearritt, D.; Wolf, R.M. 1999. *The benefits and limitations of international achievement studies.* Paris: IIEP-UNESCO; International Academy of Education.

Beaton, A.E.; Zwick, R. 1990. *The effect of changes in the national assessment: Disentangling the NAEP 1985-86 reading anomaly.* Princeton NJ: Educational Testing Service.

Chinapah, V. 1997. *Handbook on monitoring learning achievement. Towards capacity building.* Paris: UNESCO.

Chinapah, V.; H'ddigui, E.M.; Kanjee, A.; Falayajo, W.; Fomba, C.O.; Hamissou, O.; Rafalimanana, A.; Byamugisha, A. 2000. *With Africa for Africa. Towards quality education for all.* Pretoria: Human Sciences Research Council.

Greaney, V.; Kellaghan, T. 1996. *Monitoring the learning outcomes of education systems.* Washington, DC: World Bank.

Guthrie, J.W. 1991. "Globalisation of educational policy and reform". In: T. Husén, T.N. Postlethwaite (Eds.), *The international encyclopedia of education.* 2nd Ed., pp. 2495-2500. Oxford: Pergamon.

Keeves, J.P. 1994. *National examinations: design, procedures and reporting.* Paris: IIEP-UNESCO.

Kellaghan, T. 1996. "Can public examinations be used to provide information for national assessment?" In: P. Murphy, V. Greaney, M.E. Lockheed, C. Rojas (Eds.), *National assessments: testing the system,* pp. 33-48. Washington, DC: World Bank.

Kellaghan, T.; Greaney, V. 1992. *Using examinations to improve education. A study in fourteen African countries.* Washington, DC: World Bank.

Kellaghan, T.; Greaney, V. 2001a. "The globalisation of assessment in the 20th century". In: *Assessment in Education, 8,* 87-102.

Kellaghan, T.; Greaney, V. 2001b. *Using assessment to improve the quality of education.* Paris: IIEP-UNESCO.

Kellaghan, T.; Madaus, G..F. 1982. "Trends in educational standards in Great Britain and Ireland". In: G.R. Austin and H. Garber (Eds.), *The rise and fall of national test scores,* pp. 195-214. New York: Academic Press.

Kellaghan, T.; Madaus, G..F. 2003. "External (public) examinations". In: T. Kellaghan, D.L. Stufflebeam (Eds.), *International handbook of educational evaluation,* pp. 577-600. Dordrecht: Kluwer Academic.

Kudjoh, A.; Mingat, A. 1993. "Towards a better understanding of the functioning of school systems for better decision-making: The case of primary schools in Togo". In: D.W. Chapman and L.O. Mählck (Eds.), *From data to action: information systems in educational planning,* pp.147-174. Paris: IIEP-UNESCO.

Kulpoo, D.; Coustère, P. 1999. "Developing national capacities for assessment and monitoring through effective partnerships". In: *Partnerships for capacity building and quality improvements in education,* pp. 131-138. Paris: Association for the Development of Education in Africa.

Linn, R.L. 1983. "Testing and instruction: Links and distinctions". In: *Journal of Educational Measurement, 20,* 179-189.

Ross, K.N.; Saito, M.; Leite, S. 2000. *Translating educational assessment findings into educational policy and reform measures: lessons from the SACMEQ initiative in Africa.* Paris: UNESCO.

UNESCO. 1990. *World Declaration on Education for All: meeting basic learning needs.* New York: UNESCO.

UNESCO. 2000. *Education for All. Status and trends 2000. Assessing learning achievement.* Paris: UNESCO.

UNESCO. 2002. *Education for All. Is the world on track? EFA global monitoring report.* Paris: UNESCO.

UNESCO. 2003a. *Monitoring Learning Achievement (MLA) Project. Update.* Paris: UNESCO.

UNESCO. 2003*b*. *Southern Africa Consortium for Monitoring Educational Quality (SACMEQ)*. Harare: UNESCO.

Willmott, A.S. 1977. *CSE and GCE grading standards: the 1973 comparability study*. London: Macmillan.

Chapter 4
What are the main cross-national studies?

Aletta Grisay and Patrick Griffin

Introduction

The main objective of this article is to describe the characteristics of the most important large-scale cross-national studies that have been conducted since the 1960s. These studies have been designed to assess student achievement at different levels of the school systems, in different subjects, and in different countries. The focus is on the similarities and differences in the design of these studies, and on the conceptual and operational constraints within which they have been implemented.

The article has been limited to international comparative studies using strictly equivalent instruments, common definitions of target populations, and standardized procedures, in order to measure student achievement in each of the participating countries. Some examples of these studies include: (a) studies of mathematics and science achievement conducted by the International Association for the Evaluation of Educational Achievement (IEA); (b) the Programme for International Student Assessment (PISA) conducted by the Organisation for Economic Co-operation and Development (OECD); and (c) the educational policy research studies conducted by the Southern and Eastern Africa Consortium for Monitoring Education Quality (SACMEQ).

This article will not include international surveys that contain little or very marginal assessment components (such as the IEA Classroom Environment Study or the IEA Preprimary Project). Multi-national programmes mainly focused on assistance to the development of national assessments, such as the Monitoring Learning Achievement (MLA) project conducted by UNESCO and UNICEF, the Assessing Basic Competencies (ABC) studies conducted by the World Bank in South Asia, the Programme d'analyse des systèmes éducatifs (PASEC) conducted by the CONFEMEN (Conférence des ministres de l'Éducation des pays francophones), and the studies conducted by the Latin American Laboratory for Assessment of the Quality of Education (LLECE) are not within the scope of the article either, since their sampling designs and/ or the data collection instruments used could not be considered strictly equivalent across countries.

References to all of the research programmes listed above have been presented in the *Appendix*.

National and international assessments of student achievement

School systems around the world have experienced unprecedented quantitative and organizational changes over the past fifty years. In industrialized countries, a dramatic increase in enrolments occurred during the 1950s and 1960s, due to the combined effects of the post-war baby boom, and swift rises in educational demand from families and labour markets. These trends resulted in pressures to achieve universal secondary schooling and large increases in enrolments in tertiary education.

This shift from 'elite' to 'mass' education, particularly in secondary schools, not only required huge public investment, but also enormous adaptation efforts in school systems. The length of compulsory schooling was extended; and there were extensive reforms of organizational structures, curricula, and teaching methods as many education systems were required to switch from strict selectivity, highly tracked study programmes, and discrimination against disadvantaged minorities, towards retentivity and more comprehensive instruction for all.

In developing countries, the same period was characterized by a movement of many nations to independence, accompanied by the expansion of enrolments in primary and secondary education, and reforms intended to replace colonial school systems with new national institutions and curricula. In a number of countries, this was also the period when a variety of large-scale innovations were attempted (from Paulo Freire's 'Popular Education' and the Colombian 'Escuela Nueva', to technology-based programmes using television and radio), often with support from international organizations, to face the many challenges posed by launching literacy programmes in countries with limited economic and human resources.

The 1990 Jomtien Conference (UNESCO, 1990), the 2000 Dakar Framework for Action (UNESCO, 2000), and the Millennium Development Goals – MDG (United Nations, 2000) confirmed the near universal engagement of governments in extending to all children the provision of basic primary education by improving access, quality and equity through the 'Education for All' programme.

The worldwide movement towards expanded access to basic education has generated, both in political spheres and among the scientific community, concerns that large and rapid enrolment increases might result in reduced quality and the possibility of an unequal distribution in the standard of instruction delivered by schools. This issue has been raised particularly in developing countries that have been struggling to achieve the (sometimes competing) goals of the Dakar Framework for Action (UNESCO, 2000).

Concerns about the potential for trade-offs among access, equity and quality have created a need for empirical information on student achievement and its relation with the resources invested and the characteristics of the educational environment. First conducted as large (but isolated) surveys aimed at addressing major policy concerns such as the well-known 'Study on Equality of Educational Opportunities' (Coleman, 1966), assessments of students' achievement became a regular component of national monitoring systems in some countries. For example, in the United States, the National Assessment of Educational Progress (NAEP) was initiated in 1969.

In a number of countries, the implementation of high-quality national assessments drew much of its impetus and many of its techniques from the research undertaken at international level by the IEA. This organization was established in 1958 by a group of the world's leading educational research institutions under the auspices of the UNESCO Institute for Education in Hamburg. The IEA members wanted to measure the achievement of comparable samples of students in different subjects and in different school systems, with the aim of investigating the relationships between differences in achievement and differences in educational inputs, processes and contexts.

Since then, both the IEA and several other international agencies have undertaken a large number of cross-national studies. The results of these widely publicized surveys have generated great interest in the implementation of national assessments, and it was through participation in these studies that many national research teams developed the complex technical skills needed to conduct their own national assessments. In a reciprocal fashion, theoretical and technical advances made in a number of outstanding national research centres were also taken up by international studies. By the beginning of the twenty-first century, this cross-fertilization process had resulted in an impressive knowledge base about the functioning of school systems, and in a largely shared set of scientific standards, methods and procedures for the conduct of valid and rigorous assessments. One of the important benefits of the common 'assessment culture' among experts in charge of international surveys and of national monitoring systems was the shift of international studies towards a more policy-oriented focus.

Most of the funding at the national and international level in the early IEA surveys came from ministries of education and foundations interested in fundamental research. The national research teams were almost exclusively composed of university scholars and, although the goal of providing useful data to education authorities was considered important, the main orientation of the studies was clearly scientific. The idea, as expressed by Benjamin Bloom, one of the founding fathers of IEA, and often echoed in the earliest IEA study reports, was that school systems around the world could be considered as a sort of natural 'experimental laboratory', where the effects on student achievement of different 'treatments' (differences in school organization, in instructional resources, and in teaching practices) could be explored more effectively than in single national studies, because of the larger diversity that could be expected at the international level for each of these factors.

In an increasing number of countries participating in the IEA studies, and in virtually all of those participating in the PISA programme, the responsibility for project implementation progressively shifted from 'independent' university departments to governmental agencies, or to university centres directly subcontracted by ministries of education to conduct the research. While contributing to advances in scientific knowledge remains a fundamental concern, most recent international studies go to great lengths to carefully identify policy issues that can be addressed through the study results, and to systematically devise strategies for disseminating the information collected among stakeholders at all levels of educational systems.

In this respect, international comparative studies can be considered as complementary to national monitoring systems:

- National assessments are better able than international studies to provide information that is tailored to the specific characteristics of a school system. For instance, they are more appropriate than international surveys to inform educational authorities on: (a) whether all aspects of a new curriculum were implemented effectively in schools; (b) the proportion of students that meet specific national standards; and (c) possible local negative effects of an otherwise beneficial nationwide innovation. They may also be used to address questions such as 'How much does our education system cost?' 'Who pays for education?' and 'Do they get good value for money?'

- On the other hand, only international assessments can: (a) inform national authorities about the extent to which other school systems 'do better' than their own system, in terms of student outcomes, and areas such as instructional delivery, teachers' qualifications, and/or effectiveness of resource use; (b) indicate whether school organization in other countries results in fewer disparities in the quality of instruction delivered, and in a lower impact on student's outcomes of social background, gender, or ethnicity; and (c) show whether the evolution over time of any of these indicators is positive (or negative) across several countries.

Most international studies routinely allow for both international analyses of the pooled data set and for replicated analyses of each country's data. Then cross-national generalizations about education can be made, as well as statements with more specific national analyses. These studies also encourage the use of national options whereby a country can add extra country-specific questions to the cross-national data collection.

For some countries, participation in international studies is not a complement to national assessments, but indeed a substitute for them. This sometimes occurs in very small countries, or countries with limited human and financial resources that have neither the research budgets nor the highly specialized experts needed to conduct rigorous assessments. Sharing with other countries the development of valid sampling frames, assessment frameworks, and test instruments is an efficient way for these countries to obtain policy-relevant information at a reasonable cost and to give their national research teams access to international expertise.

Finally, in some federal nations, it may happen that international comparative studies appear more 'politically acceptable' than national assessments. This is the case in countries such as Belgium, where both the Flemish- and French-speaking communities participate in the IEA and PISA studies as if they were separate 'countries'. In this case, Belgium education authorities considered these two sets of studies to be 'neutral', whereas any national assessment, including the two linguistic areas, would be considered too politically sensitive.

Main cross-national assessments

More than 20 international assessments have been conducted by several agencies during the past fifty years, in a range of subjects and in a large number of both industrialized and developing countries (see *Appendix*).

The IEA studies

The International Association for the Evaluation of Educational Achievement (IEA), a non-governmental organization (NGO), founded in the late 1950s, was the first agency to conduct cross-national studies of student achievement, and remains the outstanding model in terms of the number of participating countries (from 12 countries in the first IEA Mathematics study to around 50 by the year 2000), the variety of subjects explored, and the range of student ages and/or grades covered.

Most of the IEA comparisons are based on so-called 'age/grade' samples. That is, in each participating country, the target population is defined as all students attending the grade where most of the students in a given age cohort can be found. For example, in the IEA/Reading Literacy Study conducted at the primary school level (Elley, 1992), a probability sample of primary schools was drawn in each country; then in each sampled school, one intact class was randomly selected from Grade 4 classes (or from Grade 3 classes, depending on which of these grades was the modal grade attended by 9-year-old students in that particular country).

Other IEA studies have used pure 'age' or pure 'grade' definitions. For example, in the First International Mathematics Study (FIMS) (Husén, 1967), conducted in 1964, there were separate grade and age samples at the lower secondary level: an age sample (all 13 year-olds wherever they were in the system and in whichever grade they were) and a grade sample (the modal grade for 13 year-olds), and in this case one or two intact classes were selected. On the other hand, all IEA assessments conducted at the upper secondary level defined their target population as students attending the last year of secondary school, irrespective of their age. In the Third International Mathematics and Science Study (TIMSS), (Beaton *et al.*, 1996) a complex variant of the 'age/grade' design was used for the lower secondary level; the sample included intact classes drawn from the two contiguous grades where the majority of 13-year-old students were enrolled (that is, in most countries, Grades 7 and 8).

These different designs are related to variations in the focus of the comparison. If the main goal is to compare educational systems in terms of yield (that is, what has a system achieved with an age cohort – the cumulative effect of students' instructional experiences in and out of school), then the most appropriate sample is an age-based sample. All students assessed have the same age, and variations in grade (resulting from across-country differences in the regulations concerning age of entry in compulsory education, or in the policies concerning grade repetition) are just considered as one of the system-related factors affecting their learning experience.

If, on the other hand, the focus is on comparing systems in terms of the effects on achievement of differences in resources, curricula and instructional practices, then it is more appropriate to assess intact classes in grades that are as comparable as possible across systems. The IEA 'age-grade' design is generally considered as a reasonable compromise between these two perspectives.

The IEA studies covering main curriculum subjects (reading, mathematics, and science) were loosely structured in large 'cycles' of approximately 10 to 15 years, with a first cycle in the 1960s and early 1970s (FIMS) (Husén, 1967) in 1966, First International Science Study (FISS) in 1971 (Comber and Keeves, 1973), and a first Reading Comprehension Study (RCS) also in 1971 (Thorndike, 1973). A second cycle took place in the 1980s and early 1990s (Second International Mathematics Study (SIMS) (Travers and Westbury, 1989) and Second International Science Study (SISS) respectively in 1982 and 1984 (Rosier and Keeves, 1991); and a Reading Literacy Study (RLS) in 1991(Elley, 1992). However, a number of changes in the definitions of populations assessed, in the instruments used, and in the sets of participating countries, prevented the development of rigorous time-series comparisons. This aspect has been improved in the third cycle of IEA studies, where repeated data collections were implemented using a four-year pattern, both in the joint Third Mathematics and Science Study (TIMSS in 1995 and TIMSS-Repeat in 1999) and in a new Reading study (Progress in International Reading Literacy Study (PIRLS) in 1999 and PIRLS-Repeat in 2004) (Mullis *et al.*, 2004).

The first IEA 'cycle' also included assessments in some conceptually and/or operationally challenging domains – civic education, literature, foreign languages (English and French). A second civic-education study was conducted in the third cycle, while lack of financial support prevented the completion of a new foreign-languages assessment. A computer education study was conducted in the second cycle, and a second one is currently being conducted.

All of these studies were cross-sectional. A strict longitudinal component (where the same sample of students was tested twice in order to assess achievement growth over one school year) was included as an option only in SIMS and TIMSS. Due to the high costs of longitudinal data collections, only a small subset of countries participated in these options. However, cross-sectional studies such as TIMSS, RLS or PIRLS used test instruments that were anchored over successive age-grade samples, which allowed reasonable estimations of gains in students' achievement obtained in a given period.

The IAEP studies

The International Assessment of Educational Progress (IAEP) (Lapointe *et al.*, 1989) was a two-phase study conducted in the late 1980s by the American agency Educational Testing Services (ETS). It was an offspring of the National Assessment of Educational Progress (NAEP) conducted in the United States on a regular basis since 1969. It received strong financial support from the United States federal authorities, in a context where the publication of the famous report entitled *A nation at risk* (National Commission on Excellence in Education, 1983) had created a disturbing turmoil in public opinion towards school education in America. The report, based on data drawn from IEA and NAEP, as well as from national examinations, pictured a dramatic decline in mathematics and science achievement of American students, and major gaps between American students and students of other nations (particularly Japan). The United States Government was therefore very interested in seeking additional cross-country comparative information to explore these issues further.

This 'American' origin was probably the major weakness of the IAEP studies, which may explain why they were discontinued after the second round. Contrary to most other international assessments, where the test materials are usually contributed co-operatively by various countries and carefully reviewed for cultural and curricular suitability in each participating country, the assessment items used in the IAEP study were drawn from the NAEP item bank (all of them in IAEP I, and a large majority of them in IAEP II). In this respect, the study was questionable both in terms of content validity and of political acceptability for countries other than the United States.

Some aspects of the IAEP study were nevertheless innovative. In particular, it was the first occasion where international results were reported as 'described scales' based on Item Response Theory (IRT), rather than as raw test scores or mean percentages of correct answers (see below a discussion of this technique). Described scales had been first used in some of the most advanced national assessments during the 1980s. They progressively became a standard form of reporting achievement results in virtually all international surveys. Another important (strictly technical) innovation, also applied by the IAEP for the first time in an international survey, was the use of so-called plausible values in order to increase the accuracy of the estimation of country means and other statistical parameters. Similarly, the use of plausible values has been applied to most subsequent international studies.

The IALS studies

The International Adult Literacy Study (IALS) (Tuijnman *et al.*, 1994) was a household survey aimed at assessing reading literacy and computational skills among adults aged 16 to 65 years. It was conducted by Statistics Canada (STATCAN) and sponsored by the Organisation for Economic Co-operation and Development (OECD). It comprised two assessments in 1995 and 1998 (Tuijnman, 2000), in which twenty countries participated.

The main characteristics of IALS were: (a) a focus on an assessment perspective oriented towards human capital and lifelong learning (rather than on an evaluation of school systems), and a strong interest in the relationship between individuals' knowledge and skills and outcomes in the labour markets; (b) the functional nature of the tasks used in the assessment – all of them were based on authentic materials drawn from situations that individuals encounter in everyday life; (c) comprehensive household-based samples, representing the whole of the active population in each country; and (d) in contrast with school-based assessments where multiple-choice items are often predominant, all IALS items were open-ended, in order to maintain the authenticity of the test materials and of the cognitive processes assessed.

IALS is a typical example of an international study that benefited from theoretical and technical advances made during the implementation of previous national surveys, both in the United States and Canada. The framework used to assess reading literacy, in particular, had strong theoretical and empirical foundations derived from years of research conducted at ETS and at STATCAN for the National Adults Literacy Study (NALS), the national study from which IALS was initially derived as an international extension.

Household surveys are costly, labour-intensive, and operationally complex; they are also challenging in terms of institutional responsibilities. In many countries, studies like IALS cannot be conducted without effective co-operation among a number of ministries. This often prevents countries from participating, which is regrettable. Due to the comprehensive age group assessed, IALS has a unique feature: it is the only international study that allows comparison of the global outcomes of education over a range of generations across a variety of cultures.

The PISA studies

The Programme for International Student Assessment (PISA) (OECD, 2001, 2004; OECD-UNESCO, 2003) was initially developed as part of the Strategic Plan implemented by the Organisation for Economic Co-operation and Development (OECD) in order to provide their International Indicators of Education Systems project (INES) with regular indicators of students' achievement towards the end of compulsory schooling.

A specificity of PISA is that the programme is primarily intended to provide indicators to governments of a specific group of countries – the industrialized nations that make up the membership of the OECD. All but two of the thirty OECD countries participated in the first assessment in 2000, and all of them in 2003. While a number of non-OECD countries also joined in the assessments (about sixty countries will participate in the 2006 survey), their delegates serve on the PISA Governing Board as observers, not with a decisional status.

PISA uses a 'pure' age-based definition of its target population, which consists of 15-year-old students, irrespective of the grade attended. This is the oldest age group where nearly 100 per cent of students are still attending school in most OECD countries.

PISA was conceived as a periodic programme, where each 9-year cycle includes three assessments of student performance, in reading, mathematics and science, conducted in the third, sixth and ninth year of the cycle. Each of the three data collections includes all three domains, but with a special focus on one of them, and lighter test instruments for the two others. In the first PISA assessment, conducted in 2000, reading literacy was assessed as the major domain, while mathematical and scientific literacy were the minor domains. In 2003, mathematical literacy was the major domain, and reading and science were included as minor domains. In 2006, the focus will shift to science literacy, with reading and mathematics as minor domains. In 2009, it has been proposed that a new nine-year cycle will start, with reading again as the major domain. This design allows trends in achievement in all three areas to be monitored on a regular basis.

Each assessment also includes an additional 'experimental' domain, which is not part of the rotation described above. In PISA 2000, the experimental domain was self-regulated learning; in PISA 2003, problem-solving; in PISA 2006 it will be computer assessed science.

Like the IEA studies, PISA studies are school-based; but like the IALS study, they are mainly literacy-oriented rather than school-curriculum oriented. The intention is 'to provide policy-relevant information on the cumulative yield of education systems towards the end of compulsory schooling, measured in terms of the performance of students in applying knowledge and skills they have acquired in key subject areas'. The PISA test instruments are similar to those used in IALS in that they are focused on the students' ability to apply their competencies in functional situations and authentic contexts.

The SACMEQ studies

The Southern and Eastern Africa Consortium for Monitoring Education Quality (SACMEQ) is a collaborative network of fifteen ministries of education. It was launched in 1995, with assistance from UNESCO's International Institute for Educational Planning (IIEP). Its major focus is on 'capacity building' in the area of educational policy research. It uses participation in cross-national studies as vehicles for the delivery of training programmes. Its comprehensive programme of intensive-training workshops includes project design, instrument construction, sampling, data collection, data entry and data cleaning, computer-based data analyses, data archive production and dissemination of research results. SACMEQ aims at providing continuous assessment and monitoring of education quality and learning achievement, resulting in informed policy suggestions leading to improvements in the provision of quality education through: (a) assessing learning achievement at the end of primary school, and factors affecting learning achievement for children at a specific level of education; (b) the collection of data and information for assessment of the conditions of schooling and how they compare with the ministry's benchmark standards, and to inform policy and education planning; and (c) the determination of the relative effects of educational inputs that have significant impacts on learning achievement, and establishing their level of distribution (including textbooks and teaching resources).

The first SACMEQ survey (SACMEQ I) in 1995-1999 focused on reading achievement. The second phase, in 2000-2004 (SACMEQ II), focused on reading and numeracy. An interesting feature of the SACMEQ II Project was that samples of teachers were assessed using test instruments that 'overlapped' with their own students' tests. This permitted results for both students and teachers to be mapped on to the same proficiency scales.

SACMEQ differs from other studies in that it has created a systematic strategy for consulting with governments and policy-makers in order to identify the policy concerns and the research questions they wish to have answered. It is these research questions obtained from senior decision-makers in ministries of education that form the basis of the SACMEQ studies.

The SACMEQ studies are also innovative in their reporting procedures, which include a well-balanced combination between international comparisons and 'customized' national indicators. In particular, while the studies use strictly equivalent instruments and common IRT-based described scales that allow for international comparisons, accurate procedures are also developed to map the common scales against country-specific standards of 'acceptable' or 'desirable' student proficiency, as defined in each country by panels of national experts. This represents a quite effective model for other developing countries that are facing similar educational challenges and are interested in learning from the experience of neighbouring countries.

Challenges to the validity of cross-national studies

The OECD, IEA and SACMEQ studies have all aimed to: (a) provide policy-makers and educational practitioners with information about their education system in relation to other systems; and (b) assist policy-makers and educational practitioners to understand the reasons for observed differences in the achievement of students from different educational systems.

In order to deliver on these aims, these studies have been required to ensure that they produce valid data that can be used to make meaningful cross-national comparisons. Critics of cross-national studies usually challenge the validity of cross-national data with respect to three main dimensions:

- *Student achievement tests*: Are they equally appropriate for all participating countries, and have they been designed to cope with variations in culture and curricula?
- *Target populations and sampling*: Are the target population definitions consistent across countries, and have these populations been sampled in a manner that avoids bias?
- *Reporting the results*: Have the research results been oversimplified in the form of 'league tables', or have they been reported in a manner that informs and improves classroom teaching?

Student achievement tests

    Different curricula

Critics of international studies have been active ever since the IEA studies began. Perceived problems with international studies have centred on the nature of the measures, the influence of background variables, curriculum links, validity and reliability of the scores, and inferences made as a result of the common approach. Russell (1981, 1982, in press) has consistently criticized the use of a 'total test score' in tests that are applied in many different countries to report student achievement across countries. He argued that the IEA tests could not be valid because the coverage of the curriculum is less than perfect, and is uneven across participating countries.

Other researchers (for example, Goldstein and Wood, 1999; Blum *et al.*, 2001) were concerned that the tests may not be consistent measures of the same curriculum outcomes for each participating country. That is, that students in participating countries may not have all had the same opportunity to learn the skills being assessed, and that tasks may match the curriculum of some countries better than others. This is addressed by the tests focusing on a body of knowledge and skills agreed to by participating countries.

Russell drew support from Freudenthal's (1975) criticism based on curriculum relevance and opportunity to learn in the IEA's First International Mathematics Study (FIMS) (Husén, T., 1967). He pointed out that too little progress had been made to address these concerns by the time of the second study (SIMS) in 1982 (Travers and Westbury, 1989). In SIMS, a single comprehensive pool of items was developed for the mathematics tests, but critics saw this as exacerbating the issue of opportunity to learn and curriculum coverage rather than providing a solution. The comprehensive item pool contained items that were relevant to as few as two countries.

By the time when the TIMSS study was conducted, new technologies related to the field of modern item response theory provided a technique by which student scores on the same underlying construct (for example, mathematics) could be obtained – even though the students completed different (but overlapped) sets of items. This approach removed the constraint that every pupil must be assessed with the same test in order for valid comparisons to be made among students.

Russell's views have been rejected by the TIMSS researchers (Beaton *et al.*, 1996). They showed that, when the participating countries were scored by using items focused on their own curricula, there were negligible differences between these country specific scores and the overall TIMSS test scores. Similarly the SACMEQ tests were shown to have high validity because the correlation between student scores based on items that each SACMEQ national co-ordinator said were focused on his/her own national curriculum, and the scores obtained from all items using the whole test ranged between 0.98 and 1.00.

Similar research findings were obtained by the PISA researchers by comparing student scores on the whole set of international items with students' scores computed only using the subset of items that were considered as 'most appropriate in their national context' by national experts. The correlations among the scores approached 1.00 for each country, confirming the high cross-national validity of the assessment instruments for all participating countries.

■ Different languages

Translation errors can be a source of equivalence problems in cross-national studies of the quality of education. Most studies employ one of two basic approaches to prevent them. The most popular approach uses forward translation by two or more independent translators. Each translator translates the source materials (usually developed in English) into the target language; then the independent versions are compared and reconciled into a final national version. Alternatively, a single forward translation into the target language is completed first, and then a second translator translates back into the source language. The original source materials and the back-translations are then compared, and possible deviations are corrected in the target version. PISA has introduced a more rigorous version of the multiple forward translation approach whereby parallel English and French source versions of the test are first prepared under the supervision of the group of international test developers. These two source versions are then provided to the translation teams in each participating country, who develop their target versions by independently translating the instruments from each source language, then by comparing the two versions obtained and reconciling them into a final national version.

In a number of current studies (PISA, TIMSS, PIRLS), the translation process (be it multiple forward translations or back translation) is followed by a central verification stage, where all countries submit their target version to translators appointed by the international study centre, who check the final equivalence of the various national versions against the source version. The goal is to ensure consistency and accuracy of translation across all participating countries.

However, even with accurate translation, items may differ in difficulty across languages. To intercept problems in this area, a psychometric technique known as Differential item Functioning (DIF) is used to identify test items that are susceptible to language and cultural influences. These items are then excluded from the study.

Target populations and sampling

■ Retention

Most cross-national studies of the quality of education have been focused on populations of students attending compulsory education, either at primary or lower secondary levels. In many countries, (but not in all of them, and certainly not in most of the developing countries that have participated in these studies) this means that the target populations correspond to age groups that are still 100 per cent (or almost) enrolled in schools, thereby providing a reasonably sound basis for cross-national comparisons.

81

However, cross-country differences in retention rates remain a serious comparability problem – both for studies conducted at the upper secondary level in industrialized countries, and for all populations assessed in developing countries. Researchers need to be very cautious when interpreting comparisons in student achievement across school systems where, for example, in one school system only 50 per cent of the children in the target age group attend school and, in another, up to 95 per cent are enrolled.

Low retention rates are likely to result in upward biases in the estimation of the overall mean achievement (since the assessed sample tends to contain a smaller proportion of low-achievement children). It also results in distorted estimation of achievement variance (since the enrolled group who sits the test is most probably more homogeneous in their proficiency than the whole age population).

In some earlier IEA studies, adjustment formulas were developed to permit approximate judgements on the effects of differences in retentivity on the estimation of country means. The later TIMSS approach, at the upper secondary level, was to define a sub-sample of students taking advanced mathematics or advanced science subjects (5-hour courses or more). Countries could then compare not only the mean achievement of their 'general' enrolled population, but also the level of proficiency attained by the group of students that were considered in each system as the 'elite group' preparing for future mathematics and science-oriented careers. This approach to analysis and reporting provided policy-relevant information because it is important for a country to know about the size and performance of their elite groups of students.

■   Differences between age-based and grade-based populations

Countries have different policies with regard to school-age entry, grade repetition, promotion, retention rates, enrolments and graduation. Cross-country variations in age and length of time in school can be expected to influence achievement, and hence are a threat for the comparability of target populations.

This problem is mainly addressed in cross-national studies by accurately defining the target population of students on a basis which is consistent with the aims of the study – that is, by using either an 'age/grade', or a 'pure grade' or a 'pure age' target population definition.

In the TIMSS study, for example, three populations of students were selected using two slightly different 'age/grade' definitions for the primary and lower secondary levels: students attending the modal grade where most of the 9-year-old students could be found; students attending the two contiguous grades where most of the 13-year-old students could be found, and (using a 'pure grade' definition for the upper secondary level) students completing the last year of secondary school. In SACMEQ, the target populations were defined as the students in Grade 6, also a 'pure grade' definition.

In PISA, a 'pure age' definition was used: students aged 15 at the time of testing. This definition resulted in the selection of students across several grade levels in some countries, and in some cases, across primary/secondary education levels. The PISA results therefore need to be interpreted with care when reporting information about the 'average student', and when comparing research results across countries with high and low levels of grade repetition. The choice between age-based or grade-based population affects the kinds of data analyses that can be undertaken, and also upon the interpretation of the data analyses.

   ▓   Differences in 'exclusion rules'

Sometimes countries exclude sections of the defined target population for a variety of reasons. Definitions of disability (physical, emotional and intellectual), for example, may differ across countries and result in the exclusion of different percentages of students. In others, the target population may exclude remote and inaccessible groups of students. Most studies have now developed clear standards governing population exclusions, in order to reduce them to a minimum (usually less than 5 per cent of the sampled students) and to ensure that all participating countries accurately document any deviation of their national sample from the internationally defined population.

   ▓   Differences in response rates

In most large-scale educational research surveys, there are some schools and some students who do not wish to participate. For cross-national studies, this can be a problem if response rates vary substantially across countries, because large amounts of non-response may lead to biases in research results. Most studies (for example, IEA, PISA, SACMEQ) require that participating countries document the actual response rates obtained as well as the effect of non-response on the nature of the sample.

These studies ensure that sampling requirements are well known to participating countries, and countries not conforming to those requirements are excluded from reports or their results are reported with caveats.

Reporting the results of cross-national studies

'League tables' and 'horse races'

A much-criticized aspect of international comparative studies is that they are deemed to encourage 'horse-race' interpretations of the results by publishing league tables in which countries are ranked in order of mean achievement scores. This encourages superficial (and often misleading) interpretations of the results, based on ranks, rather than on the magnitude and the statistical and pedagogical significance of the observed differences.

This type of presentation is often used, particularly in the media, to 'support' unwarranted conjectures about possible causal explanations for differences among the 'high' and 'low' ranking countries. In some cases, these 'explanations' grasp at a particular contextual variable and put this forward as the (only) reason for observed cross-national differences. For example, in the 1990s, when the first TIMSS results were published, a number of 'experts' in the United Kingdom claimed that the reason for the high mathematics and science achievement of East Asian countries was mainly due to the use of more 'whole class teaching'.

While whole class teaching may (or may not) impact positively on learning, it must always be recognized that the educational environment is formed from a complex inter- locking network of inputs, processes and contexts – which cannot be summarized by simply appealing to a one-dimensional explanation.

Multiple comparisons

To prevent misuse of the reported mean country scores, some studies have put great effort into designing information displays where tabulated data on student achievement levels are reported, and confidence limits are 'incorporated' in the layout of the table. An example from the TIMSS study is presented in *Figure 4.1*.

Figure 4.1   Multiple comparisons of national mean scores of the TIMSS mathematics scale

COUNTRY	Singapore	Czech Republic	Japan	Korea	Bulgaria	Netherlands	Slovenia	Austria	Hungary	England	Belgium (Fl)	Australia	Slovak Republic	Russian Federation	Ireland	Sweden	United States	Germany	Canada	Norway	New Zealand	Thailand	Israel	Hong Kong	Switzerland	Scotland	Spain	France	Greece	Iceland	Romania	Latvia (LSS)	Portugal	Denmark	Lithuania	Belgium (Fr.)	Iran, Islamic Rep.	Cyprus	Kuwait	Colombia	South Africa
Singapore		△	△	△	△	△	△	△	△	△	△	△	△	△	△	△	△	△	△	△	△	△	△	△	△	△	△	△	△	△	△	△	△	△	△	△	△	△	△	△	△
Czech Republic	▼		●	●	●	●	●	●	△	△	△	△	△	△	△	△	△	△	△	△	△	△	△	△	△	△	△	△	△	△	△	△	△	△	△	△	△	△	△	△	△
Japan	▼	●		●	●	●	△	△	△	△	△	△	△	△	△	△	△	△	△	△	△	△	△	△	△	△	△	△	△	△	△	△	△	△	△	△	△	△	△	△	△
Korea	▼	●	●		●	●	△	△	●	△	△	△	△	△	△	△	△	△	△	△	△	△	△	△	△	△	△	△	△	△	△	△	△	△	△	△	△	△	△	△	△
Bulgaria	▼	●	●	●		●	●	●	●	●	●	●	△	△	△	△	△	△	△	△	△	△	△	△	△	△	△	△	△	△	△	△	△	△	△	△	△	△	△	△	△
Netherlands	▼	●	●	●	●		●	●	●	●	●	●	△	△	△	△	△	△	△	△	△	△	△	△	△	△	△	△	△	△	△	△	△	△	△	△	△	△	△	△	△
Slovenia	▼	●	▼	▼	●	●		●	●	●	●	△	△	△	△	△	△	△	△	△	△	△	△	△	△	△	△	△	△	△	△	△	△	△	△	△	△	△	△	△	△
Austria	▼	●	▼	▼	●	●	●		●	●	△	△	△	△	△	△	△	△	△	△	△	△	△	△	△	△	△	△	△	△	△	△	△	△	△	△	△	△	△	△	△
Hungary	▼	▼	▼	●	●	●	●	●		●	●	●	●	●	△	△	△	△	△	△	△	△	△	△	△	△	△	△	△	△	△	△	△	△	△	△	△	△	△	△	△
England	▼	▼	▼	▼	●	●	●	●	●		●	●	●	●	●	△	●	△	△	△	△	△	△	△	△	△	△	△	△	△	△	△	△	△	△	△	△	△	△	△	△
Belgium (Fl)	▼	▼	▼	▼	●	●	●	▼	●	●		●	●	●	●	●	●	●	△	△	△	△	△	●	△	△	△	△	△	△	△	△	△	△	△	△	△	△	△	△	△
Australia	▼	▼	▼	▼	●	●	▼	▼	●	●	●		●	●	●	●	●	●	●	△	△	△	△	●	△	△	△	△	△	△	△	△	△	△	△	△	△	△	△	△	△
Slovak Republic	▼	▼	▼	▼	▼	▼	▼	▼	●	●	●	●		●	●	●	●	●	●	△	△	△	△	●	△	△	△	△	△	△	△	△	△	△	△	△	△	△	△	△	△
Russian Federation	▼	▼	▼	▼	▼	▼	▼	▼	●	●	●	●	●		●	●	●	●	●	●	△	△	△	●	△	△	△	△	△	△	△	△	△	△	△	△	△	△	△	△	△
Ireland	▼	▼	▼	▼	▼	▼	▼	▼	▼	●	●	●	●	●		●	●	●	●	●	●	△	△	●	△	△	△	△	△	△	△	△	△	△	△	△	△	△	△	△	△
Sweden	▼	▼	▼	▼	▼	▼	▼	▼	▼	▼	●	●	●	●	●		●	●	●	●	●	△	●	△	△	△	△	△	△	△	△	△	△	△	△	△	△	△	△	△	△
United States	▼	▼	▼	▼	▼	▼	▼	▼	▼	●	●	●	●	●	●	●		●	●	●	●	●	△	△	△	△	△	△	△	△	△	△	△	△	△	△	△	△	△	△	△
Germany	▼	▼	▼	▼	▼	▼	▼	▼	▼	▼	●	●	●	●	●	●	●		●	●	●	●	●	●	△	△	△	△	△	△	△	△	△	△	△	△	△	△	△	△	△
Canada	▼	▼	▼	▼	▼	▼	▼	▼	▼	▼	▼	●	●	●	●	●	●	●		●	●	●	●	●	●	△	△	△	△	△	△	△	△	△	△	△	△	△	△	△	△
Norway	▼	▼	▼	▼	▼	▼	▼	▼	▼	▼	▼	▼	▼	●	●	●	●	●	●		●	●	●	●	●	△	△	△	△	△	△	△	△	△	△	△	△	△	△	△	△
New Zealand	▼	▼	▼	▼	▼	▼	▼	▼	▼	▼	▼	▼	▼	●	●	●	●	●	●	●		●	●	●	●	△	△	△	△	△	△	△	△	△	△	△	△	△	△	△	△
Thailand	▼	▼	▼	▼	▼	▼	▼	▼	▼	▼	▼	▼	▼	●	●	●	●	●	●	●	●		●	●	●	△	△	△	△	△	△	△	△	△	△	△	△	△	△	△	△
Israel	▼	▼	▼	▼	▼	▼	▼	▼	▼	▼	▼	▼	▼	▼	●	●	●	●	●	●	●	●		●	●	△	△	△	△	△	△	△	△	△	△	△	△	△	△	△	△
Hong Kong	▼	▼	▼	▼	▼	▼	▼	▼	▼	▼	▼	▼	▼	▼	▼	●	●	●	●	●	●	●	●		●	●	△	△	△	△	△	△	△	△	△	△	△	△	△	△	△
Switzerland	▼	▼	▼	▼	▼	▼	▼	▼	▼	▼	▼	▼	▼	▼	▼	▼	●	●	●	●	●	●	●	●		●	△	△	△	△	△	△	△	△	△	△	△	△	△	△	△
Scotland	▼	▼	▼	▼	▼	▼	▼	▼	▼	▼	▼	▼	▼	▼	▼	▼	●	●	●	●	●	●	●	●	●		●	△	△	△	△	△	△	△	△	△	△	△	△	△	△
Spain	▼	▼	▼	▼	▼	▼	▼	▼	▼	▼	▼	▼	▼	▼	▼	▼	▼	●	▼	▼	●	●	●	●	●	●		△	△	△	△	△	△	△	△	△	△	△	△	△	△
France	▼	▼	▼	▼	▼	▼	▼	▼	▼	▼	▼	▼	▼	▼	▼	▼	▼	▼	▼	▼	▼	▼	▼	▼	▼	▼	▼		●	●	△	△	△	△	△	△	△	△	△	△	△
Greece	▼	▼	▼	▼	▼	▼	▼	▼	▼	▼	▼	▼	▼	▼	▼	▼	▼	▼	▼	▼	▼	▼	▼	▼	▼	▼	▼	●		●	●	△	△	△	△	△	△	△	△	△	△
Iceland	▼	▼	▼	▼	▼	▼	▼	▼	▼	▼	▼	▼	▼	▼	▼	▼	▼	▼	▼	▼	▼	▼	▼	▼	▼	▼	●	●	●		●	●	●	△	△	△	△	△	△	△	△
Romania	▼	▼	▼	▼	▼	▼	▼	▼	▼	▼	▼	▼	▼	▼	▼	▼	▼	▼	▼	▼	▼	▼	▼	▼	▼	▼	▼	●	●	●		●	●	●	●	△	△	△	△	△	△
Latvia (LSS)	▼	▼	▼	▼	▼	▼	▼	▼	▼	▼	▼	▼	▼	▼	▼	▼	▼	▼	▼	▼	▼	▼	▼	▼	▼	▼	▼	●	●	●	●		●	●	●	△	△	△	△	△	△
Portugal	▼	▼	▼	▼	▼	▼	▼	▼	▼	▼	▼	▼	▼	▼	▼	▼	▼	▼	▼	▼	▼	▼	▼	▼	▼	▼	▼	●	●	●	●	●		●	●	△	△	△	△	△	△
Denmark	▼	▼	▼	▼	▼	▼	▼	▼	▼	▼	▼	▼	▼	▼	▼	▼	▼	▼	▼	▼	▼	▼	▼	▼	▼	▼	▼	●	●	●	●	●	●		●	●	△	△	△	△	△
Lithuania	▼	▼	▼	▼	▼	▼	▼	▼	▼	▼	▼	▼	▼	▼	▼	▼	▼	▼	▼	▼	▼	▼	▼	▼	▼	▼	▼	●	●	●	●	●	●	●		●	●	△	△	△	△
Belgium (Fr.)	▼	▼	▼	▼	▼	▼	▼	▼	▼	▼	▼	▼	▼	▼	▼	▼	▼	▼	▼	▼	▼	▼	▼	▼	▼	▼	▼	▼	●	●	●	●	●	●	●		●	●	△	△	△
Iran, Islamic Rep.	▼	▼	▼	▼	▼	▼	▼	▼	▼	▼	▼	▼	▼	▼	▼	▼	▼	▼	▼	▼	▼	▼	▼	▼	▼	▼	▼	▼	●	▼	●	●	●	●	●	●		●	△	△	△
Cyprus	▼	▼	▼	▼	▼	▼	▼	▼	▼	▼	▼	▼	▼	▼	▼	▼	▼	▼	▼	▼	▼	▼	▼	▼	▼	▼	▼	▼	▼	▼	▼	▼	●	●	●	●	●		△	△	△
Kuwait	▼	▼	▼	▼	▼	▼	▼	▼	▼	▼	▼	▼	▼	▼	▼	▼	▼	▼	▼	▼	▼	▼	▼	▼	▼	▼	▼	▼	▼	▼	▼	▼	▼	▼	▼	▼	▼	▼		△	△
Colombia	▼	▼	▼	▼	▼	▼	▼	▼	▼	▼	▼	▼	▼	▼	▼	▼	▼	▼	▼	▼	▼	▼	▼	▼	▼	▼	▼	▼	▼	▼	▼	▼	▼	▼	▼	▼	▼	▼	▼		△
South Africa	▼	▼	▼	▼	▼	▼	▼	▼	▼	▼	▼	▼	▼	▼	▼	▼	▼	▼	▼	▼	▼	▼	▼	▼	▼	▼	▼	▼	▼	▼	▼	▼	▼	▼	▼	▼	▼	▼	▼	▼	

Source: Beaton *et al.*, 1996

Similar tables are used in PISA and PIRLS. In these so-called multi-comparison tables, specific icons are used to show, for each pair of countries, whether the mean score of country X was significantly higher (upward triangle ?) or significantly lower (downward triangle ?) than the mean score of country Y, or whether the difference was not statistically significant (circle ?).

This way of reporting country results helps to indicate that ranks or average scores alone do not tell the whole story. That is, while differences may be observed among the rankings of countries, they may only be

85

attributable to uncertainties associated with sampling stability and therefore the use of ranking may be questionable.

It is important to note that in some national and cross-national studies the inappropriate use of standard statistical software (where the default option assumes that data were collected using simple random sampling) has resulted in serious underestimation of standard errors. Consequently, differences between countries or between regions within countries, or between specific groups of students, may have been considered as significant, when they actually were not.

Graphical displays

Other sophisticated graphical presentations are used in international studies in order to report differences (or similarities) between national mean scores in a manner that draws attention to differences (or similarities) in their dispersion, and to their precision as estimates of population values. An example from the TIMSS study is presented in *Figure 4.2*.

Figure 4.2 shows several pieces of information. Apart from the mean and standard error on the scaled score, it also indicates the grade attended, the average age of pupils and the distribution of scores. The black zone in the centre of each bar represents the mean and standard error range. The grey shaded zone surrounding this represents the locations of the middle 50 per cent of students, and the limits of the bar represents the range from 5 per cent to the 95 per cent of the sample for each country.

Described scales

While there has been a continuing trend to report test score distributions and standard errors, there is also an emerging trend to report distributions in terms of levels of competence. This has far greater utility in terms of policy development.

Competency continua are established using item response modelling, and then obtaining from domain experts a detailed description of the skills required to answer the test items corresponding to various score points on the continuum. These 'item maps' enable an interpretation of the underlying variable measured by the tests. By setting cut-points on the scale, different levels of proficiency can be established, and results can be reported in a much more meaningful manner. This approach provides policy-makers with information on the percentages of students in their population who are proficient at each competency level, and with information on knowledge and skills that students at each level have actually mastered.

Figure 4.2   Comparisons of countries' results in mathematics in TIMSS, illustrating the use of distribution of scores as a basis for comparison

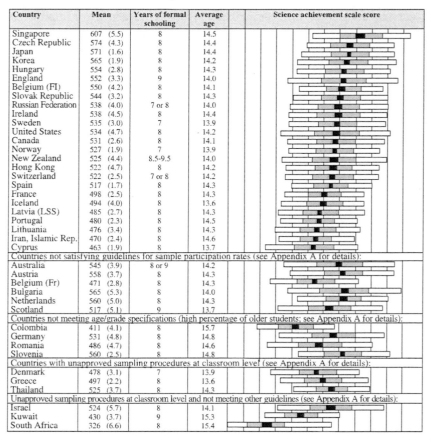

Country	Mean	Years of formal schooling	Average age	Science achievement scale score
Singapore	607 (5.5)	8	14.5	
Czech Republic	574 (4.3)	8	14.4	
Japan	571 (1.6)	8	14.4	
Korea	565 (1.9)	8	14.2	
Hungary	554 (2.8)	8	14.3	
England	552 (3.3)	9	14.0	
Belgium (Fl)	550 (4.2)	8	14.1	
Slovak Republic	544 (3.2)	8	14.3	
Russian Federation	538 (4.0)	7 or 8	14.0	
Ireland	538 (4.5)	8	14.4	
Sweden	535 (3.0)	7	13.9	
United States	534 (4.7)	8	14.2	
Canada	531 (2.6)	8	14.1	
Norway	527 (1.9)	7	13.9	
New Zealand	525 (4.4)	8.5-9.5	14.0	
Hong Kong	522 (4.7)	8	14.2	
Switzerland	522 (2.5)	7 or 8	14.2	
Spain	517 (1.7)	8	14.3	
France	498 (2.5)	8	14.3	
Iceland	494 (4.0)	8	13.6	
Latvia (LSS)	485 (2.7)	8	14.3	
Portugal	480 (2.3)	8	14.5	
Lithuania	476 (3.4)	8	14.3	
Iran, Islamic Rep.	470 (2.4)	8	14.6	
Cyprus	463 (1.9)	8	13.7	
Countries not satisfying guidelines for sample participation rates (see Appendix A for details):				
Australia	545 (3.9)	8 or 9	14.2	
Austria	558 (3.7)	8	14.3	
Belgium (Fr)	471 (2.8)	8	14.3	
Bulgaria	565 (5.3)	8	14.0	
Netherlands	560 (5.0)	8	14.3	
Scotland	517 (5.1)	9	13.7	
Countries not meeting age/grade specifications (high percentage of older students; see Appendix A for details):				
Colombia	411 (4.1)	8	15.7	
Germany	531 (4.8)	8	14.8	
Romania	486 (4.7)	8	14.6	
Slovenia	560 (2.5)	8	14.8	
Countries with unapproved sampling procedures at classroom level (see Appendix A for details):				
Denmark	478 (3.1)	7	13.9	
Greece	497 (2.2)	8	13.6	
Thailand	525 (3.7)	8	14.3	
Unapproved sampling procedures at classroom level and not meeting other guidelines (see Appendix A for details):				
Israel	524 (5.7)	8	14.1	
Kuwait	430 (3.7)	9	15.3	
South Africa	326 (6.6)	8	15.4	

Source: Beaton *et al.*, 1996

Since the end of the 1980s most international studies have used described scales (IAEP to IEA/RLS, IALS, TIMSS, SACMEQ, and PISA) to report achievement or proficiency levels. This presentation emphasizes that there is a complementary reporting approach to the use of means and standard errors, and that the use of standards referenced scales is a method of communicating to policy-makers that 'intervention programmes only based on means can be misinterpreted'.

In the SACMEQ study, teachers were assessed using a test that overlapped with the test taken by their own students; this permitted their results to be mapped on to the same scale – a quite relevant source of information for the country authorities. The percentages of pupils and teachers at each reading competency level are presented in *Figure 4.3*.

Figure 4.3   Competency levels of Grade 6 pupils and their teachers in the SACMEQ II project

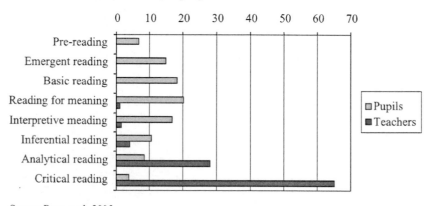

Source: Ross *et al.*, 2005.

SACMEQ's main objective was to assist in capacity building within each country, and to help to build policy aimed at improving performances. It has now released data archives for both SACMEQ I and SACMEQ II projects. International comparisons are planned, and some are beginning to emerge. In addition, intra-national studies are using descriptive scales.

As a further example, the described scale used in the IAEP study as a basis for reporting cross-country results in science is presented in *Box 1*.

This form of reporting enables more interesting reflections on the relations between achievement and teaching. Benchmarks can be set, but, more importantly, intervention strategies can be developed for students at every level – not just for the students below the expected levels of achievement. This has far-reaching implications for curriculum and policy developers.

Box 1.   The IAEP competency levels for science

Level 700   Integrate scientific information and experimental evidence

Students at this level can interpret experimental data that involve several variables. They also can interrelate information represented in a variety of forms –text, graphs, figures, and diagrams. Students can make predictions based on data and observations and are aware of limitations of extrapolations. Students demonstrate a growing understanding of more advanced scientific knowledge and concepts, such as the definition of a calorie or the concept of chemical change.

Level 600   Understand and apply intermediate scientific knowledge and principles

Students at this level demonstrate an understanding of intermediate scientific facts and principles and can apply this understanding in designing experiments and interpreting data. They also can interpret figures and diagrams used to convey scientific information. Students at this level can infer relationships and draw conclusions by applying facts and principles, particularly from physical science.

Level 500   Use scientific procedures and analyse scientific data

Students at this level have a grasp of experimental procedures used in science, such as designing experiments, controlling variables, and using equipment. They can identify the best conclusions drawn from data on a graph and the best explanation for observed phenomena. Students also understand some concepts in a variety of science content areas, including the Life Sciences, Physical Sciences, and Earth and Space Sciences.

Level 400   Understand and apply simple scientific principles

Students at this level exhibit growing knowledge in the Life Sciences, particularly human biological systems, and can apply some basic principles from the Physical Sciences, including force. They also display a beginning understanding of some of the basic methods of reasoning used in science, including classification and interpretation of statements.

Level 300   Know everyday science facts

Students at this level know some general science facts of the type that can be learned from everyday experiences. For example, they exhibit some rudimentary knowledge concerning the environment and animals.

Source: Lapointe *et al.*, 1989

The manner in which international study results are reported can have a substantial impact on generating public opinion and policy decisions. It is also important to recognize that despite all efforts deployed in the subtle presentations of the data, little can be done to prevent the media from focusing on the most 'visible' results of international comparisons – the 'horse-race' aspects. However, well-conducted studies provide information that goes well beyond spectacular rankings and their shortsighted impact on national egos. A merit of comparisons is that, by illustrating the high levels of achievement that have been attained in some of the participating countries, the researchers are able to provide empirical evidence that such levels are 'within reach by other education systems'. In this respect, comparative results have often proved to be a powerful impetus to encourage countries to investigate why their students were less proficient, and to show what could be done to improve their own education systems.

Conclusion

In a number of countries, results from international studies (such as those conducted by the IEA and the OECD) have had a strong impact on the public by bringing the issue of excellence to the fore. In many school systems, people tend to hold a comfortable opinion that their school system is 'the best in the world', and shocks are created when empirical evidence indicates that this is perhaps a questionable point of view. As noted by Beaton *et al.* (1999) and by Postlethwaite (2004), cross-national studies have often played a significant role by encouraging improvements in educational investments, the implementation of curriculum reviews, the establishment of new standards, the review of teacher training programmes, and have often forced increased consideration of disparities in school resources, school organization, and teaching practices.

For example, the impact of IEA studies both in Sweden and the United States have resulted in changes to curriculum and school-based practices. Hungary's participation in IEA studies led to curriculum reform in reading, and the finding that home factors were more influential than school factors has led to a review of curricular ideologies in a number of Eastern European countries. In Norway, the TIMSS results have informed policy regarding curricula for upper secondary education, resulted in increased attention being given to guidelines in response to gender differences in achievement, and caused revisions in curriculum for teacher education because it became apparent that primary teachers' backgrounds in mathematics and science needed to be strengthened.

At the primary-school level, between-school differences are quite large in developing countries where dramatic disparities are observed in schooling conditions, teacher qualifications, provision of textbooks, and other instructional materials. In industrialized countries, where instructional inputs and resources tend to be uniform across primary schools in a given system, variables such as teacher qualifications or availability of textbooks are generally associated with only negligible variations in achievement.

Cross-country exploration of factors associated with achievement progressively challenged the *Coleman report*'s famous finding that "school resources and processes had little impact on students' achievement after taking into account the differences attributable to student's home background". Certainly, home background characteristics remain a universal determinant of achievement differences, both in industrialized and developing countries. However, the strength of correlations between students' socio-economic background and achievement varies across countries, suggesting that some systems may be more effective than others in moderating the effects of disadvantage, and in providing more equal learning opportunities to the various social groups composing their population.

Similarly, the magnitude and patterns of gender gaps in achievement differs across countries, and seems to be dependent upon cultural and organizational differences. While male/female disparities have been reduced over time in mathematics (and to a lesser extent in science), new concerns have emerged as regards reading, a domain in which boys tend to achieve less well than girls in a majority of countries. Specific programmes aimed at the reduction of gender gaps have been shown to be effective in a number of cases (Keeves, 1995).

While the cross-national studies have identified a number of school variables that seem to 'work' in producing higher levels of proficiency (for example, student achievement has been found to be positively related both to the time given to the study of the subject at school and to the time spent on homework), the most important message conveyed to policy-makers by international comparisons seems to be that, in general, the impact of any single school variable is small, and often linked to a variety of other aspects of the educational context. No spectacular progress in achievement can probably be expected by just implementing some 'miracle' innovation, copied from a specific aspect found in high-achieving school systems. By contrast, much can be learned by carefully examining how important positive and negative factors interact in a variety of other systems, in order to redesign national reforms.

Governments have shown increasing interest and financial support for these research efforts, based on the general assumption that progress in literacy and numeracy among the working population will yield a better quality of life and improved economic competitiveness. For example, OECD and the World Bank have often based their arguments in favour of better monitoring of education on the relationship between educational achievement and productivity growth at a national level (OECD, 1989). Whether the nature of this relationship is causal or not is, however, a much-debated issue. McKenzie and Wurzburg (1998) have argued that the evidence relies on comparisons between countries at different stages of development, and the relationship may well be spurious. IEA publications indicate that there is "little firm evidence to support the widely held view that there is a strong and direct causal connection between mean student test scores for nations and their economic competitiveness" (Beaton *et al.*, 1999).

The authors of a recent synthesis of related literature have (Hannum and Buchman, 2003) proposed a more balanced view. They concluded that the evidence about the effects of education on the economic growth of nations is indeed mixed, with some of the studies showing positive effects, and some indicating no short-term effects. At the individual level, the effects are almost universally positive, although with huge variations in the magnitude of economic returns per additional year of schooling, depending upon a variety of national factors. Further, there is strong evidence that education has positive effects on overall health, decrease of mortality, and moderation of demographic growth. There also seems to be some clear evidence that education contributes to reducing gender inequality – but not other types of inequality, such as relative socioeconomic or ethnic disadvantage.

Thus, the debate on long-term outcomes of education appears far from closed, and it will likely continue to fuel – rather than reduce – the interest of policy-makers in international comparisons of the outputs of their school systems.

References

Beaton, A.; Martin, M.; Mullis, I.; Gonzalez, E.; Smith, T.; Kelly, D. 1996. *Science achievement in the middle school years.* Boston: IEA, TIMSS International Study Center.

Beaton, A.; Postlethwaite, T.N.; Ross, K.; Spearritt, D.; Wolf, R. 1999. *The benefits and limitations of international educational achievement studies.* Paris: IIEP-UNESCO.

Blum, H.; Goldstein, H.; Guérin-Pace, F. 2001. "IALS: An analysis of international comparisons of adult literacy". In: *Assessment in Education, 8*(2), 225-246.

Coleman, J.S. 1966. *The equality of educational opportunity study.* Washington, DC: U.S. Department of Health, Education, and Welfare, Office of Education.

Comber, L.C.; Keeves, J.P. 1973. *Science education in nineteen countries.* Stockholm: Almquist & Wiksell.

Elley, W. 1992. *How in the world do students read?* Hamburg: International Association for the Evaluation of Educational Achievement (IEA).

Freudenthal, H. 1975. "Pupils' achievements internationally compared". *Educational Studies in Mathematics, 6,* 126-186.

Goldstein, H.; Wood, R. 1989. "Five decades of response modelling". *British Journal of Mathematical and Statistical Psychology, 42,* 139-167.

Griffin, P. (In press). Total test-score variable. An approach to the validity issue: A comment on Russell's zero-sum hypothesis. *Curriculum Inquiry.*

Griffin, P. 2001. *New directions in the measurement of literacy and numeracy: The SACMEQ tests and their linkages to levels of competence.* Paper presented at the UNESCO Policy Forum for the SACMEQ Assembly of Ministers. Paris: IIEP-UNESCO. October.

Hannum, E.; Buchmann, C. 2003. *The consequences of global educational expansion.* Cambridge, MA: American Academy of Arts and Sciences.

Husén, T. (Ed.). 1967. *A comparison of twelve countries: international study of achievement in mathematics.* Vols. 1-2. Stockholm: Almquist & Wiksell.

Keeves, J. 1995. The world of school learning: selected key findings from 35 years of IEA research. Fundamentals of Educational Planning 071. The Hague: IEA.

Lapointe, A.; Mead, N. A.; Phillips, G. W. 1989. *A world of differences: An international assessment of mathematics and science.* Princeton NJ: Educational Testing Service.

Martin, M.O., Kelly, D.L. (Eds.). (1996). *TIMSS technical report: Vol.1. Design and development.* Chestnut Hill, MA: Boston College.

McKenzie, P.; Wurzburg, G. 1998. *Lifelong learning and employability.* *OECD Observer*, *207*, 13-17.

National Commission on Excellence in Education (1983). *A nation at risk: The imperative for educational reform superintendent of documents*. Publication no. 20402. U.S. Government Printing Office: Washington, DC.

Mullis, I.V.S.; Kennedy, A.M.; Martin, M.O.; Sainsbury, M. 2004. *PIRLS (Programme in International Reading Literacy Study) 2006: Assessment framework and specifications*. International Association for the Evaluation of Educational Achievement (IEA): Chestnut Hill, MA.

OECD. 1989. *Employment outlook.* Paris: OECD.

OECD. 1996. *Lifelong learning for all.* Paris: OECD.

OECD. 2001. *Knowledge and skills for life: First results from PISA 2000.* Paris: OECD.

OECD. 2004. *Learning for tomorrow's world: First results from PISA 2003.* Paris: OECD.

OECD; UNESCO. 2003. *Literacy skills for the world of tomorrow: Further results from PISA 2000.* Paris: OECD; UNESCO-UIS.

Peaker, G. 1975. *An empirical study of education in 21 countries: A technical report.* Stockholm: Almqvist & Wicksell.

Plomp, T. (1999, August). *The relevance of IEA type international comparative assessments of educational achievement.* Paper presented at the 40th General Assembly of IEA Oslo.

Postlethwaite, T.N. 2004. *What do international assessment studies tell us about the quality of school systems?.* Retrieved 5 July 2005 from: http://portal.unesco.org/education/en/ev.php-URL_ID=36356&URL_DO=DO_PRINTPAGE&URL_SECTION=201.html

Rosier, M.J.; Keeves, J.P. 1991. *Science education and curricula in twenty-three countries: The IEA study of science.* Oxford: Pergamon Press.

Ross, K.; Saito, M.; Dolata, S.; Ikeda, M. 2005. *SACMEQ data archive.* Paris: IIEP-UNESCO.

Russell, H. 1981. *Validity patterns and the total test score variable.* Mimeo. Toronto: OISE.

Russell, H. 1982. *Total score. Subscore group: Comments.* Memorandum IEA (Maths-NZ) A./362. Wellington: Department of Education.

Russell, H. In press. Connecting issues in education. *Curriculum Inquiry.*

Thorndike, R.L. 1973. *Reading comprehension education in fifteen countries.* Stockholm: Almquist & Wiksell.

Travers, K.J.; Westbury, I. (Eds.). 1989. *The IEA study of mathematics: Analysis of mathematics curricula.* Oxford: Pergamon.

Tuijnman, A. 2000. *Benchmarking adult literacy in America: An international comparative study.* Ottowa: Statistics Canada.

Tuijnman, A.; Kirsch, I.S.; Jones, S.; Murray, T.S. 1994. *Literacy, economy, and society: Results of the first International Adult Literacy Survey.* Paris: OECD.

UNESCO. 1990. *World declaration on education for all.* New York: UNDP, UNESCO, UNICEF, World Bank.

UNESCO. 2000. *Education for all. Status and trends 2000. Assessing learning achievement.* Paris: UNESCO.

United Nations. 2000. *United Nations millennium declaration.* (Resolution adopted by the General Assembly A/RES/55/2). New York: United Nations.

Appendix: International studies published since the 1960s

Study	Domains assessed	Countries	Target populations	Main publications
1964. IEA/FIMS First International Mathematics Study	Mathematics	12 countries: Australia, Belgium, England, Finland, France, Germany (FRG), Israel, Japan, Netherlands, Scotland, Sweden, United States.	Students attending the modal grade for 13 year olds (11 countries); Students attending the last year of secondary education (10 countries)	Husén, T. (Ed.). 1967. *A comparison of twelve countries: International study of achievement in mathematics* (Vols. 1-2). Stockholm: Almquist & Wiksell.
1970-71. IEA/FISS First International Science Study	Science	19 countries: Australia, Belgium (Flemish), Belgium (French), Chile, England, Germany (FRG), Finland, France, Hungary, India, Iran, Italy, Japan, Netherlands, New Zealand, Scotland, Sweden, Thailand, United States.	Pop. I: 10-year-old students (16 countries);Pop II:14-year old-students (18 countries); Pop IV: Students attending the last year of secondary education (18 countries).	Comber, L.C.; Keeves, J.P. 1973. *Science education in nineteen countries.* Stockholm: Almquist & Wiksell; New York: John Wiley & Sons.
1970-71. IEA/RCS Reading Comprehension Study	Reading	15 countries: Belgium (Flemish), Belgium (French), Chile, England, Finland, Hungary, India, Iran, Israel, Italy, Netherlands, New Zealand, Scotland, Sweden, United States.	Pop. I:10-year-old students (14 countries); Pop II:14-year old-students (15 countries); Pop IV: Students attending the last year of secondary education (15 countries).	Thorndike, R.L. 1973. *Reading comprehension education in fifteen countries: An empirical study.* Stockholm: Almquist & Wiksell.
1970-71. IEA/Literature Study	Literature	10 countries: Belgium (Flemish), Belgium (French), Chile, England, Finland, Iran, Italy, New Zealand, Sweden, United States.	Pop II:14-year old-students; Pop IV: Students attending the last year of secondary education.	Purves, A.C. 1973. *Literature education in ten countries.* Stockholm: Almquist & Wiksell; New York: John Wiley & Sons.
1970-71. IEA/French as a foreign language Study	French as a foreign language	8 countries: Chile, England, Netherlands, New Zealand, Romania, Scotland, Sweden, United States.	Pop II:14-year old-student Pop IV: Students attending the last year of secondary education.	Carrol, J.B. 1975. *The teaching of French as a foreign language in eight countries.* Stockholm: Almquist & Wiksell; New York: John Wiley & Sons.

Study	Domains assessed	Countries	Target populations	Main publications
1970-71. IEA/English as a foreign language Study	English as a foreign language	10 countries: Belgium (French) Chile, Federal Republic of Germany (FRG), Finland, Hungary, Israel, Netherlands, Sweden, Thailand.	Pop II: 14-year old-students; Pop IV: Students attending the last year of secondary education	Lewis, E.G.; Massad, C.E. 1975. *The teaching of English as a foreign language in ten countries.* Stockholm: Almqvist & Wiksell; New York: John Wiley.
1971. IEA/First Civic Education Study	Civic Knowledge and attitudes	10 countries: Finland, Germany (FRG), Iran, Ireland, Israel, Italy, Netherlands, New Zealand, Sweden, United States.	Pop II: 14-year old-students; Pop IV: Students attending the last year of secondary education	Farnen, R.F., Oppenheim, A.N., Torney, J. 1976. *Civic education in ten countries: An empirical study.* Stockholm: Almqvist & Wiksell; New York: John Wiley.
1982. **IEA/SIMS** Second International Mathematics Study (SIMS)	Mathematics	20 countries: Belgium (Flemish), Belgium (French), Canada (British Columbia and Ontario), England and Wales, Finland, France, Hong Kong, Hungary, Israel, Japan, Luxembourg, Netherlands, New Zealand, Nigeria, Scotland, Swaziland, Sweden, Thailand, United States	Pop A: Students attending the modal grade for 13-year old students; Pop B: Students in the last year of secondary education and attending about 5 hours of Maths courses per week.	Robitaille, D.F.; Garden. R.A. (Eds.). 1989. *The IEA study of mathematics II: Context and outcomes of school mathematics.* Oxford: Pergamon Press.
1983-84. **IEA/SISS** Second International Science Study	Science	23 countries: Australia, Canada, China, England, Finland, Ghana, Hong Kong, Hungary, Israel, Italy, Japan, Korea, Netherlands, Nigeria, Norway, Papua New Guinea, Philippines, Poland, Singapore, Sweden, Thailand, United States, Zimbabwe.	Pop 1 (15 countries): Students attending the modal grade for 10 year old students; Pop 2 (17 countries): Students attending the modal grade for 13-year old students; Pop 3 (13 countries): Students in the last year of secondary education.	Postlethwaite, T.N.; Wiley, D.E. (Eds.). 1992. *Science achievement in twenty-three countries: The IEA study of science II.* Oxford: Pergamon Press.

Study	Domains assessed	Countries	Target populations	Main publications
1988. **ETS/IAEP-1** First International Assessment of Educational Progress (IAEP-I, Mathematics and Science)	Mathematics, science	6 countries: Canada (4 provinces), Ireland, Korea, Spain, United Kingdom, and United States.	13-year-old students.	Lapointe, A.E.; Mead, N.A.; Phillips, G.W. 1989. *A world of differences: An international assessment of mathematics and science. Report of the First International Assessment of Educational Progress.* Report No. 19-CAEP-01. January. Educational Testing Service, Princeton, New Jersey.
1991. **ETS/IAEP-2** Second International Assessment of Educational Progress (IAEP-II, Mathematics and Science)	Mathematics, science, geography	20 countries: Brazil (2 cities), Canada (9 provinces), China (20 provinces), England, France, Hungary, Ireland, Israel (Hebrew), Italy (Emilia-Romagna), Jordan, Korea, Mozambique (2 cities), Portugal, Scotland, Slovenia, Soviet Union (14 republics), Spain (Spanish schools), Switzerland (15 cantons), Taiwan, United States.	Pop 1 (14 countries): Age 9 students; Pop. 2 (20 countries): Age 13 students	Lazer, S. 1992. *Learning about the world. report of the international assessment of educational progress.* Report No. 22-CAEP-05. June. Educational Testing Service, Princeton, New Jersey.
1990-91. **IEA/RLS** Reading Literacy Study	Reading	32 countries: Belgium (French), Botswana, Canada (British Columbia), Cyprus, Denmark, Finland, France, Germany (East), Germany (West), Greece, Hong Kong, Hungary, Iceland, Indonesia, Ireland, Italy, The Netherlands, Nigeria, New Zealand, Norway, Philippines, Portugal, Singapore, Slovenia, Spain, Sweden, Switzerland, Thailand, Trinidad and Tobago, the United States, Venezuela, Zimbabwe.	Pop A (28 countries): Students attending the modal grade for 9-year-old students; Pop. B (31 countries): Students attending the modal grade for 14-year old students.	Elley, W.B. 1992. *How in the world do students read? IEA study of reading literacy.* The Hague: IEA.

Study	Domains assessed	Countries	Target populations	Main publications
1988-92. **IEA/COMPED** Computers in Education Study	ICT education; ICT familiarity and attitudes	Phase 1: 22 countries Phase 2: 12 countries. Austria, Belgium-Flemish, Belgium-French, Bulgaria, Canada-British Columbia, China, France, Germany, Greece, Hungary, India, Israel, Italy, Japan, Latvia, Luxembourg, Netherlands, New Zealand, Poland, Portugal, Slovenia, Switzerland, Thailand, and the United States of America.	Population 1: students attending the modal grade for 10 years-old students. Population 2: students attending the modal grade for 13 years-old students. Population 3: students in the next-to-last year of secondary education.	Pelgrum, W.J.; Plomp, T. 1991. *The use of computers in education worldwide: Results from the IEA computers in education survey in 19 education systems.* Oxford, UK: Pergamon Press.
1994-98. **OECD-STATCAN /** **IALS** International Adult Literacy Survey	Reading literacy, numeracy	20 countries: Australia, Belgium-Flemish, Canada, Chile, Czech Republic, Denmark, Finland, Germany, Hungary, Ireland, Netherlands, New Zealand, Norway, Poland, Portugal, Slovenia, Sweden, Switzerland, United Kingdom, United States of America.	Adults aged 16-65.	OECD-STATCAN. 2000. *Literacy in the information age: final report of the international adult literacy survey.* Paris and Ottawa: OECD and Statistics Canada.
1994-95. **IEA/TIMSS** Third International Mathematics and Science Study	Mathematics, science	46 countries: Argentina, Australia, Austria, Belgium (Flemish), Belgium (French), Bulgaria, Canada, Colombia, Cyprus, Czech Republic, Denmark, England, France, Germany, Greece, Hong Kong, Hungary, Iceland, Indonesia, Iran, Ireland, Israel, Italy, Japan, Korea, Kuwait, Latvia, Lithuania, Mexico, Netherlands, New Zealand, Norway, Philippines, Portugal, Romania, Russian Federation, Scotland, Singapore, Slovak Republic, Slovenia, South Africa, Spain, Sweden, Switzerland, Thailand, United States.	Pop 1.Students enrolled in the two grades containing the largest proportion of nine-year-old students (29 countries); Pop. 2: Students enrolled in the two grades containing the largest proportion of 13-year-old students (46 countries); Pop 3: Students in their final year of secondary education (General population: 22 countries; students taking advanced courses in mathematics : 17 countries; students taking advanced courses in physics : 18 countries).	Beaton, A.E.; Martin, M.O.; Mullis, I.V.S.; Gonzales, E.J.; Smith, T.A.; Kelly, D.L. 1996. *Science achievement in the middle school years: IEA's TIMSS.* Chestnut Hill, MA: Boston College. Beaton, A.E.; Mullis, I.V.S.; Martin, M.O.; Gonzales, E.J.; Kelly, D.L.; Smith, T.A. 1996. *Mathematics achievement in the middle school years: IEA's TIMSS.* Chestnut Hill, MA: Boston College.

Study	Domains assessed	Countries	Target populations	Main publications
1997-98. **IEA/TIMSS-R** Third International Mathematics and Science Study-Repeat	Mathematics, science	Albania, Australia, Belgium (Flemish), Bulgaria, Canada, Chile, Chinese Taipei, Cyprus, Czech Republic, England, Finland, Hong Kong (SAR), Hungary, Indonesia, Islamic Republic of Iran, Israel, Italy, Japan, Korea, Jordan, Latvia, Lithuania, Republic of Macedonia, Malaysia, Moldova, Morocco, Netherlands, New Zealand, Norway, Philippines, Romania, Russian Federation, Singapore, Slovak Republic, Slovenia, South Africa, Thailand, Rep. of Tunisia, Turkey, United States.	Grade 8 students.	Martin, M.O.; Mullis, I.V.S.; Gonzales, E.J.; Gregory, K.D.; Smith, T.A.; Chrostowski, S.J.; Garden, R.A.; O'Connor, K.M. 2000. *TIMSS 1999 international science report: findings from IEA's repeat of the third international mathematics and science study at the eighth grade*. Chestnut Hill, MA: Boston College. Mullis, I.V.S., Martin, M.O., Gonzales, E.J., Gregory, K.D., Garden, R.A., O'Connor, K.M., Chrostowski, S.J., Smith, T.A. (2000). *TIMSS 1999 international mathematics report: findings from IEA's repeat of the third international mathematics and science study at the eighth grade*. Chestnut Hill, MA: Boston College.
1999. **IEA/CIVED** Second Civic Education Study	Civic knowledge and attitudes	28 countries: Australia, Belgium (French), Bulgaria, Chile, Colombia, Cyprus, Czech Republic, Denmark, England, Estonia, Finland, Germany, Greece, Hong Kong (SAR), Hungary, Italy, Latvia, Lithuania, Norway, Poland, Portugal, Romania, Russian Federation, Slovak Republic, Slovenia, Sweden, Switzerland, and the United States.	Phase 1: qualitative case study in 24 countries; Phase 2 Assessment in 28 countries: Pop 2 : Students attending the modal grade for 14-year olds. Optional older population: upper secondary school students.	Torney-Purta, J.; Lehmann, R.; Oswald, H.; Schulz, W. 2001. *Citizenship and education in twenty-eight countries: civic knowledge and engagement at age fourteen*. Amsterdam: International Association for the Evaluation of Educational Achievement (IEA).

Study	Domains assessed	Countries	Target populations	Main publications
2001. **IEA/PIRLS** Progress in International Reading Literacy Study	Reading	35 countries: Argentina, Belize, Bulgaria, Canada, Colombia, Cyprus, Czech Republic, England, France, Germany, Greece, Hong Kong SAR, Hungary, Iceland, Iran, Israel, Italy, Kuwait, Latvia, Lithuania, Republic of Macedonia, Moldova, Morocco, The Netherlands, New Zealand, Norway, Romania, Russian Federation, Scotland, Singapore, Slovak Republic, Slovenia, Sweden, Turkey, and the United States.	Students attending grade 4.	Mullis, I.V.S.; Martin, M.O.; Gonzalez, E.J.; Kennedy, A.M. 2003. *PIRLS 2001 international report: IEA's study of reading literacy achievement in primary schools.* Chestnut Hill, MA: Boston College.
2000. **OECD/ PISA 2000** Programme for International Student Assessment	Reading, mathematics, science	Phase 1 (PISA): 32 countries: Australia, Austria, Belgium, Brazil*, Canada, The Czech Republic, Denmark, Finland, France, Germany, Greece, Hungary, Iceland, Ireland, Italy, Japan, Korea, Latvia*, Liechtenstein, Luxembourg, Mexico, The Netherlands, New Zealand, Norway, Poland, Portugal, The Russian Federation*, Spain, Sweden, Switzerland, The United Kingdom, The United States. Phase 2 (PISA+): 11 additional countries: Albania, Argentina, Bulgaria, Chile, Hong Kong, Indonesia, Israel, FYR Macedonia, Peru, Romania, Thailand	15-year-old students	OECD. 2001. *Knowledge and skills for life: first results from PISA 2000.* Paris: OECD. OECD-UNESCO. 2003. *Literacy skills for the world of tomorrow: further results from PISA 2000.* Paris: OECD/UNESCO-UIS.

Study	Domains assessed	Countries	Target populations	Main publications
2003. OECD/ PISA 2003 Programme for International Student Assessment	Reading, mathematics, science, problem solving	41 countries: Australia, Austria, Belgium, Brazil*, Canada, The Czech Republic, Denmark, Finland, France, Germany, Greece, Hong Kong, Hungary, Iceland, Indonesia, Ireland, Italy, Japan, Korea, Latvia*, Liechtenstein, Luxembourg, Macau, Mexico, Netherlands, New Zealand, Norway, Poland, Portugal, The Russian Federation*, Serbia Republic of Yugoslavia, Slovak Republic, Spain, Sweden, Switzerland, Thailand, Tunisia, Turkey, United Kingdom, United States, Uruguay.	15-year-old students	OECD. 2004. *Learning for tomorrow's world. First results from PISA 2003.* Paris: OECD.
1997-1999. SACMEQ Southern Africa Consortium for Monitoring Educational Quality	Reading, mathematics	15 countries: Botswana, Kenya, Lesotho, Malawi, Mauritius, Mozambique, Namibia, Seychelles, South Africa, Swaziland, Tanzania (Mainland), Tanzania (Zanzibar), Uganda, Zambia, Zimbabwe.	Grade 6 students	Kulpoo, D. 1998. Mauritius: *The quality of education: some policy suggestions based on a survey of schools.* SACMEQ Policy research: Report No.1. Paris: IIEP-UNESCO. Machingaidze, T.; Pfukani, P.; Shumba, S. 1998. *Zimbabwe: the quality of education: some policy suggestions based on a survey of schools.* SACMEQ Policy research: Report No.3. Paris: IIEP-UNESCO. Milner, G.; Chimombo, J.; Banda, T., Mchikoma, C.2001. *The quality of education: some policy suggestions based on a survey of schools: Malawi.* SACMEQ Policy research: Report No.7. Paris: IIEP-UNESCO.

Nassor, S.; Mohammed, K.A. 1998. *Zanzibar: the quality of education: some policy suggestions based on a survey of schools.* SACMEQ Policy research: Report No. 4. Paris: IIEP-UNESCO.

Nkamba, M.; Kanyika, J. 1998. *Zambia: the quality of education: some policy suggestions based on a survey of schools.* SACMEQ Policy research: Report No. 5. Paris: IIEP-UNESCO.

Nzomo, J.; Kariuki, M.; Guantai L. 2001. *The quality of education: some policy suggestions based on a survey of schools: Kenya.* SACMEQ Policy research: Report No. 6. Paris: IIEP-UNESCO.

Voigts, F. 1998. *Namibia: the quality of education: some policy suggestions based on a survey of schools.* SACMEQ Policy research: Report No. 2. Paris: IIEP-UNESCO.

Chapter 5
What is a 'good' cross-national study?

T. Neville Postlethwaite

Introduction

Over the past decades, there has been a major expansion of interest in cross-national studies of the quality of education. This trend has been fuelled by the widespread belief that the relative cross-national achievement levels of students in a nation are highly predictive of future national economic development. Unfortunately, however, some cross-national studies of the quality of education have limitations associated with either their technical design and implementation or their capacity to deliver information that can be used for informed decision-making. As a result, it is important for both – researchers (especially technicians within the ministry of education's research and planning division) and decision-makers (especially ministers and senior members of ministries of education) – to be able to judge whether their nation should join a particular study. Such judgements require that they are able to identify the main features of a 'good' cross-national study.

A problem arises here because these two groups of people – researchers and decision-makers – usually base their judgement of what is 'good' on different sets of criteria. The following discussion has aimed to list, comment and occasionally answer the most salient questions that arise among members of each group. This framework has been adopted in the hope that a better elaboration and understanding of the concerns of researchers and decision-makers will enable these stakeholders to: (a) work together more effectively; (b) make sound judgements concerning whether to participate in cross-national studies; and (c) make such studies more responsible to both political and scientific demands.

From a decision-maker's point of view

Senior members of ministries have to balance the aspirations and needs of a wide diversity of stakeholders – and at the end of the day retain personal credibility and sustain confidence in government policies and programmes. This represents a challenging task, and from a day-to-day viewpoint, can sometimes appear to resemble a form of 'crisis management'. Ministries are therefore just as interested in the political ramifications of the results of cross-national studies of the quality of education as they are interested in the policy and practice reforms that can flow from the research results.

Are the results based on valid data and sound data analyses?

The decision-maker's main concern will be that the results emanating from a cross-national study of the quality of education should be based on high-quality data and that the data analyses have been conducted in a sound manner. It is often the case that senior ministry officials will reject a piece of research when the research findings contradict (a) what is 'generally believed' in the ministry, or (b) what is 'currently specified as official government policy'. It is therefore incumbent on the researchers to show that the data and research results are trustworthy. This is normally achieved through the researchers' demonstrating that appropriate technical standards were applied during the research.

In some cases, it is hard for the researchers to convince the ministry's senior staff of the accuracy of the research results. A few real examples based on the author's recent experience should illustrate the point.

In one ministry, there was a policy that there should be 18 books per pupil in a primary school library. However, the research results showed that in one region there was only an average of two books per pupil in the average school library. Not surprisingly, the ministry officials stated that 'the data were wrong'. This illogical conclusion required the research team to visit a large number of schools in the region, and conduct a careful 'hard count' of the library books. The expensive and time-consuming follow-up data collection produced the same results as the original survey – and finally the ministry officials believed that the research data were accurate.

In another ministry the officials were shocked because the average reading literacy score for students in that country was much lower than they expected, and also much lower than in several other countries that were perceived to have less effective education systems. They assumed that these other countries must have excluded certain less able groups of students from their testing sessions. A scientific judgement of data quality in this area requires, among other things, that the research report for a study contains a very clear description of the 'defined target population' for the testing programme – including a precise definition of which students were 'excluded' prior to the selection of the final study sample.

Are the results related to the major policy concerns of the ministry?

Ministers of education are always interested to know how students in their own school systems compare with students in other 'similar' countries – on achievement in different subject areas and attitudes towards learning different subjects towards school in general.

Most ministers are also interested in the levels of educational provision, and whether or not these have been equalized across regions within the country, and across schools within regions. In a cross-national study, these 'interests' must be known in advance so that the data collection can take as many of them as possible into consideration. The best approach in this area is to commence a cross-national study with a 'preliminary interview phase' in which the minister and the most senior officials are asked about their policy concerns with respect to the conditions of schooling and the quality of education. If the data collection focuses on these concerns then it is more likely that the final research report and recommendations will be read and used for decision-making.

In some cross-national studies, it is common for the researchers to make 'policy suggestions' that outline agendas for action based on the research findings. For example, the research reports produced by the Southern and Eastern Africa Consortium for Monitoring Educational Quality (SACMEQ). The SACMEQ researchers provide lists of policy suggestions (based on evidence) that are classified by timeframe: a short time (some six months), a medium time (around one or two years), or a long time (more than two years) to implement. They are also classified by cost: low cost, medium cost, or high cost. These kinds of suggestions should always be checked for their feasibility through discussions with the appropriate people in the ministry before they are published.

Are the research results delivered in a timely fashion?

It can happen that a problem arises quickly in parliament or in the public domain about some aspect of education. It is then fortuitous if the research results throw some light on the problem. However, if the policy concerns of the minister and his or her senior staff have guided the research design, then the research results should be available to inform policy debates.

When accurate information can be provided rapidly to decision-makers, there is always a greater likelihood that it will be used to make informed decisions. Therefore, in planning a study of the quality of education, due consideration should be given to providing sufficient resources to deliver the data in a timely fashion. Experience shows that many studies lose a great deal of time at the data entry, data cleaning, and data management phases – just prior to the main data analyses. Researchers need to be aware of this danger and plan accordingly.

Are the research results useful for guiding concrete reform actions?

Senior members of ministries who have limited knowledge of the complexities of educational research often look for simple unidimensional solutions as pathways to educational reform. This can sometimes be exacerbated by researchers who present cross-national research results in the form of aggregate tabulations of national percentages or mean scores. Such tabulations often ignore the dangers associated with the 'Ecological Fallacy' (Ross, 1997) whereby, for example, a relationship between two variables at the national mean level of data analyses might be very different (or even reversed) within a country at the student level of data analysis.

Researchers also need to aim at presenting results that acknowledge the complexity of the educational environment, and at the same time are not made inaccessible to decision-makers due to technical jargon and analytic complexities. Such a balance is not easy to strike!

Are the research results 'dangerous' for the government?

The senior ministry staff must have adequate prior warning and briefings if any of the research results are likely to be 'dangerous' in the sense that they show, for example, that a government promise has not been kept, or that educational provision and/or student achievement is much lower than expected for the country as a whole, or for particular parts of it. Different ministers react differently to 'bad news' received from the results of a cross-national study. Their reactions may arise from a general dislike of criticism, a feeling that the performance of a whole education system is a barometer of their intellectual capacities, uncertainties among ministerial colleagues about the proximity of a general election, and so on.

Over the past decade there have been several examples, in both developed and developing countries, where ministers have withdrawn their nation's data from a study because they did not like the results, and/or banned the publication of research results because they considered that comparisons made in the research report reflected poorly on their country. In one famous incident in the 1990s, a minister withdrew from a cross-national study just before the first research report was due to be printed. In this case, the particular country's data had to be deleted from the international data set, all analyses based on the pooled data had to be rerun, and the final research report had to be completely re-written. This cost a great deal in terms of extra time and money. Cross-national studies now usually require ministers to agree to the publication of results and data before the study commences.

Researchers in this area need to adopt a 'no surprises' strategy with respect to their minister when the final research report is published. That is, even if the news is 'not so good', it is better to provide a clear and factual briefing for the minister well in advance of a wider release of the research results. This briefing should include some diplomatic, succinct and technically sound explanations for the research findings.

Are the samples of students and schools of high quality?

When 'very good' or 'very bad' or 'unusual' research results are obtained for a country, it is common for senior ministry staff to question the sampling procedures. Responding to such questions can be fraught with difficulties – because the correct answers are sometimes 'counter-intuitive'. For example, it is difficult to explain to many people that 'sample size is not necessarily a benchmark for sampling accuracy', or that 'for most countries, the size of the student population has no impact upon the size of the sample that must be selected' (because the finite population factor is negligible for most countries), or that 'in poor developing countries (where the variations between primary schools tend to be large), the required sample size for a given level of accuracy is generally much higher than in a rich developed country', or that 'a simple random sample of schools followed by the within-school selection of a simple random sample of a fixed number of students results in a biased sample' (because students in large schools have a smaller chance of selection).

The only scientific benchmark for a sample is the size of the sampling error (or sampling uncertainty) for a statistic that is generated from the sample data as an estimate of a population value. The sampling error provides 'boundaries' for the uncertainty in sample estimates – and these, in most cases, are quite meaningful to most people, whether or not they have had training in the field of statistics.

Are the tests 'fair'?

When the minister asks if the tests are 'fair', he or she is asking whether the tests are 'valid for the purposes that they were intended for'. In many cross-national studies of the quality of education, the validity levels of the tests are governed by the extent to which the tests are constructed from test items that have a representative coverage of the official curriculum content and the official description of skills that students are supposed to demonstrate for a particular age or grade level.

In the past, cross-national studies tried to address this requirement by developing cross-national 'content by skills' grids that reflected commonality in curricula across the participating countries. This approach tended to reject interesting, but not universal, aspects of the various curricula. In recent years, with the emergence of modern test-scaling techniques, it has become possible to use 'rotated' test booklets – that permit more test items to be used, and allow each school system to be scored separately for all curriculum frameworks across all participating countries.

From a researcher's point of view

It would be possible to write a very detailed 'Guidebook for researchers' about all of the technical standards that should be respected when conducting cross-national studies of the quality of education. Indeed, a good case could be made that such a book should be written for the benefit of all such studies. However, what follows is but a selection of the more important technical features of a 'good' cross-national study of the quality of education.

Ten features have been listed. These were prepared with two purposes in mind. The first was to provide a framework for judging the scientific value of a study that has been completed and published. The second was to sensitize those responsible for commissioning and managing cross-national research within countries to the technical issues that need to be addressed if a country is to derive valid information for planning the quality of education.

It must be acknowledged that all large-scale cross-national research studies differ with respect to their objectives and methodologies. It is impossible, therefore, to address technical requirements in terms of detailed prescriptive statements. Instead, the approach has been to identify the key areas of concern and then raise (and where appropriate comment on), questions that need to be addressed by researchers as they design, implement and report a cross-national study.

What are the aims of the study?

What are the specific aims of a cross-national study of the quality of education? Have they been clearly stated? Has evidence been presented in documents or reports to show that the research questions that have been developed address important policy and theory-oriented issues in many of the participating education systems? (If this is not the case, then there is a danger that the research issues are the favourite topics of the researchers rather than those of the practitioners.) Is there evidence to show that the design of the study was specifically developed to permit policy and theory-oriented questions to be answered?

Have the policy issues specified for the study been used to guide the preparation of 'dummy' or 'blank' tabulations that can form a 'results reporting framework' for the variables that are required and the data analyses that must be conducted? Such an approach establishes firm connections between policy concerns and recommendations arising from the research.

It is sometimes stated that the interests of different systems of education are too different to be able to specify a set of research questions to guide a cross-national study. However, experience shows that there are many policy concerns in the field of education that are both perennial and shared across most education systems. For example, almost all ministers of education are interested in levels of educational provision and attainment, and in the equity of these levels across administrative units, such as regions within a country as well as among schools.

Have the aims of the study been linked to its design?

Was the research design for a cross-national study appropriate for answering the questions posed? Did the data collection instruments (questionnaires, tests and attitude scales) cover all of the research questions? Were unnecessary questions avoided in the data collection instruments?

In some cases, it is possible to see that there are questions in the data collection instruments that are not related to the questions posed for the study – which can mean that the researchers have inserted questions based on their own personal research interests. A major mismatch between the policy concerns of the senior staff of the ministry of education and the focus of a research design almost certainly consigns any resulting research report to the bookshelf.

Research specialists who wish to have their research results used in policy evaluation and policy development need to recognize the importance of improving the dialogue between the producers and consumers of information. That is, providing evidence to decision-makers represents 'meaningful communication' only when the decision-maker is actively listening and reflecting on a related problem. Researchers who ignore this lesson often present evidence and answers to an audience that may be asking unconnected questions.

What are the target population definitions?

When comparisons were made across countries in a cross-national study, was like being compared with like? For example, if students in a specific grade group were being compared for their achievement, were all of the students in the grade included in the target population, or were some students excluded? It is usual to have some students excluded either because they are small in number (and it would be exorbitantly expensive to collect data from them – for example, in very isolated areas), or because they are in special education schools (for example, for the blind or deaf). These students are normally referred to as the 'excluded population'. It is normal to have an 'excluded population' that is less than 5 per cent of the total number of students in the 'desired target population'. What is not desirable is to have situations, where, for example, 2 per cent of students have been excluded in some countries and 15 per cent in others.

Were the different extents of school and student level exclusions reported, and the likely impact of these exclusions on comparisons of means and distributions across countries discussed? What makes the reader extremely suspicious is when no excluded students have been reported. The experienced researcher will always report the extent of the excluded population with the reasons for such exclusions. If information has not been reported on this matter, then it is likely that no attention was paid to it and the reader therefore has no idea what is being compared with what. This is a sign that the related research results might be questionable.

The same argument applies when age groups are being compared. One argument for using age groups rather than grade groups for within-school sampling is to discover the achievement level of students born between certain dates (for example, a calendar year). This approach seeks to examine how systems of education have coped with the education of an age cohort.

Where school systems have high rates of grade repetition it is possible to have students of a particular age spread across several grades. Some systems will argue that in this case the tests are too difficult for those students who are three grades behind the others, and that these students should therefore be 'excluded'. These issues need to be addressed in association with test construction procedures because there are good ethical (as well as research) reasons why students in lower grades should not be subjected to the experience of sitting for a test that is unrealistically beyond their capabilities.

Have scientific sampling procedures been used?

Has the study employed scientific sampling procedures (that include the application of probability sampling, the use of sampling weights to avoid bias, and the calculation of errors of sampling that allow for the complexities of the sample design)?

All high-quality cross-national studies are based on scientific probability samples whereby each member of the defined target population has a known, non-zero, chance of selection. Probability sampling is required in order to be able to calculate the correct measures of sampling error associated with estimates of population characteristics. So the first issue in the area of sampling is to ask: Has true probability sampling been applied?

A second major issue is the question of sampling weights – which are required in most 'real' surveys in order to adjust for (a) variations in probabilities of selection (for example, caused by employing different sampling rates across strata), and/or (b) loss of data due to less than perfect response rates.

Population estimates derived from samples should have sampling errors that are 'acceptable' with respect to the policy decisions that are based on the results. Since the mid-1960s, many of the major international studies have adopted the standard of having sample designs that have the same or better sampling precision as a simple random sample of 400 students for the main educational outcome measures. This level of sampling precision provides sampling errors for results on test items (percentage correct) of no more than 2.5 per cent for one standard error, and no more than 5 per cent for two standard errors. This means, for example, that for a sample estimate of 50 per cent, then one can be sure, 19 times out of 20, that the population value lies between 45 and 55 per cent. Since in nearly all countries the sample is a two-stage sample (first a sample of schools, and then a sample of students within schools), it is important that the standard error is calculated to take this into account. Many make the mistake of using 'standard' statistical software that produces standard errors that assume that the sample was a simple random sample. This assumption can lead to substantial underestimates of standard errors.

In some studies, where direct international comparisons are less important, a lower level of sampling precision may be acceptable. This is often the case where a broad analysis of the curriculum is required. Such studies often aim at discovering 'well-achieved', 'averagely achieved', and 'poorly achieved' objectives. In this case, it might be sufficient to say that 'well achieved' means about 80 per cent or more of the students that have mastered a particular objective or curriculum unit; 'averagely achieved' means about 50 per cent; and 'poorly achieved' means about 20 per cent or less. In this case, two standard errors of 10 per cent for percentage correct on test items might be adequate for the purposes of the study.

The question for the reader then is 'Was the sampling conducted in such a way as to yield standard errors of sampling that are acceptable for the purposes of the study?' It is usually the case that researchers who are knowledgeable in the area of sampling will have provided a detailed description of the steps of sampling and the correct sampling errors. If this information has not been provided, then there is a distinct possibility that the samples are suspect. It is also usual for the standard errors of sampling to be presented in the tables of results. If they are not there, then the reader should be wary.

Care also needs to be exercised when testing for 'statistically significant differences'. In some cases, a very large sample can appear to produce such differences because the calculations of sampling error are based on the assumption of simple random sampling.

Have systematic (and modern) procedures been used for instrument construction?

The construction of data collection instruments is a complex and rapidly developing field – particularly with respect to the design and development of student tests. Many questions can be raised in this area – but the answers to some of the most important questions are not always completely 'scientific' because issues of values can enter the discussion. For example, the construction of valid student tests needs to rely on the availability of clear and unambiguous descriptions of the central aims of the teaching and learning with respect to the school curriculum. In many school systems, these aims are either not made explicit, or they are presented in such a generalized form that they do not provide guidance for test construction.

Where the study aims at measuring what the students have learned at school, the test instruments must cover the intended curriculum of the participating countries. This normally involves a two-stage process.

First, a content analysis is undertaken of the curricula (via curriculum guides, textbooks, examinations, and what teachers say they teach) in the various countries. Second, this first step is used to construct an 'international blueprint' for the tests. While many of the curricular objectives will be common across countries, some objectives will be common to a subset of countries. Mathematics and science are the key subject areas in which there is considerable curricular variation among countries.

In some cases, the aim of a cross-national study will focus on other outcomes such as whether the pupils can read well enough 'to cope in society' or 'progress to the next grade'. In these cases, exercises must first be undertaken in each country to have panels define what is required for these types of outcomes. This is a laborious process, but must be convincing.

There is much less variation across countries in the curricular objectives for subjects such as reading and foreign languages. However, there must be agreement on the international blueprint and this must cover the bulk of the curricula in all countries if it is the intention of the study to focus on the common contents of national curricula.

Test items must be written to cover all cells having objectives in the blueprint. The item formats must be agreed and justified. The items must be trial-tested and analysed. Where multiple-choice items are used, then the distracters must be acceptable, not only in terms of content, but also in terms of distracting power. Free-response questions requiring students to construct answers should be pre-tested to ensure that they will yield responses that can be reliably scored. Where scaling is being used, there must be agreement on the substantive meaning of the scale in terms of student performance on specified tasks at specified points on the scale. There must be agreement on the appropriateness of the items and the tests must be shown to be reliable. Where there is an attempt to measure change over time, then there must be sufficient common items between time points in order to allow change to be reliably measured.

Items should be tested for item bias in every country. The psychometric properties of the test items should be similar over a sufficiently large number of countries. Where overlapping tests have to be used, it must be shown at the trial stage that the common items used to allow calibration on the same scale fulfil their purpose.

In some instances, 'hands-on' performance assessment tasks (often using special equipment) may be deemed necessary to cover the full range of objectives in a subject area. The design of such tasks should take into account the amount of time available for testing, the need to make use of equipment which is simple and available in multiple copies and not beyond the resources of participating countries, and the need to yield responses that can be reliably scored across countries.

The questionnaire instruments must include questions to cover all of the indicators needed to answer the policy issues raised at the outset of the study. Several of the indicators will be what are normally called 'derived variables' – that are constructed from the information obtained from several questions. The questions must be written in a simple language easily understood by all of the students (able and less able) who have to answer them. All questions must then be trial-tested and analyses undertaken to ensure that the questions are providing accurate and reliable information.

The attitude instruments, usually a part of the questionnaires, measure selected attitudinal dimensions. Attitude items are sometimes collected through special small studies from the target population members and then trial-tested and revised for the final form. Very often about three times as many items are needed for trial testing as for the final attitude scale measure. The final scale must be shown to be reliable for the purposes for which it is intended.

Do the translation procedures permit valid cross-national comparisons?

The translation of data collection instruments is not an easy business and the main question is: Was a thorough verification undertaken of the translation? Procedures must be put in place in order to ensure that there is cultural appropriateness and linguistic and psychometric equivalence of the instruments in participating countries. This task requires the assistance of bilingual research specialists, and usually requires the cross-checking of original data collection instruments against those that have been forward-translated into a second language and then back-translated into the original language.

Have the logistics of the data collection been well planned?

Many expensive large-scale cross-national studies of the quality of education experience problems at the data collection phase. Two important questions that need to be addressed in this area include: 'Are the data collection manuals sufficiently clear to ensure validity in the field work?' and 'Have the required school and student tracking forms been used effectively?'

The data collection stage in each of the countries is crucial. The object of the data collection is to have students complete every question in the questionnaires and all test items that they are able to answer. Normally, in each country, a manual is written for the persons in charge of the data collection at the national level. This manual is required to ensure that the data collection procedures proceed in a manner that will provide valid data under conditions that are uniform at each data collection site.

The data collection manual should cover every possible detail that must be taken into account when conducting the data collection. This involves 'school forms' and 'student forms' to ensure that: the correct schools are selected, the correct students are tested (and not others), and the correct teachers are selected (where questionnaires or tests are being administered to teachers). This manual should specify: (a) what each test administrator has to do and say during the actual testing sessions; (b) the procedures and timing for the administration of the instruments; and (c) how to parcel up the instruments and return them to a central point.

Have the data been cleaned?

In most cross-national studies, much more time is spent on preparing the data for computing purposes than is spent on actually doing the data analyses. This is because data recording and data cleaning requires a systematic combination of computer and manual work – in which a simple error can require several hours to detect and correct. Many questions can be raised here. For example: Have all 'wild codes' (that is, out-of-range codes) been verified so that student, teacher, and school data can be merged? Have logical cross-checks been made across appropriate variables? Have all possible efforts been made to avoid the incidence of missing data?

The data are usually recorded on computers at national research centres. Typically, the study provides data entry software that is used in all countries. Good data entry software provides a number of initial checks on the data that can be corrected immediately during the data entry process. There are always 'extra' errors in data entry no matter how good the data entry programme – and these have to be identified and corrected using 'data cleaning procedures'. For example, there is a need to check that school identification codes that are used for students, teachers and schools are accurate because these codes are required in order to 'merge' data prior to the data analyses. Errors or problems are reported back to national centres; they then contact the schools for elucidation and send the correct data back to the international data processing centre. The necessary changes are then made. This 'cleaning process' can take a long time – especially when there are many countries in the study.

It is also important for the reader of research reports to be made aware of those variables where there are so many missing data that they could not be used in the analyses. Furthermore, it is important to see which missing data were imputed, and how.

Do the data analyses address the main aims of the research?

The aim should be to ensure that the selected data analyses are clearly focused on answering the main research questions that were posed during the design of the study. The data analyses for a study should be guided by the 'dummy tables' that were prepared during the research design.

Care should be taken to include standard errors of sampling along with each summary statistic that is presented – so that the reader can have some information about the 'stability' of each sample estimate. Basic tabulations can be prepared using standard statistical software packages – but sometimes these computer programmes do not provide the correct estimates of sampling error.

Reports emanating from the study

The reports should be clearly written and deal with each of the policy issues in turn. The source of the data under discussion should always be clear, as should arguments concerning the interpretation of the analyses.

The use of 'league tables' to report results should be managed with great care – so that lists of average scores do not become the sole foundation for education policy. The main aim here is to strive to prepare accessible reports that deliver information in appropriate formats that can be used at different decision-making levels of a school system.

New and very promising approaches to show student educational achievement in the form of descriptions of 'competence levels' need to be encouraged because such techniques optimize the capacity of research to change and improve the teachers who are responsible for guiding and managing student learning. In addition, graphical methods of data summarization (as pioneered in the PISA international reports and their executive summaries) should be emphasized to present more understandable summaries of complex analyses.

Conclusion

For a ministry of education, it is of great importance to know about, and monitor, the conditions of learning and the quality of education in schools. Participation in cross-national studies of the quality of education can provide this important information. However, it should be noted that information generated from cross-national studies is most useful if it provides sound evidence to inform debate and decision-making in a meaningful manner for all stakeholders.

For a cross-national study to provide sound evidence there needs to be confidence from the 'research side' and the 'decision-making side' that the study satisfies criteria that do not always overlap. This article has sought to list, discuss and question some of these criteria – with the aim of providing 'information producers' (researchers) and 'information users' (decision-makers) with some insights into what are the key concerns – from each side – when making judgements about the capacity of a study to provide sound evidence that can be used to guide policy decisions aimed at improving an education system.

References

Ross, K.N. 1997. "Research and policy: A complex mix". In: *IIEP Newsletter, XV*(I), 1-4.

Chapter 6
What do ministers of education 'really think' about cross-national studies?

Saul Murimba
SACMEQ Co-ordinating Centre, Harare (Zimbabwe)

Introduction

Over the past decade, many ministers of education in developed and developing countries have become interested in having their school systems participate in cross-national studies of the quality of education. This trend has emerged irrespective of available facts or perceptions regarding their education systems' performance in absolute and/or relative terms. These ministers have also been prepared to invest heavily in cross-national studies, their conviction being that participation in such studies has the potential to yield benefits for their school systems.

Naturally, such participation raises both expectations and anxieties, because the results from cross-national studies may bring good or bad news. In some cases, the results may provide 'surprises', as may be the case when performance far exceeds, or falls far below, expectations.

This article examines several issues related to ministers' perceptions about cross-national studies. It has been based on practical experience gained from involvement in the research and training programmes conducted by the Southern and Eastern Africa Consortium for Monitoring Educational Quality (SACMEQ). The key sources of information were: (a) perceptions expressed by ministers in SACMEQ Assembly of Ministers' Meetings that are held in order to discuss SACMEQ's research and training programmes; (b) reports obtained from SACMEQ National Research Co-ordinators (NRCs) and their colleagues; and (c) information gathered during visits to SACMEQ ministries of education.

Understanding the role and position of ministers of education

In order to understand ministers' perceptions about cross-national studies, we have to examine their position and role within their ministries as well as the broader national framework. Their role is associated with expectations that are widely shared among a variety of stakeholders. The position they occupy also defines the boundaries of their influence on the development of their own education system, and for what they can be held accountable.

Ministers view themselves, primarily, as politicians – and this is true both for ministers who are elected and for those who are appointed. Ministers who are elected members of parliament usually see themselves as representatives of their constituencies, while those who were appointed tend to view themselves as having a 'special status' within the nation's political life. Both have the mandate to spearhead the development of their nations' education sectors, and are therefore answerable to the whole nation.

In the African context, most ministers secure their portfolios through their political parties whose development agenda is usually stated in party manifestos. The common thread that runs through the manifestos of ruling parties in post-colonial states is the promise to deliver 'free', and in some cases 'compulsory', education of high quality to all learners. These ministers therefore hope that cross-national studies will demonstrate that this goal has more or less been achieved, or that there is progress towards the achievement of this goal. Where such progress has not been registered, cross-national studies should generate practical suggestions and proposals on how this goal can be achieved. When results of cross-national studies fail to do this, but instead merely highlight weaknesses of the system, this can be perceived as a direct criticism of the minister's competence.

The fact that ministers view themselves primarily as political actors was driven home when one minister responded to a controversial issue raised by SACMEQ II results at the Fourth Assembly of Ministers' Meeting held in 2003. His remark was as follows: "What you researchers sometimes forget is that we are politicians. What will my President think when he gets hold of such information? Do you think he will retain me in the next Cabinet?" What he meant was that, when researchers failed to take due regard of political sensitivities around certain issues, they could be viewed as being irresponsible or dangerously reckless.

Education is a gigantic enterprise where the interests of a diverse set of stakeholders converge, and represents an area of prime investment by individuals, households, communities and nations. Ministers therefore want to see that cross-national studies reflect an understanding of the country's broader political context. In view of this, absolute judgemental statements about the 'quality of education' can generate highly emotive reactions since conceptions of quality may vary considerably from one context to another, and what contributes to it may be even more elusive.

Ministers' concerns about cross-national studies

In order to 'really understand' what education ministers think about cross-national studies of the quality of education, we have to take into account that their views may be influenced by different criteria at different times, in different situations, and on different issues. For example, as much as ministers may wish to exploit the political capital offered by the results of cross-national studies, they are careful to avoid relying on information that does not provide them with an honest assessment of quality. What they really want is information that provides them with a strategic vision of their education systems and what ought to be done to achieve and sustain this vision.

Ministers are public figures whose actions are subject to public scrutiny. The decision to participate in cross-national studies of quality is a risk because the publication of the results may either enhance their public image, or may erode public confidence in them as leaders. They therefore have to grapple with the tensions created by the need to know the truth (whether positive or negative) and the need to protect their image against potentially damaging messages contained in the results. Cross-national studies should be sensitive to these tensions, and they can do this by addressing the areas of concern highlighted below.

Focus of cross-national studies

When undertaking cross-national studies of the quality of education, researchers are frequently motivated by curiosity, and face the challenge of accommodating their own interests as well as the individual and collective issues and concerns of participating ministries of education. In particular, ministers have little interest, and will therefore be reluctant to invest in cross-national studies that have been formulated by outsiders, and that represent an externally driven research agenda. The manner in which SACMEQ studies have been designed shows that it is possible for cross-national studies to address those educational issues and policy concerns that are considered to be of high priority by ministers while simultaneously addressing the interests of researchers (Saito, 1999: 108).

Accountability

Ministers acknowledge that it is the primary responsibility of the state to provide a good quality education for all citizens. For this reason, their position is that school-based education should be largely state-funded. It makes sense that ministers accept the responsibility of mobilizing state and other resources for the support of education, and are accountable for the efficient transformation of these resources into educational programmes that expand learning opportunities for children. This is seen as a potent vehicle for the achievement of national goals.

Ministers have acquitted the task of resource mobilization very well, and this is borne out by the fact that, in most SACMEQ and other African countries, the education sector commands the largest proportion of the national budget. However, the availability of resources to the education sector is not always accompanied with a corresponding rise in the quality of education offered. Ministers therefore want cross-national studies to provide them with feedback on the benefits of such investment, and thus on how well they are discharging their responsibilities.

For ministers, the results from cross-national studies are valuable in several other ways. When the results of cross-national studies show that resource provisions to schools fall below benchmark standards, they frequently provide the minister with an advantage point to argue for more national resources for education. They may also be instrumental in securing external or donor funding. This, however, creates another challenge for ministers because when little or nothing has been achieved with the additional resources, they get very anxious. In one country, the SACMEQ II Project results showed a decline in learning achievement compared with the SACMEQ I Project, and the minister's reaction to his senior ministry staff was the following: "These results suggest that we fared worse than before, and this makes it very difficult for me to go to the Cabinet to defend a larger budget for education year after year."

Achieving balance

For those in charge of cross-national studies, one of the biggest challenges is how to communicate both positive and negative results in a balanced manner that constitutes 'positive feedback'. SACMEQ's experience is that, invariably, every country's education system has some positive attributes that it can be proud of, and faces some challenges that can be addressed by tapping into the experiences of its neighbours.

Ministers get concerned when cross-national studies fail to recognize this. When the focus is primarily on the negative aspects of their systems, they feel 'demonized' and when they receive only the good news, they feel deprived of opportunities for further system improvement.

The case of the minister whose country's SACMEQ II results showed a decline over SACMEQ I illustrates how 'balanced feedback' can be provided. In this case, the country's SACMEQ National Research Co-ordinator (NRC) skilfully prepared a briefing note that highlighted both the 'bad news' and the 'good news'. He explained that, while the SACMEQ II average pupil achievement scores were slightly lower, there had been impressive achievements in the equitable allocation of resources, and that, while there were fewer children performing at high levels of competence, larger proportions of children had managed to reach basic literacy levels. In fact, this actually confirmed the fact that the country had indeed made good progress in addressing some of the key challenges faced by the education sector, namely, inequities in resource allocation and low levels of literacy.

This example illustrates the need for cross-national studies to seek a careful balance, both in collecting information and in reporting results, between providing adequate information on a school system's strengths and achievements, as well as highlighting the challenges to be addressed in order to strengthen the systems and help thereby chart the way forward.

Beyond comparisons

One fundamental concern that ministers have is that cross-national studies frequently get preoccupied with the production of 'league tables' that report countries in rank order as if they had participated in the 'Cognitive Olympics'. Such tables usually focus narrowly on learning outcomes, and are viewed by ministers as an unfair basis for evaluating their own performance, and the performance of their own school system as a whole. At the level of rhetoric, ministers are quick to point out that they do not so much mind that their countries' performance was low compared against other countries' but, as one of the SACMEQ ministers has consistently and repeatedly argued, what irked them is that cross-national studies were often used as a crude way of 'comparing the incomparable'.

A pertinent question to ask is whether it is actually possible to conduct cross-national studies without indirectly making comparisons among countries. When countries' results on any quality-related variable are presented side by side (for example, in a table) there is an inherent element of comparison. Although this cannot be totally avoided, SACMEQ's experience is that it is possible to present results in a way that diverts readers' attention away from oversimplified comparisons.

When achievement levels in the SACMEQ II Project for different countries were presented in 2003, for example, the minister of one SACMEQ country had this to say:

> We are a poor country, and we have been struggling to provide education to all our people. In fact we have phenomenally expanded access to education for all our people, and it is free. You can see from the figures presented that we have made great strides in this regard. We therefore knew that quality as defined by the 'average' score was going to decline, but that is what we are focusing on now. Just how we can do this is what we hope to learn from our neighbours.

This comment suggested that ministers feel more secure with cross-national studies on quality when 'comparisons' are not the ultimate aim or the focus. That is, 'comparisons' should be considered as the starting point for more important policy messages. Additional analyses beyond simple comparisons need to provide insights into the strategic issues that countries should focus on. Ministers will accept 'their' results more readily if cross-national studies leave them to make independent decisions regarding the issues and priorities they should address as they pursue the more broadly shared goals. An example of how this can be done was presented in the article, 'Different pathways to EFA for different school systems' (Dolata *et al.*, 2004). This article provided comparative data across 14 school systems – and then showed how each system might utilize different policy 'pathways' in order to reach the same 'Education for All' goals.

The issues each education system chooses to prioritize at any one time depends on the national context. The presentation of cross-national results is less threatening to ministers when issues of national context are given sufficient prominence. Some elements of this context relate to the country's economic performance, demographic characteristics, the socio-cultural characteristics of its population, the impact of history and politics on the development path it has taken, any natural disadvantages and significant setbacks suffered (natural or man-made), and other such factors. Ministers want cross-national studies that make an effort to understand the overall circumstances of their own countries, because they feel that this is essential in order to appreciate the difficulties and challenges that they have had to contend with as they strive to improve their education systems.

Capacity building

Ministers get very worried when cross-national studies are preoccupied with research results – to the exclusion of other benefits that can accrue from the research process itself. Ministries, for example, are very interested in the capacity-building opportunities that participation in a cross-national study can have on their ministry staff. Participation in such studies provides 'hands-on' training that equips staff with valuable skills related to the design and implementation of large-scale research studies, the design and use of data collection instruments, computer-based management and analysis of data, policy analysis and development, and report preparation. All of these skills are needed in order to conduct educational policy research that provides information that can be used to make informed planning decisions in important areas such as curriculum development, enhancing pedagogical practices, monitoring of quality standards, enhancing equity in the provision of resources, and identifying teacher training needs.

Methodological issues

One assumption often made by researchers is that ministers are not interested in methodological issues, and that they lack the competence to appreciate methodological issues. These assumptions are wrong. While ministers may not be interested in the specific technicalities of areas such as sampling, test item analysis, computer-based data management, etc. They are interested to know: (a) whether acceptable scientific methodologies have been applied; (b) the nature of any technical 'weakness' in the methodologies that have been used; and (c) how reliable and valid are the major research findings. Remarks such as "As a Professor of education in my own right ..." or "As a language specialist ..." have sometimes prefaced ministers' remarks in order to dispel the misplaced assumption that they are not interested or competent in methodological issues.

It is the desire of every minister to be associated with high-quality cross-national studies that are methodologically well grounded, and that therefore stand the test of public criticism. They exhibit pride and confidence when their countries have participated in research initiatives that meet world-class standards. It is often the case that, when they are called upon to defend decisions based on the results of cross-national studies, ministers' credibility will be buttressed by the overall integrity of the cross-national studies methodology.

When cross-national studies fail to present results in a way that is sensitive to national contexts, needs and priorities, ministers may sometimes attack the integrity of the methodology, and SACMEQ has experienced this. In extreme cases, ministers may take a defensive posture by making vague reference to 'results from other research initiatives with equal or greater methodological rigor'. These attacks, ostensibly directed at 'flaws' in the methodology, may, in reality, be a reflection or expression of other deep-seated concerns, or may be a form of protest against the manner in which the results were presented. Above all, the presentation of cross-national studies has to take into account the different information needs of different stakeholders, and ministers are one category of stakeholders whose information needs have to be addressed in a careful manner (Ross and Mählck, 1990).

The question of 'ownership'

Ministers want to feel that they and their ministry officials are active players in the cross-national studies that their countries take part in. This sense of ownership is acquired in a variety of ways. To start with, there must be full, genuine involvement of the minister's officials in all stages of cross-national studies – from design to reporting. Studies that allow only limited participation by ministry officials hardly enhance a sense of ownership, however technically sound they may be.

The level of participation required may certainly slow down the pace of research activities, frequently requiring the training of ministry personnel in order to prepare them for the execution of many research tasks, but this is worth the investment. Another form of ministry involvement that enhances the sense of ownership is ensuring that it assumes the leadership role in key decisions concerning the research study, (for example, on the nature of the sampling frame, the selection of test items, and the setting of performance standards). Another benefit emerging from such involvement is that, when it is done proactively, ministers are less likely to dispute the results of the cross-national study.

Another important area where ministry involvement is important is in the formulation of policy recommendations. What may appear to be a sound 'evidence-based' policy suggestion to an outsider may be impracticable to insiders who understand better the prevailing culture and its norms, the way the system works, and the constraints it faces. At the same time, while policy recommendations should take the ministry officials' input into account, this should by no means imply that 'tough' policy recommendations based on empirical evidence should be dropped. On the contrary, ministers have often welcomed 'tough' policy recommendations because they provide a defensible basis for 'radical' actions they may institute.

Avoiding 'surprises'

The results of cross-national studies may appear to be very negative, and researchers within the ministry may be hesitant to share them with the minister and senior ministry staff. This can be very dangerous because ministers hate 'surprises'!

SACMEQ's experience is that ministers need to be appraised of the findings as they emerge so that they have a good grasp of the main 'messages' in the results, and they have had sufficient time to digest them and seek advice if they are required to 'explain' the results. Nothing is more annoying to a minister than to have a research report given (or 'leaked') to the public without his/her consent and knowledge of its contents.

SACMEQ has also found that controversial results can generate interesting debates that can hasten policy reforms. The issue is to ensure that any 'harsh truths' are communicated in the correct language. In one ministry, a SACMEQ research report indicated that the extent of private tutoring of students had, unknown to policy-makers, far exceeded acceptable limits, even though it was associated with high achievement. However, because this came as a 'surprise', it caused an unpleasant backlash on the national research team that reported it. Later, however, the research findings related to extra tuition generated a healthy national debate that initiated constructive policy reforms.

Setting agendas for action

Ministers want cross-national studies to provide them with clear agendas for action. However, many ministers over many years have received research reports that ignore the need to suggest a clear policy agenda based on research results. As a consequence, some ministers have become somewhat sceptical about the value of research, and this can create barriers to the development of a culture of employing 'evidence' to guide policy reforms. They sometimes see research studies as 'one-off' activities that invite, and require, little or no follow-up action.

Researchers must understand that ministers want to be proposed 'agendas for policy action' to be: (a) based on results of the research (and not on speculation); (b) realistic in terms of costs, time, and logistics; (c) linked with the individuals/groups responsible for taking action; and (d) presented in the form of 'options' that permit ministers to consider alternative solutions to policy questions. Research of this kind automatically provides a framework for the design of future policy research evaluations because they list areas of required reform and define the areas of expected follow-up action and the specific players within specific sections or departments of the ministry who can be held accountable for such actions.

Conclusion

This article was prepared based on experience gathered while working with ministers whose school systems were involved in cross-national studies. This experience has shown that ministers occupy difficult positions in their countries as stewards of their education systems, and that they feel personally responsible for their school systems' development. Those who design and implement such studies must understand the political and professional tightrope ministers have to walk, because the fear that cross-national studies can make or break their careers as politicians and professionals is well founded.

The main lesson gathered from this experience was that researchers who design and implement cross-national studies of the quality of education must 'build the ministers into the studies' by connecting them with the evolution of a study from initial concepts to results dissemination. There is plenty of evidence available from the SACMEQ research programme to show that this kind of partnership bears fruit in the form of research-based policy reform.

References

Dolata, S.; Ikeda, M.; Murimba, S. 2004. "Different pathways to EFA for different school systems". In: *IIEP Newsletter, XXIII*(1), 8-9, January-March.

Lockheed. M.E.; Verspoor, A.M. 1991. *Improving primary education in developing countries.* Washington, DC: World Bank.

Ross, K.N.; Mählck, L. (Eds.). 1990. *Planning the quality of education: The collection and use of data for informed decision-making.* Paris: UNESCO.

Saito, M. 1999. 'A generalisable model for educational policy research in developing countries.' In: *Journal of International Cooperation in Education, 2*(2), 107-117.

Part II
Planning the design of cross-national studies of the quality of education

Chapter 7
What should be measured in a cross-national study?

Rainer Lehmann

Introduction

Most ministries of education are complex institutions with a host of divisions and offices, in which hundreds, and sometimes thousands of individuals work. Correspondingly, it would seem to be a gross oversimplification to assume that a generalized agent called 'the Ministry' acts on the basis of a well-defined set of intentions, even in the relatively narrow domain of supporting and conducting cross-national studies. The very fact that invitations to participate in a given cross-national study can result in substantial political controversy within a ministry, let alone between rivals in party-based educational politics, is sufficient to demonstrate, and to some extent explain, the respective ambiguities in the real world. To take this empirical perspective of ministerial intentions might be considered as an application of political science, sub-discipline public administration, to a highly specialized field of educational policy-making.

The question as to which measures a ministry, situated in an ideal world, ought to request and why, refers to quite another matter. Here a concept of rational choice is assumed according to which the ministry as the governing body of an educational system successfully acquires all the information needed to arrive at fully justified decisions. The problem with this normative perspective, however, rests with the fact that its assumptions not only differ from everyday experience, but that it also leaves considerable doubt as to their philosophical soundness. This is because few such concepts, based, in fact, on the Platonic notion of the Philosopher-King, make allowance for the essential limitations of the information at hand in conjunction with the temporal constraints of the decision-making process.

For this chapter, rather than either elaborating a rich description (and possibly an explanation) of how different ministries of education relate to cross-national studies, or proposing a highly normative account of what ministries ought to demand of researchers in the field of internationally comparative surveys, an attempt will be made to analyse methodological issues of cross-national research from the perspective of its potential benefits for educational policy-making.

A taxonomy of cross-national studies: benefits and justifications

The emergence of the methodology for cross-national studies in education is not one of straightforward, linear development, but a 'long and winding road' of changing goals and opportunity structures. It may be helpful to begin with a short outline of which options have been chosen so far, of the benefits expected of and associated with them, and of the corresponding patterns of justifying cross-national research in education.

Comparisons of mean achievement, based on the assumption of variable system characteristics and fixed context-output relationships

Historically, the first approach to cross-national studies of educational achievement, connected with the early studies conducted by the International Association for the Evaluation of Educational Achievement (IEA), was that of searching for 'best practice' or 'benchmarks' in an international frame of reference. Although neither term was current at the time, the arguments upon which both the design and the funding of these studies were based are essentially the ones now associated with these two concepts. This becomes apparent in Torsten Husén's (the foundation Chairman of IEA) famous proposal that the world's education systems could collectively be considered as a natural laboratory in which the effectiveness of alternative national educational arrangements could be studied.

One of the key issues in the early international comparisons was the relative performance of integrated 'comprehensive' school systems as opposed to the traditional articulated ones. Obviously, a key element in the justification of this approach to cross-national comparisons was that of sufficient commonality in terms of the criteria to be employed, invariant against specific cultural environments, including the influence of the language of instruction. Thus, according to the rationale, it was not by chance that mathematics was the first school subject to be chosen for a systematic cross-national study of school achievement (Husén, 1967).

There were, of course, many other latent assumptions involved, if the metaphor of the 'world as a natural laboratory' was to be considered valid. For example, one had to assume that cross-national variability in terms of various factors that described the conditions of schooling (for example, societal expectations with regard to the role of public education) could be sufficiently controlled in order to justify such a quasi-experimental perspective. In any event, it is likely that at least some of the ministries involved in those studies chose to participate because they were persuaded that they would obtain 'benchmark evidence' in favour of educational reforms envisaged or already under way. Interestingly, some of the underlying justifications which were characteristic of this approach have been revived in the discourse accompanying the most recent cycle of studies for the Programme for International Student Assessment (PISA) that have been organized by the Organisation for Economic Co-operation and Development (OECD).

Comparisons of productivity, based on the assumption of fixed objectives and fixed input-output relationships

Provided that there is a well-established international core curriculum, describing the main objectives prevalent in all educational systems to be compared, it is an attractive idea to measure not only differences between countries in terms of mean achievement, but also to try to determine the differences between (international) curricular norms and attained levels of achievement as a function of variable ('manipulable') input factors. The aim here is to ascertain the overall effectiveness of education in a given country or system, usually with respect to certain domains such as reading, mathematics, or science, which have been demonstrated to follow universal curricular norms. It is here that the fundamental distinction between the intended, the implemented, and the achieved curriculum constitutes the premise under which international comparisons of this type claim relevance for educational policy-making. A noteworthy application of such principles lies in the computation of so-called 'yield curves' which describe the percentage of a target population reaching or surpassing any defined level on a set of curricular elements which are ordered by difficulty.

Even more important within this approach is the identification of those variables or factors that have demonstrable effects on the formation of a favourable achievement distribution. The objective of determining the relative importance of determinants of school achievement was a characteristic of the second generation of IEA studies (such as the Six-Subject-Survey (Passow *et al.*, 1976; Walker, 1976) and has also been applied in recent IEA studies (Torney-Purta *et al.*, 2001; Amadeo *et al.*, 2002). As a research strategy, this approach has subsequently developed into an elaborate paradigm, primarily due to developments in the group led by Walberg (1990).

Comparisons of literacy distributions, based on the assumption of educational achievement as a determinant of economic growth

In the previous paradigms, the criteria to be measured were accepted as given 'universals'. In contrast, some recent international comparisons have attempted to justify the choice of criteria in terms of their economic relevance. This perspective was first implemented on a large scale in the field of adult literacy surveys (NCES, 1993, 1998) and was subsequently transferred to the area of international comparisons of school achievement by the OECD (2001). It also had linkages with much earlier work conducted by economists of education (Becker, 1964; Schultz, 1961) who had suggested that educational attainment should be considered as an important input factor explaining economic growth. Instead of such rough proxies as years of schooling, however, measures of educational achievement – fundamental qualifications often summarized under the term 'literacy' – are now entered as predictors in the equations used to explain economic states and tendencies.

The challenge embedded in this rather recent educational perspective obviously lies in the linkage of measurable educational output to measurable economic outcome. Since the existing programmes for cross-national studies of the quality of school-based education do not yet include longitudinal investigations up into the stages of vocational or professional training, employment and work, this particular perspective exists, to this day, more in the domain of desirable research than in the realm of available studies. It may be noted, however, that corresponding arguments, plausible as they are, are frequently made to justify the implementation of cross-national comparisons and to motivate countries to participate in them.

Multi-criterial comparisons, based on the assumption
of educational achievement as a determinant of social cohesion
and peace

Despite the acute attention currently paid to economic issues, many educators argue that education should not be reduced to economically profitable qualification processes. While the individualist version of this argument – education as a process leading to autonomy and self-fulfilment – does not lend itself easily to cross-national comparisons, it is undeniable that the intergenerational maintenance and development of humane societies requires that the respective essentials also be conveyed through education – if not informally by families and the immediate social environment, then in ways institutionalized in formal systems of education. There seems to be a consensus worldwide that historical competence (not just 'historical knowledge'!) and civic competence, along with certain desirable attitudes and behavioural characteristics, are among such aims that transcend the sphere of economic 'usefulness'.

Indeed, civic education has been an early subject of cross-national comparisons (Torney *et al.*, 1975). A case for international comparisons had also been made for the historical domain through the rather comprehensive 'Youth and history' study (Angvik and von Borries, 1997). Both of these domains stand out for the reason that it cannot be assumed that the educational aims that are to be evaluated are universally valid. Quite to the contrary, it seems certain that several 'important' notions of civic competence do not apply to all known societies, and in the case of history, it is even more obvious that national and/or regional curricula are highly context-specific because they are expected to contribute towards, and be conducive to, the formation of a collective identity.

Comparisons of equity, based on the assumption of variable
background-output-relationships

While the first four approaches discussed here all had in common that countries were assumed to compete with each other in terms of maximizing the selected criteria, a more recent development in cross-national comparisons has been centred around the notion of minimizing the influence of background characteristics on educational achievement. It is assumed here that equity, understood as a balanced educational opportunity structure for all social groups, is differentially attained in different systems of education. Although this perspective has notable predecessors in research on the (in-)equalities of educational opportunities in individual countries, PISA appears to be the first major internationally comparative study where this aspect is treated as an important criterion. The concept used is that of the 'social gradient', defined as the regression line which links social background to individual educational achievement, including implications for the proportion of variance explained in these terms (OECD, 2001: 184).

It is worth noting that this perspective differs substantially from earlier notions of investigating the relationship between social background and institutional affiliation (school type or track). In fact, despite the correlations between social background and track or school type membership, which are often quite high, and despite high correlations between track or school type membership and educational achievement, it is not necessarily the case that one of these effects is simply a duplicate of the other. As it turns out, there may well be a significant difference between the two rank orders so generated for systems, even if they operate under comparable internal structures (for example, the 16 German federal states or *Länder*).

Explanatory variables to be measured

The taxonomy presented above has demonstrated that cross-national comparisons differ in their assumptions as to relevant explanatory components. In particular, statistical advances over the last decades have facilitated analytic distinctions of multiple levels of antecedents to educational achievement.

System-level explanatory variables

Proponents of the productivity approach in cross-national comparisons tend to believe that educational expenditure is an important determinant of aggregate educational achievement, at least potentially, if not actually. The same holds true for many economists of education who compute rates of return to educational investments. It has become routine practice, therefore, to collect standardized information on educational expenditure, on the assumption that additional investments in education should be accompanied by higher levels of achievement (OECD, 1992). Obviously, a high degree of differentiation is in order with respect to this point, because it is unreasonable to assume that there will be equal returns to investments into buildings, learning materials, or teacher salaries, to name but some of the available options.

In the case of expenditure for personnel (teachers), there may be differences depending on the intended effects. For example, an increase in the size of the teaching force in order to improve the teacher-student ratio (or diminish average class sizes), or an increase in teacher salaries in order to attract better-qualified candidates for the teaching profession. Another measure, which is more directly related to learning processes, would be the official allocation of instructional time for a given school subject or topic, with the expectation that more hours of instruction will be correlated with higher achievement.

The latter example shows that such expectations need not be supported by the evidence available at the system level. Thus, various analyses of the TIMSS data set have failed to confirm the expectation at the system level (Baumert *et al.*, 2000), but it may well be that intra-system (class-level) variations in the relationship between officially allocated and effectively used instructional time are responsible for the attenuation of the expected effect. This case may help to demonstrate the necessity of carefully distinguishing the levels of analysis with respect to any one of the predictors mentioned here (Ross, 1997).

Ministries that are in the process of selecting potential explanatory variables at the system level in order to establish a sound educational monitoring system may be well advised to consult the respective lists of indicators that have emerged over time. The OECD's annual 'Education at a glance' reports are a good example.

Similarly, the European Union (2001) has defined a (somewhat more parsimonious) list of educational indicators. These include six system-level variables that could be taken to function as antecedents to educational 'productivity': (a) parent co-operation; (b) system evaluation and governance; (c) educational expenditure per pupil; (d) pre-service and in-service teacher education; (e) participation in pre-primary education; and (f) number of pupils per computer in school.

School and class-level explanatory variables

Most cross-national comparisons have used school-level variables in order to provide accurate descriptions of the context under which the investigated teaching-learning processes take place. It has always been difficult, however, to relate this information to aggregate achievement. The incorporation of class-level data – in particular, teacher-related data – has been accompanied by even more serious difficulties in terms of shaping robust explanatory arguments that are generalizable across systems of education. Much of this experience has been derived from the earlier IEA studies, and it would appear to have been the basis for the decision not to include teacher questionnaires in the PISA research programme.

There is, however, a sizeable body of research evidence accumulated under the label 'school effectiveness research' (Scheerens and Bosker, 1997).

Promising constructs that have emerged from a series of meta-analyses in this line of research are, among others: (a) explicitness and ordering of goals and content; (b) structure and clarity of content; (c) use of material for evaluation of student outcomes, (including the provision of feedback and corrective instruction); (d) mastery learning; (e) differentiated teaching materials; (f) effective class management; (g) use of homework; and (h) high teacher expectations (Creemers *et al.*, 2000).

In the current situation, it seems highly advisable to collect such information, which appears to be reasonably accessible through questionnaires, and incorporate it into cross-national analyses at the appropriate level.

Individual level explanatory variables

At the individual level, superior educational achievement appears to flow from powerful antecedent experiences that have been proven indispensable for any theoretically meaningful analysis. It is therefore imperative that these be included in the respective data collection and analysis. As there is a high degree of commonality across existing cross-national comparisons in this respect, suffice it to include here a list of indicators, grouped into appropriate clusters:

• Basic demographics: (a) age; (b) gender; (c) ethnicity (or immigrant) background; and (d) family situation.
  Socio-cultural and socio-economic background: (a) parents' education; (b) parents' occupation; (c) language(s) spoken in the home; (d) educationally relevant resources (for example, books) in the home; and (e) home possessions/resources.

In the case of the socio-cultural and socioeconomic indicators, these are often combined into a simple construction that is generally described as a 'socioeconomic index'.

Educational outputs to be measured

In its catalogue of educational indicators, the European Union lists the following six domains: (a) mathematics; (b) reading; (c) science; (d) foreign languages; (e) independent learning in the domain of ICT; and (f) civic education. When this list is compared to the sequence of IEA studies since the 1960s, it is obvious that this association has established the feasibility of constructing such indicators beyond any reasonable doubt. By contrast, it will be noted that the OECD has not included all of these areas in its own Programme for International Student Assessment (PISA) although some of the IEA findings beyond PISA have been reported in *Education at a glance.*

It is not by chance that the PISA core programme includes a notion of literacy applied to the first three domains: mathematics, reading and science. Not only does this correspond to the fact that these three subjects appear to be taught and cultivated in all school systems and tracks and in (almost) all grades. This choice also alludes to the assumption that the respective competencies are required for, and conducive to, national economic success. It has already been mentioned, however, that the concept of literacy tends to loosen the link to particular school subjects in favour of an assumed close relationship to 'authentic' situations in everyday (adult) life.

While a similar (though more general) case could be made for information and communication technologies (ICT) and civic competencies and attitudes, the OECD has not progressed very far in the elaboration of respective assessment designs. Yet it appears safe to predict that ICT will eventually form an integral part of the OECD testing programme, and there have been several initiatives to include civic education also (at times classified as a 'cross-curricular competency').

It is even more surprising to find that foreign-language competencies have not received much attention since the IEA studies of English as a foreign language (Massad and Lewis, 1975) and French as a foreign language (Carroll, 1975) in the early 1970s. This contradicts the belief inherent in the school curricula of many European countries that ministries should launch and/or support both teaching and research efforts in this area. For example, the German Standing Conference of Ministers of Education has decided to call for (and fund) a study intended to supplement PISA in the domains of English as a foreign language and German as the language of instruction ('DESI: Assessment of proficiency in German and English as a foreign language', cf. Beck and Klieme, 2003).

The inclusion of German as the language of instruction in this example points to the fact that curricular arguments and references to the increasing significance of foreign languages (most notably English) in the movement towards a global society are not the only, and perhaps not even the most important, sources of justification for cross-national comparisons focused on language beyond reading literacy. Due to a lack of attention (and funds) over the last decades, the measurement of language competencies has not kept up technically with measurement in other domains. However, the existence of school systems with multiple languages of instruction (for example, Belgium and Switzerland) and the occurrence of substantial migratory movements accompanied by the emergence of linguistic minorities clearly demonstrate the need for empirical evidence and a better theoretical understanding of the respective phenomena. It seems safe to infer that the existence of a public language such as English, French or Spanish, which requires pupils to substitute it in school for their vernacular, implies comparable problems in many African and some Latin American countries.

In this situation, it seems fortunate that the Council of Europe (1998) has developed a hierarchical classification of language competencies that is meant to be applicable to both mother tongue and foreign language. If the current attempts to validate this hierarchy of competencies and to demonstrate its usefulness for assessing instructional effectiveness succeed, the respective methodology may develop into an extremely valuable tool for all those ministries of education whose systems have to address, in one way or another, problems of language instruction.

'Higher order thinking skills' to be measured

Conceptual and theoretical foundations

In contexts where simple factual knowledge is losing importance – because it is subject to rapid change, because it is easily available due to ubiquitous modes of information access, and because employment requirements have changed correspondingly – the term 'higher order thinking skills' has gained significance and public attractiveness. However, it is not always quite clear what is meant by this.

One of the best known approaches to distinguishing between simple and more complex or 'higher order' thinking skills has been introduced to the field of educational measurement and, indeed, to the internationally comparative assessment of educational achievement by Benjamin Bloom's *Taxonomy of educational objectives: cognitive domain* (Bloom *et al.*, 1956). It was argued here that, for any subject-matter domain, mastery of a higher level of mental activities requires the individual to have mastered three lower levels: 'knowledge/recall', 'comprehension', and 'application', in that order. That is, the three higher order skills – 'analysis', 'synthesis' and 'evaluation' – were said to require mastery of the three lower levels.

During the first decades of comparative surveys of student achievement, this taxonomy proved to be quite useful as a framework for designing 'test blueprints'. A perusal of these test instruments does show that meaningful test items of higher difficulty can, and should, be generated by aiming at higher order mental processes rather than by concentrating test items on the recall of isolated pieces of information. It has to be noted, however, that test theory in its classical form had rendered little support for instruments designed to operate under such schemes of systematically varied levels of difficulty.

As test models were developed, which were specifically geared towards such frameworks, it became evident that a mastery of 'higher order skills' in one subject-matter area did not necessarily refer to 'general' or 'cross-curricular competencies'. Transferability was limited, and the likelihood of solving a 'higher-order problem' in a given domain was highly correlated with the ability to recall both declarative and procedural knowledge in that field, with a demonstrable level of comprehension and the ability to apply that knowledge to a novel context. The widely held expectations that schools might be able to develop a 'general problem solver' have not been fulfilled (Weinert, 2001).

What does emerge from an analysis of item difficulties in modern tests is that the demand for speedy and complex mental operations increases, as well-designed test items become more difficult. Another way of expressing this is that, within a given domain, the complexity and difficulty of an item is not independent of demands on general intelligence. Even so, mastery of lower competency levels is a good predictor, if not a necessary requirement, for a person to find the solution for a difficult item. In that sense, school-based learning generates important predispositions for students to excel in specific areas, even if not all mental processes involved are directly teachable.

Available evidence

The test design for PISA 2000 included a component on metacognitive abilities, which is of relevance here. Although these abilities were only measured by way of student self-reports, they were highly correlated with the available measures of achievement – above all reading comprehension. Strategically, this is an important finding, suggesting the necessity of further research in this area: Provided that adequate metacognitive abilities prove to be trainable, respective programmes may one day facilitate more efficient institutional learning. Interactive relationships between metacognitive abilities and differential performance, according to the difficulty level of tasks, would be of particular concern here.

PISA has also experimented with problem solving skills, as have some preceding regional studies. More specifically, 'problem solving' here refers to the ability to take acceptable decisions under more or less complex constraints in predefined sequences of action. Current extensions attempt to link such abilities to school-based and extra-curricular skills such as manipulation of functions and computer-handling skills. Should the respective experiments be successful and their outcomes generalizable cross-nationally, it will be the next important step to investigate their relationships with more specifically school-related competencies. One study that was conducted in the very special setting of schools for extremely low-performing students has produced some evidence that reading literacy and structural insight as evidenced by the results of a mathematics test function as necessary conditions for dealing successfully with this type of problem-solving exercise.

Affective areas to be measured

Attitudes as criterion variables

It has been mentioned above that cross-national assessments of civic and historical competencies have included affective measures as criteria. Some examples include: tolerance with respect to immigrants, support for women's rights, attitudes of solidarity with oppressed agents in historical settings, and allegiance to national symbols and tenets of the constitutive national narrative (for example, accounts of the wars of 1812 in the Russian or the American cases). Although these subject-matter areas have received relatively little attention in the course of cross-national comparisons of student achievement, there is valuable evidence available that demonstrates the applicability of elaborate scaling techniques to this type of data. These techniques have been used to investigate the existence of item-by-country interaction affects, so-called 'differential item functioning', in order to answer the question of whether or not these attitudes can be compared internationally (Schulz, 2004). So far, little evidence has been found that might induce significant scepticism in this respect.

Attitudes as covariates

The tradition of including attitudinal variables as 'predictors' or, phrased somewhat more carefully, as 'covariates' of educational achievement refers to an entirely different practice. Generally, this assessment strategy is built upon the robust relationship between motivational and achievement variables, and there is an abundance of scales (shown to 'work' in earlier studies) which can be used for this purpose. The following is a list of dimensions that might be considered here: (a) subject-related interest; (b) subject-related self-efficacy; (c) general self-confidence; (d) general motivation to study; (e) general satisfaction with school; (f) test-anxiety; (g) perception of school climate; and (h) perceptions of classroom and instruction. The comparability of such measures across countries has generally been assumed, although it has seldom been tested. Here, too, dimensional analyses, intended to ascertain the construct validity of these measures, as well as investigations into the psychometric properties of items and scales including potential differential item functioning, will have to be conducted.

New trends in assessment

Scaling methods

Beginning with IAEP (Lapointe *et al.*, 1992*a*, *b*) and the IEA Reading Literacy Study (Elley, 1994), the application of probabilistic test models derived from Item Response Theory (IRT) have become standard in the field of cross-national comparisons of student achievement. Although this technique was first suggested as early as 1960 (Rasch, 1960), and although it remained largely ignored for a number of years, there are a number of reasons why this paradigmatic shift took place:

- IRT scores express student abilities in terms of probabilities to solve items of known difficulty. Item difficulties and person abilities are defined on the same scale.

- Tests to be scaled with IRT can be tailored to specific ability groups, if there is some overlap of items between the test versions used ('horizontal anchoring'), and they can also be used longitudinally to monitor changes over time, if this condition is met ('vertical anchoring').

- IRT offers a number of options to deal with missing data, including the case of systematically omitted data in rotated designs. The most elaborate of these techniques to date is the so-called 'plausible-values approach' (Beaton, 1987) where even background information is taken into account when computing optimal estimates of ability distributions.

- IRT models are available for a considerable variety of conditions, distinguishing, for instance, the cases of dichotomous v. polytomous variables. For the case of dichotomous variables, the classical Rasch model (that is, the one-parameter logistic model) estimates only item difficulty parameters, while Birnbaum's two-parameter logistic model (Lord and Novick, 1968) adds a separate parameter for item discrimination. The three-parameter logistic model (3PL) also estimates a corrective term for guessing.

- Over and above the estimation of 'latent traits' (such as student abilities), models have been proposed to indicate also the existence of 'latent classes' with specific response patterns (McCutcheon, 1987).

It is clear that this is not the place to discuss the relative merits of each of these models. The decision in favour or against a particular model depends in part on certain psychometric fit indices that may rule out one or more of the available options. At the same time, a data analyst may decide on a particular model because of secondary advantages of a given option among the ones that are justifiable in principle. Such a consideration may refer to the robustness of estimates across replications, a point that certainly merits significant attention in a cross-national context. The latter consideration generally leads to decisions in favour of relatively simple, robust and parsimonious models.

A particularly important point in this respect refers to the construction of 'hierarchies of competencies' or 'performance scales' (Kelly, 2002), as they are sometimes called. This special area is currently very much under development, with several approaches to the definition of 'competency levels' developed. Once more, TIMSS had a pioneer role in this field of development. It seems to be a generalizable experience that the definition of such levels greatly enhances the dissemination of assessment results, and it renders an important starting point for the formulation of theories explaining the cognitive demand structures in the respective subject-matter area.

Types of assessment

Partly because of these new approaches to analysing test data, hitherto rarely applied or entirely new methods of assessing student achievement have begun to be common in the field:

- Increasingly, achievement tests display variable item formats, including closed formats such as multiple choice and open formats such as short answers and extended responses, as was already the case in TIMSS. In the case of such combinations, by virtue of IRT scaling techniques, dichotomous and polytomous items (to be scored in the 'partial credit mode') can be freely combined.

- Standardized tests can be complemented by more flexible tasks, such as essay-type assignments. There are promising approaches to combine expert rating techniques with IRT-based methods to ascertain the psychometric qualities of the implicit rating standards. At the same time, text-related data can be coded in dichotomous form and included in the analysis.

- 'Practical' or 'hands-on' tests are increasingly used to enhance the aspect of authenticity in the assessment exercise. Again, TIMSS has played a major role in introducing such elements into the field of cross-national achievement comparisons. Although pragmatic aspects may, in some cases, be counter-indicative of such extensions – cost, for instance, or the difficulties involved in ensuring comparable ratings/codes for the students' work results or products, there can be little doubt that this area merits further exploration.

- It is of special interest to accompany experiments where conventional paper-and-pencil techniques are complemented or even substituted by computer-based testing techniques (Lietz and Kotte, 2000). As computers become more readily available, this may become an affordable and efficient option, even in less developed countries. The advantageous aspect of using this approach to enhance access to the more remote segments of an educational system hardly needs elaboration here.

Curricular versus contextual validity

It has been discussed above that the adult literacy studies and, in their sequel, PISA have to a certain extent uncoupled the assessment of educational achievement from the rather narrow considerations of curricular validity which had featured so prominently in the early international comparisons, above all, the early IEA studies.

TIMSS had an intermediate role in this respect: In order to test the effects of deviations from curricular equivalence across countries, a special checking routine, the 'test-curriculum matching analysis' (TCMA) (Beaton and Gonzales, 1997) was designed. Within this special routine, performance in each participating country was scaled according to a vector representing that country's own curriculum, as well as all the vectors for the other participating countries. The results showed that, at least in the area of mathematics, there were few differences attributable to such distinctions. It is possible, of course, that in other areas of comparison, such effects would be larger.

In the case of the IEA civic education study, it had been assumed that considerable item-by-country interaction affects would be evident for the cognitive test, due to differential influences of surrounding political cultures. In fact, it was hoped to find such instances that could have been taken as empirical evidence for the cross-national variance of political cultures. As it turned out, extremely few such effects could be identified. Where they were noted, they were not large enough to justify the exclusion of the respective items from the country-related analyses.

Countries with different sub-systems of education and/or different languages of instruction are, in principle, in a situation that is not different from that in international comparisons. Several decades of experience in that field have produced a wealth of methods and techniques that facilitate fair comparisons, taking all sorts of contextual influences into account. It may have become clear, however, that the notion of comparisons is second to the dominant objectives of identifying benchmarks of commendable student achievement and system productivity, as well as mechanisms where the effectiveness and efficiency of educational systems can be changed for the better. Undoubtedly, most ministries of education subscribe to these aims and are willing, for that very reason, to continue to invest in the conduct of cross-national studies of the quality of education.

Conclusion

No single investigation can meet all questions, concerns, and intentions that are potentially behind the initiative of a ministry of education to conduct an assessment study. This is not only because of the possibility of diverging interests within any given ministry, but even more so because of the wide array of alternatives to be considered and eventually implemented by the researchers. A lesson to be drawn from the taxonomy of studies presented above may be that the choice is not likely to be an easy one. Above all, decision-makers in the ministry are required to specify, with maximum precision, the issues to be investigated, obviously a necessary step before any design can rationally be defined.

While the basic assumptions of some of the older paradigms – for example, the assumption of context-output relationships which are invariant across countries or the assumption of fixed input-output-relationships – appear to be both oversimplified and overoptimistic; more recent approaches with their emphasis on contextual heterogeneity and multiple criteria present a significant challenge to context knowledge and methodological judgement. Thus, decision-makers in the ministries will have to be familiar both with the political issues as part of the domain for which they are responsible, and with the potential of current approaches to educational research.

It is, perhaps, realistic to assume that this familiarity does not necessarily include high levels of specialized competence in terms of test theory and data analysis. What seems to be more relevant here is an acute awareness of the factors that are potentially influencing the criteria under scrutiny. Such awareness will be crucial to the selection of relevant constructs and valid indicators, respectively, and thus be essential to the usefulness of the study undertaken.

References

Amadeo, J.-A.; Tourney-Purta, J.; Lehmann, R.; Husfeldt, V.; Nikolova, R. 2002. *Civic knowledge and engagement. An IEA study of upper secondary students in sixteen countries.* Amsterdam: IEA.

Angvik, M.; von Borries B. (1997). *Youth and history. A comparative European survey on historical consciousness and political attitudes among adolescents.* Hamburg: Körber-Stiftung.

Baumert, J.; Bos, W.; Lehmann, R.L. 2000. *TIMSS/III. Dritte Internationale Mathematik- und Naturwissenschaftsstudie – Mathematische und naturwissenschjaftliche Bildung am Ende der Schullaufbahn.* 2 Bde. Oplade: Leske + Budrich.

Beaton, A.E. 1987. *Implementing the new design: The NAEP 1983-84 technical report.* Princeton, NJ: Educational Testing Service, National Assessment of Educational Progress.

Beaton, A.E.; Gonzales, E.J. 1997. "TIMSS test curriculum matching analysis". In: M.O. Martin and D.L. Kelly (Eds.), *Third international mathematics and science study. Technical report. Vol. II: Implementation and analysis.* pp.187-193. Chestnut Hill, MA: Boston College.

Beck, B.; Klieme, E. 2003: DESI – Eine Längsschnittstudie zur Untersuchung des Sprachunterrichts in deutschen Schulen. *Empirische Pädagogik, 17*(3), 380-395.

Becker, G.S. 1964. *Human capital.* New York: National Bureau of Economic Research.

Bloom, B.S.; Engelhart, M.D.; Furst, E.J.; Hill, W.H.; Krathwohl, D.R. (Eds.). 1956. *Taxonomy of educational objectives. Handbook 1: Cognitive domain.* New York, NY: McKay.

Carroll, J.B. 1975. *The teaching of French as a foreign language in eight countries. International Studies in Evaluation V.* Uppsala: Almquist & Wiksell.

Cattell, R.B. 1960. *Culture fair intelligence test, scale 2.* 3rd Ed. Champaign, IL: IPAT.

Council of Europe (1998). *Modern languages: Learning, teaching, assessment. A common European framework of reference.* Strasbourg: Council for Cultural Co-operation.

Creemers, B.; Scheerens, J.; Reynolds, D. 2000. "Theory development in school effectiveness research". In: C. Teddlie and D. Reynolds (Eds.), *The international handbook of school effectiveness research.* pp. 283-298. London & New York: Falmer.

Deutsches *PISA*-Konsortium (Ed.). 2002. *PISA 2000 – Die Länder der Bundesrepublik Deutschland im Vergleich.* Opladen: Leske + Budrich.

Elley, W.B. (Ed.). 1994. *The IEA study of reading literacy: Achievement and instruction in thirty-two school systems.* Oxford: Pergamon.

European Union – Directorate General for Education and Culture. 2001. *European report on the quality of school education. Sixteen quality indicators. Report based on the working committee on quality indicators.* Luxembourg: European Union.

Husén, T. 1967. *International study of achievement in mathematics. A comparison of twelve countries.* Vols. 1-2. Uppsala: Almquist & Wiksell.

Kelly, D.L. 2002. "Application of the scale anchoring method to interpret the TIMSS achievement scales". In: D.F. Robitaille and A. Beaton (Eds.), *Secondary analysis of the TIMSS data.* pp. 375-390. Dordrecht: Kluwer Academic Publishers.

Lapointe, A.E.; Mead, N.A.; Askew, J.M. 1992a. *Learning mathematics. Report of the international assessment of educational progress.* (Report No. 22-CAEP-01.) Princeton, NJ: Educational Testing Service.

Lapointe, A.E.; Askew, J.M.; Mead, N.A. 1992b. *Learning science. Report of the international assessment of educational progress.* (Report No.22-CAEP-02.) Princeton, NJ: Educational Testing Service.

Lietz, P.; Kotte, D. 2000. *The importance of economic literacy.* Frankfurt am Main: Peter Lang.

Lord, F.M.; Novick, M. R. 1968. *Statistical theories of mental test scores.* Reading, MA: Addison-Wesley.

Massad, E.G., Lewis, C.E. 1975. *The teaching of English as a foreign language in ten countries. International studies in evaluation IV.* Uppsala: Almquist & Wiksell.

McCutcheon, A.L. 1987. *Latent class analysis.* Newbury Park, CA: Sage.

NCES. 1993. *Adult literacy in America. A first look at the results of the national adult literacy survey.* Washington, DC: NCES.

NCES. 1998. *Adult literacy in OECD countries. Technical report on the first international adult literacy survey.* Washington, DC: NCES.

OECD. 1992. *Education at a glance. OECD indicators.* Paris: OECD.

OECD. 2001. *Knowledge and skills for life. First results from PISA 2000.* Paris: OECD.

Passow, A.H.; Noah, H.J.; Eckstein, M.A.; Mallea, K.R. 1976. *The national case study: An empirical comparative study of twenty-one education systems.* New York: Wiley.

Rasch, G. 1960. *Probabilistic models for some intelligence and attainment tests.* Copenhagen: Nielsen & Lydiche (2nd Ed., Chicago: University of Chicago Press, 1980).

Ross, K.N. 1997. Research and policy: a complex mix. *IIEP Newsletter, XV*(1), 1-4.

Scheerens, J.; Bosker, R.J. (1997). *The foundations of educational effectiveness.* London: Pergamon

Schultz, T. 1961. "Investment in human capital". *American Economic Review, 51*(1), 1-17.

Schulz, W. 2004. "Scaling procedures for likert-type items on students' concepts, attitudes, and actions". In: W. Schulz and H. Sibberns (Eds.), *The IEA civic education study. Technical report,* pp. 93-126. Amsterdam: IEA.

Torney, J.V.; Oppenheim, A.N.; Farnen, R.F. 1975. *Civic education in ten countries. international studies in evaluation VI.* Uppsala: Almquist & Wiksell.

Torney-Purta, J.; Lehmann, R.; Oswald, H.; Schulz, W. (2001). *Citizenship and education in twenty-eight countries. Civic knowledge and engagement at age fourteen.* Amsterdam: IEA.

UNESCO. 1997. *International standard classification of education.* November. Retrieved 28 January 2005, from: http://www.unesco.org/education/information/nfsunesco/doc/isced_1997.htm.

Walberg, H.J. (Ed.). 1990. *Educational productivity. The evaluation of educational efficiency: constraints, issues, and policies (Vol. 1).* Greenwich and London: JAI Press.

Walker, D.A. 1976. *The IEA six subject survey: an empirical study of education in twenty-one countries.* Uppsala: Almquist & Wiksell.

Weinert, F. 2001. "Concept of competence: A conceptual clarification". In: D.S. Rychen and L.H. Salganik (Eds.), *Defining and selecting key competencies,* pp. 45-65. Seattle, Toronto, Bern, Göttingen: Hogrefe & Huber.

Chapter 8
Whom should be measured in a cross-national study?

Pierre Foy

Introduction

Sampling is an important and integral part of any international comparative assessment. It is only through the selection of proper samples that researchers and policy analysts alike can be assured that the assessments of the quality of education are applied to comparable populations of students, resulting in unbiased and reliable survey estimates. This is accomplished by correctly defining the target population, relying on sound sampling methodology, determining an appropriate sample size, computing and applying sampling weights, and correctly estimating the standard errors.

One of the primary purposes of international comparative studies in education is to compare student achievement across countries. Sampling is an important activity in such studies. Samples must be drawn based on sound methods from well-defined populations that will ultimately be comparable. Several recent international assessments have taken action to control and monitor sampling activities among participating countries. Well-designed scientific sampling procedures are the only means of assuring that the assessments will be applied to comparable groups of students in all participating countries.

This article has examined the many factors that should be considered when drawing a proper sample. It is not meant to be a detailed technical presentation, because most international assessments provide sampling manuals for this purpose (Foy and Joncas, 2001, 2004). Rather, it is meant to provide a more pragmatic discussion of these sampling procedures for researchers and policy analysts. Through these discussions, they should be in a better position to formulate their policy-relevant questions and, more importantly, be able to translate these questions into appropriate specifications of the sampling procedures.

Target population definition

The goal of international assessments is to make comparisons of interest to researchers, parents, the public and governments. Target populations must therefore be chosen so as to address the main research questions, and to permit valid comparisons across participating countries. There are two general approaches used to define target populations in cross-national studies of the quality of education: the coverage of an age cohort, or the coverage of a target grade. The study's research questions will generally lean towards one or the other, thereby making the choice relatively straightforward. However, making this choice can become complicated when multiple national policy interests and differences in national education systems manifest themselves.

Age-based definitions

Age-based target population definitions focus on the coverage of a specific age cohort, for example all 15-year-old students in an education system, as implemented by PISA (Programme for International Student Assessment) (Adams and Wu, 2002). Such a definition has definite appeal to policy analysts for its simplicity and straightforward interpretation. For instance, it can be of great policy interest to know what students have learned by the time they reach a certain age, such as the maximum age of compulsory education.

Despite the apparent simplicity of an age-based definition, getting international agreement on a common age cohort can be difficult because of structural differences among national education systems. Principally, countries will argue that a 15-year-old pupil in a given country will have been exposed to more, or fewer, years of schooling, than a 15-year-old pupil in another country. Fluctuations in age of entrance requirements, grade repetition policies, and curriculum coverage can also be drawn into the debates.

A suitable sample design for an age-based population definition would be to simply identify all age-eligible students in selected schools and draw a random sample of them. In sampling terms, this is a rather efficient design, minimizing clustering effects within schools and thereby producing more reliable student-level estimates. Analytically, an age-based definition does have its limitations. For example, it would be nearly impossible to develop explanatory models involving classroom structure and instructional practices, mostly because the age-based population would be likely to cross several grades and the sampled students would be too thinly spread across grades and classrooms in each sampled school.

An age-based target population also presents operational challenges. The students sampled within each school need to be taken out of their regular classes and assembled in an available classroom for testing. Some jurisdictions find this too disruptive of normal school operations. In addition, there may not be a suitable room to assemble the sampled students for testing. Having said this, several international assessments have managed to implement such designs – for example IAEP (International Assessment for Educational Progress) (Lapointe *et al.*, 1989) and PISA (Adams and Wu, 2002).

Grade-based definitions

Grade-based target population definitions focus on a specific grade, or a specific set of grades, as implemented in TIMSS (Third International Mathematics and Science Study) (Beaton *et al.*, 1996*a*, 1996*b*, 1996*c*, 1996*d*) and PIRLS (Progress in International Reading Literacy Study) (Martin *et al.*, 2003). For example, a definition could focus on the eighth year of schooling in an education system when counting from the start of primary schooling. Such a definition generally has great appeal, particularly since assessment instruments are usually developed based on curriculum coverage. In addition, because classrooms are organized by grade, sampling classrooms becomes practical and relevant.

Achieving an international consensus on a suitable target grade can be elusive for similar reasons that are raised in debates on age–based definitions. In addition, student ages in a given grade will vary across jurisdictions – the mean age of students in a grade can vary by as much as a full year, sometimes more, across countries – depending on age of entrance requirements and grade repetition policies.

The main advantage of a grade-based definition is its greater range of available contextual information. Whereas an age-based population can generally only offer contextual information for schools and students, a grade-based population will also offer contextual information for classrooms and teachers.

Units of analysis

The units of analysis are the entities we wish to analyse. In an international assessment, it is generally quite clear that our primary units of analysis will be the students themselves. International assessments, however, also study the contextual frameworks that can influence student achievement. Therefore, we might want to consider schools as the units of analysis by collecting information from schools. These data will allow us to describe the school-level environment in which our students learn.

School-level analyses can be approached from two perspectives. The first is simply to analyse schools as a population in their own right. We can then describe the population of schools based on the data that we collected from them. The second is to consider school-level data as contextual information to describe our population of students. For the first approach, we would make statements such as 'the percentage of schools with a library'. For the second approach, we would make statements such as 'the percentage of students who attend a school with a library'. The distinction between the two can be an important one, and may lead to different findings from a policy perspective. For example, we may learn that only 20 per cent of schools have a library, but that 80 per cent of students attend such schools.

It is important to note the distinction between units of analysis and sampling units, although we will often find that both concepts tend to overlap. Whereas we have already defined the units of analysis, sampling units are the units we actually sample in our pursuit of the units of analysis, and may not necessarily be units we wish to analyse. In general, international assessments sample schools and students for the operational convenience of sampling clusters of students within sampled schools. Thus, schools and students are both considered as sampling units. With a grade-based target population, we may wish to sample a classroom of students from sampled schools. In this case, schools, classrooms and students are the sampling units, while schools and students are the units of analysis. Classrooms may also become units of analysis if the contextual framework of the research requires this.

Coverage and exclusions

International assessments define what is generally termed the international desired target population. All participating countries are then expected to define their national desired target population in accordance with this international standard. For example, the PIRLS international desired target population definition reads as follows:

The PIRLS 2006 target population is defined as all students enrolled in the grade that represents four years of schooling, counting from the first year of ISCED level 1, providing the mean age at the time of testing is at least 9.5 years.

The international desired target population should clearly describe the primary units of analysis. All elements of the definition need to be stated clearly for all participating countries to implement properly, leading to comparable populations across countries. The national desired target population thus becomes a country's implementation of the international desired target population in its national context.

A country that wishes to consider a different age cohort, or a different target grade, in its national desired target population than what is spelled out in the international desired target population, should be immediately advised of the inappropriateness of their choice. Clearly, this kind of decision would severely compromise the comparability of this country's data with respect to all other participating (and complying) countries.

The exclusion of certain subgroups of students from all those students covered by the international desired target population is referred to as reduced national coverage. Examples could be private schools, a minority language group or a geographical region. If substantial numbers of students are excluded from the national desired target population, then the results from the study cannot be deemed representative of the whole national education system. Therefore, international assessments encourage all participating countries to strive for complete coverage in their national desired target populations. Countries with significant levels of reduced coverage are identified in the final analyses to inform the researchers and policy analysts of potential shortcomings in making comparisons from the data.

National coverage should not be limited to schools under the jurisdiction of the Ministry of Education. National coverage should include private schools, even though they may be fully autonomous and not under the direct supervision of the ministry. National coverage should in fact include all schools that operate within the mainstream of regular schooling, regardless of where their locus of responsibility lies. This could include, for example, schools administered by the ministries of agriculture, commerce, industry, or national defence.

Using their national desired target population as a general framework, participating countries will then define their national defined target population – in essence, their school sampling frame. All schools and students from the national desired target population excluded from the national defined target population are referred to as the excluded population. These exclusions can occur at the school-level, in which case the schools are removed from the sampling frame, or within sampled schools, where sampled students within sampled schools are excluded from the assessment.

International assessments set minimum standards for allowable exclusions. For example, TIMSS and PIRLS allow a maximum of 10 per cent of excluded students from the national desired target population, although most countries maintain exclusion rates below 5 per cent. In general, practical reasons are invoked for excluding schools and students from the national defined target population, such as increased survey costs, increased complexity in the sample design, and difficult testing conditions. Typical reasons for excluding schools from the sampling frame are: (a) schools in geographically remote regions; (b) schools of extremely small size; (c) schools that offer a curriculum, or structure, that is different from the mainstream education system; and (d) schools that provide instruction only to students in the exclusion categories defined as within-sample exclusions.

The exclusion of eligible students can also occur within sampled schools, generally because of impractical testing conditions for those students. The main reasons invoked for such exclusions are: (a) students with mental disabilities that would make it difficult, even impossible, for them to follow the general instructions of the test; (b) students with physical disabilities that would make it impossible for them to perform in the testing situation; and (c) students unable to read or speak the language of the test, generally newly arrived immigrants.

The distinctions between international desired, national desired, and national defined target populations can be nebulous. As their main objective, international assessments strive to achieve full coverage of the international desired target population among all participating countries and to keep all types of exclusions to a minimum. The difference between international and national desired target populations is generally referred to as exclusions from national coverage. Only a sizeable exclusion of the target population would be considered in this regard. All other sources of exclusions would constitute exclusions from the national desired population, consisting of school-level exclusions and within-sample exclusions. Exclusions, therefore, describe the difference between the national desired and national defined target populations.

Figure 8.1   Coverage and exclusions

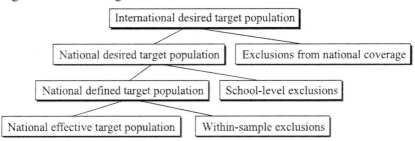

The relationships between the many levels of target populations and the possible reductions in coverage and exclusions are illustrated in *Figure 8.1*. Ultimately, the national effective target population is the population that the sample of participating students effectively represents, after all sources of exclusions have been taken into account.

The main aspects of sample design

International assessments usually make use of complex sample designs for selecting their student samples. They are generally referred to as multi-stage stratified cluster sample designs. They are called multi-stage because the sample of students is selected in multiple stages; for example schools in a first stage, classrooms in a second stage, and students in a final and third stage. They are called stratified because schools in the sampling frame are usually divided, or stratified, into homogeneous groups prior to the commencement of the sampling. Finally, the term 'cluster' is used to highlight the fact that the final sample consists of clusters of students, either at the school level, or the classroom level, or both. This clustering of students, although practical in operational terms, leads to sampling inefficiencies, which will need to be compensated, usually through the selection of larger samples.

Sampling stages and sampling units

If our sole purpose were to select a sample of students to measure overall student achievement, then the most efficient sample design would

161

consist of directly sampling students from a list of all eligible students. By efficient, we mean obtaining the most reliable survey results from the smallest possible sample size. Rarely, however, does such an efficient design meet our analytical objectives, or our operational constraints. First, a complete list of all eligible students may not be readily available. Even if such a list were available, the sample of students would be likely to be found in as many different schools (that is, one student per school) spread out all over the country, making this a potentially costly enterprise.

International assessments usually plan to analyse more than just student achievement. They will include in their analytical objectives research questions related to the context in which students learn, which would include the schools that students attend. Therefore, the need to consider schools as units of analysis, as well as sampling units, makes multi-stage sample designs attractive for analytical and operational considerations.

International assessments with age-based target populations, such as PISA, will generally make use of a two-stage sample design, with schools and students as the two sampling stages. International assessments with grade-based target populations, such as TIMSS and PIRLS, will apply a three-stage sample design, where schools, classrooms and students are the sampling stages, although two-stage sample designs can also be considered.

Classrooms as sampling units present a particular challenge. Classrooms are not always stable and homogeneous units in terms of the students they contain. For example, students in a language class might not go to the same mathematics or science class. It is therefore very important to clearly state what is meant when using the term classroom, both as a sampling unit and a unit of analysis, and to ensure that all grade-eligible students in a given school will be accounted for in the retained classroom partitioning.

The school sampling frame

The school sampling frame is a list of all eligible schools from which we select the school sample. The existence of a sampling frame of good quality is crucial if we are to draw valid samples that are meant to represent our defined target population properly. The school sampling frame is generally derived from administrative records, usually located at the ministry of education. A well-constructed school sampling frame provides complete coverage of all eligible schools, contains no ineligible schools, no duplicate entries, and is constructed from up-to-date information.

The school sampling frame should provide a complete coverage of all eligible schools, in accordance with the national defined target population. All schools with either age-eligible or grade-eligible students should be included in the school sampling frame. Eligible schools that are not present in the school sampling frame will have no chance of being included in the school sample, and consequently are considered as part of the excluded population.

The school sampling frame should have no ineligible schools. That is, schools with no age-eligible or grade-eligible students. This includes schools that have been identified for exclusion. The presence of ineligible schools in the school sampling frame may lead us to select some of them in the sample, with the consequence of reducing our effective sample size.

The school sampling frame should have no duplicate schools. That is, schools appearing more than once. The presence of duplicate schools may mask the true selection probabilities of these schools. This could also lead us to select the same schools more than once, thereby reducing our effective sample size.

The school sampling frame should have up-to-date information on all eligible schools. The school measures of size need to be as accurate as possible, as well as the stratification information. Outdated information will result in less efficient samples, possibly the inclusion of ineligible schools, the exclusion of eligible schools, and inappropriate selection probabilities.

Stratification

Stratification consists of grouping schools prior to sampling by using one, or several, stratification variables. Stratification is generally used for the following reasons: (a) to improve the efficiency of the sample design, thereby making survey estimates more reliable; (b) to apply a disproportionate sample allocation to specific groups of schools, in order to produce reliable estimates for each group; and (c) to ensure proportional representation of specific groups in the sample. International assessments will emphasize the need for stratification in an effort to improve the efficiency of national sample designs. After all, their main objective is to obtain accurate national estimates. For example, if urban schools are known to perform better than rural schools in a particular country, then defining rural and urban strata will improve the accuracy of the survey results for this country.

National researchers and policy analysts, however, are likely to have specific national requirements to report research results for subgroups of students in order to make sub-national comparisons. Therefore, they will be more inclined to stratify according to the subgroups they plan to report. For example, if a particular country was interested in reporting achievement levels for each of its states, or provinces, then state or provincial strata could be constructed in order to ensure adequate numbers in the sample from each stratum. Although 'accuracy' and 'reporting' requirements can sometimes be in conflict, they can generally both be accommodated.

■ Explicit stratification

International assessments will usually implement two types of stratification: explicit and implicit. Explicit stratification consists of building separate school lists, or school sampling frames, according to a set of explicit stratification variables. For example, if geographic region is an explicit stratification variable, then separate school sampling frames are constructed for each geographic region. Different sample designs can then be applied to each list in order to select the sample of schools.

The major reason for considering explicit stratification in international assessments is to implement a disproportionate allocation of the school sample to the explicit strata. For example, the same number of schools could be sampled from each explicit stratum, regardless of the relative size of each stratum. The objective in this scenario is to produce equally reliable estimates for each explicit stratum.

■ Implicit stratification

Implicit stratification consists of sorting the school sampling frame by a set of implicit stratification variables. This type of stratification is very effective for the school sample selection method usually employed in international assessments: a probability proportional to size (PPS) systematic method. The concept of implicit stratification is rarely seen with other sample selection methods. It is a very simple way of ensuring a strictly proportional sample allocation of schools across all implicit strata. It can also lead to improved accuracy of survey estimates, provided the implicit stratification variables being considered are known to have a significant between-strata variance component.

▒   Stratification guidelines

Stratification is a tool that allows us to improve the efficiency of our sample design and to better control the reliability of our data for subgroups of the population. There is often a temptation to define as many strata as possible, in the hopes of fully controlling the sample selection process. However, it is nearly impossible to have all segments of the population adequately represented in a sample. For example, we might want to ensure that all regions, all school districts, all school types, both rural and urban, be represented and controlled in the sample. This can quickly lead us to a very large number of strata and consequently a very large and very expensive sample size. Two to four stratification variables are usually sufficient for most surveys. More stratification variables can be considered, but this will likely lead to larger sample sizes.

The following guidelines should be considered when selecting stratification variables: (a) each school in the school sampling frame must belong to one, and only one, stratum; (b) when using a continuous variable for stratification, a few divisions of that variable, (say around 2 to 5) usually provides most of the gains in sampling precision available from that variable, and at the same time avoids creating too many strata; (c) defining very small strata, especially explicit strata, should be avoided because this is unlikely to improve the overall level of sample precision; and (d) at least two schools must be sampled in each explicit stratum to permit the computation of sampling errors. This important criterion usually sets an upper limit to the number of strata that can be defined.

Measures of size

International assessments usually employ a PPS systematic methodology to select the sample of schools. The challenge in applying PPS sampling is to have accurate (or reasonably accurate) measures of school size. Thus, for each school on the school sampling frame we need a reliable 'measure of size' (often known as 'MOS') which provides an estimate of the number of students in each school who are members of the defined target population. The word 'estimate' is used here because for most medium to large school systems the actual enrolment of students within the defined target population is obtained from a school census – which is usually 'out of date' several months after the data are collected.

For a grade-based population, we would need to know how many students in the target grade are found in each school. For an age-based population, we would need to know how many students of the required age are found in each school. However, enrolment by age cohort is not often available at the school level. If this is the case, then school-level enrolment in the target grade that has most of the required age cohort can be a substitute. If grade enrolment is also not available at the school-level, then alternate measures of size at the school-level, expected to be highly correlated with the desired MOS, should be considered: (a) average student enrolment per grade; or (b) number of classrooms in the target grade; or (c) total student enrolment. The enrolment data used as a MOS needs to be as current as possible. If a suitable MOS cannot be found, or if the available enrolment data is too out of date, then it would be wise to rely on equal probability sampling, rather than use unreliable measures of size. Using unreliable measures of size can lead to instability in sample estimates (due mainly to large fluctuations in sampling weights).

PPS systematic sampling

The PPS approach results in school selection probabilities that are proportional to the school MOS. As a result, larger schools have a greater chance of being sampled than smaller schools. The PPS systematic sampling method is very easy to implement, hence its popularity in international assessments. A section of a sampling frame is presented in *Figure 8.2* – which lists the first 42 schools from a school sampling frame with a total of 2,119 schools. Each school is uniquely identified and is reported with a suitable measure of size. From one school to the next, the MOS is cumulated since this is necessary to identify the sampled schools. The sum of the MOS for all 2,119 schools in the sample frame was 59,614. In this example, it was necessary to sample 50 schools. Thus, the 'sampling interval' was computed as the total measure of size divided by the required school sample size:

$$59,614 \div 50 = 1,192.2800$$

The PPS sampling began by determining a random start as a random number between zero and the sampling interval. In our example, this random start was 653.4887. The first sampled school was therefore the one that contained the 653rd student, as determined in the cumulative MOS column. This actually occurs with school 1718 – which is marked in *Figure 8.2* with a tick. The next sampled school is determined by adding the sampling interval to the random start:

$$653.4887 + 1,192.2800 = 1,845.7687$$

This selection number identifies school 0067 as the second sampled school, which is also marked with a tick in *Figure 8.2*. All subsequent sampled schools are identified by adding the sampling interval to the previous selection number and locating this selection in the cumulative MOS column.

Replacement schools

Some additional schools in *Figure 8.2* were identified as 'replacement schools' with the labels R1 and R2. Replacement schools are used as replacement alternatives when sampled schools refuse to participate. It is always advisable to get all, or most, sampled schools to participate, and international assessments set strict standards in this regard, since high-school participation rates are the only assurance of low response biases. We generally suspect that a school's reasons for not participating are somehow related to its performance level. Therefore, as the school participation rate drops, the risk of response bias increases. The use of replacement schools does not entirely remove the risk of response bias; it is principally a mechanism for sustaining the sample size.

As illustrated in *Figure 8.2* below, replacement schools were identified as being adjacent to the sampled schools they were meant to replace. Replacement schools will tend to have similar characteristics to their corresponding sampled school, based on the explicit and implicit stratification variables used. Although this will not necessarily avoid response bias, it may tend to minimize the potential for bias. Furthermore, this approach is better than any haphazard use of alternate schools as replacements, – especially the application of 'over-sampling' to compensate for non-response.

Very large schools

Very large schools are schools whose MOS is greater than the computed sampling interval. This phenomenon is rather unusual, but can occur when dealing with relatively small target populations, or when high sampling rates are applied. These very large schools can be problematic because they can potentially be sampled more than once if we apply the PPS systematic sampling method as described earlier. In theory, this is not a major problem, but in practice, this can be problematic since we would be requesting a larger sample of students from schools sampled more than once.

167

The solution to this problem consists of treating all very large schools as 'certainty schools', that is to say that they are included in the sample with certainty, (i.e. with a probability of 1). The remaining sample of schools is then selected from the schools that remain on the school sampling frame, after having removed all certainty schools.

Figure 8.2   PPS Systematic Sampling Method

Sampling parameters	School identifier	School MOS	Cumulative MOS	Sampled schools
Total number of schools: 2 119	0829	110	110	
Total measure of size: 59 614	0552	101	211	
School sample size: 50	1802	98	309	
Sampling interval: 1 192.2800	1288	98	407	
Random start: 635.4887	2043	95	502	
	0974	94	596	R2
	1718	94	690	✓
	1807	93	783	R1
	0457	93	876	
	0244	93	969	
	1817	91	1 060	
	1741	90	1 150	
	1652	89	1 239	
	0121	89	1 328	
	0309	89	1 417	
	0032	89	1 506	
	0021	89	1 595	
	0609	88	1 683	
	0399	86	1 769	R2
	0067	86	1 855	✓
	0202	86	1 941	R1
	0063	86	2 027	
	1467	86	2 113	
	1381	86	2 199	
	1043	84	2 283	
	1318	84	2 367	
	0659	84	2 451	
	0612	83	2 534	
	1696	82	2 616	
	0867	82	2 698	
	0537	81	2 779	
	1794	80	2 859	
	0695	80	2 939	
	0031	80	3 019	R2
	0333	79	3 098	✓
	0051	79	3 177	R1
	0384	79	3 256	
	1391	79	3 335	
	1189	79	3 414	
	0731	78	3 492	
	0634	78	3 570	
	1230	77	3 647	

Small schools

Small schools are schools whose MOS is less than the number of students we intend to sample within each school. For the PISA study, a sample of 35 15-year-old students was required per school, with any school having less than 35 students considered a 'small school'. If we now consider the TIMSS example, where one classroom of grade-eligible students is sampled per school, then any school with less than a full classroom of grade-eligible students is considered a small school. To be clearer, if the average class size is 25, then any school with less than 25 grade-eligible students is considered a small school.

The presence of small schools can cause a variety of sampling problems. First is the operational inefficiency of sampling schools with very few eligible students. Most international assessments introduce the notion of 'very small schools', for example schools with less than five eligible students, and allow their exclusion, provided this does not compromise the overall exclusion rate. This, however, does not entirely solve the issue of small schools. Any small school that is selected in the school sample may not allow us ultimately to sample a sufficient number of students. The resulting shortfall in sample size may lead to lower reliability of survey estimates. This can be of concern in countries with large rural populations and consequently many small rural schools. The solution to this problem is to consider defining an explicit stratum of small schools and selecting proportionately more schools in that stratum than we would otherwise.

Finally, small schools generally cause havoc with the sampling weights if we persist in applying a PPS sampling method. Furthermore, they are generally plagued with volatile measures of size. A sample with 10 eligible schools one year may have 5, or 15, the next year, causing wild fluctuations in the sampling weights. As a result, small schools are usually sampled with equal probabilities in order to stabilize their sampling weights.

Student sampling

Having selected a sample of schools, the next task is to sample students within sampled schools. How this is done will depend on the target population definition and the analytical objectives. With an age-based population, we draw up a list of all age-eligible students in a sampled school and randomly select a fixed number of students from that list. For example, PISA selects a simple random sample of 35 15-year-old students from each sampled school.

With a grade-based population, we have more student sampling options available. We can in fact apply the same approach as with an age-based population. In each sampled school, we draw up a list of all grade-eligible students and randomly select a fixed number of students from each school list. This is the most efficient way to sample students within schools, but not necessarily the most practical one with a grade-based population. Sampling classrooms instead is a more pragmatic, and less disruptive, sampling method. The method consists of drawing up the list of all classrooms in the target grade for each sampled school, and randomly selecting usually one classroom per school. It is of course possible, and sometimes advisable, to sample more than one classroom per school.

A third student sampling approach available for a grade-based population consists of sub-sampling students within sampled classrooms. This method is applied in two steps. First, we sample classrooms within sampled schools as just described, and secondly we select a random sub-sample of students within sampled classrooms. This approach is somewhat more complex, and may prove disruptive in a classroom setting. However, it can be considered when class sizes are very large and it would prove too costly to test all students in the sampled classrooms. For example, in a school system with class sizes of 50 students, it could be cost effective to select randomly 30 students per sampled classroom.

The determination of sample size

The biggest challenge in developing a sample design is determining the sample size (Foy, 1998). How big a sample do we need? This is the question on the lips of most researchers and policy analysts. Alas, the answer to this question is rather complex and requires elements of information from both the sampling experts and the researchers and policy analysts. Resource constraints must also be considered, and may further cloud the answer. When a sampling expert is asked what should be the sample size, he promptly hears what should be the sampling error. The answer to both questions lies somewhere in the analytical requirements of the study.

Analytical requirements

The general objective of any international assessment, or any type of assessment, is to make comparisons. These can consist of comparisons between countries, comparisons between regions in a country, comparisons between boys and girls, and so on. The kinds of comparisons that are required for a study can affect the sample size, and that therefore needs to be stated explicitly before final sampling decisions are taken. This can be illustrated by considering the information needs of a policy analyst for whom a comparison between two or more groups could lead to a policy change if the observed differences are 'too large'. The main issue here is to determine what is meant by 'too large'. In policy relevant terms, how big a difference between two regions, between rural and urban schools, between boys and girls, would lead to us to revise, or reform, some aspect of the education system?

International assessments have traditionally set achievement scales with a mean of 500 points and a standard deviation of 100 points. These figures are arbitrary, an artefact of how survey results are ultimately presented, but they can give us some context as to what could be considered a big difference. Although we find country variations, past studies such as TIMSS (Beaton *et al.*, 1996*a*; Martin *et al.*, 2000) have demonstrated that the performance gap between two adjacent grades is in the range of 50 to 70 points in the primary grades, and 20 to 40 points in the lower secondary grades (Beaton *et al.*, 1996*a*, 1996*b*, 1996*c*, 1996*d*). For example, based on TIMSS 1995 data, grade 8 students in Canada scored 33 points more than their grade 7 counterparts in mathematics. This is by no means a fixed and standard quantity, but merely a point of reference that is sometimes useful for gaining a better feel for the magnitude of score differences.

If we were to observe a difference of 30 points in favour of urban schools at the eighth grade level, for example, then we might interpret this by saying that children in rural schools are one full school year behind their counterparts in urban schools. Admittedly, this would be a dramatic gap calling for some remedial action. The question is would a 20-point difference also require remedial action? How about a 15-point difference? ... A 10-point difference? ... Assuming that as policy analysts, we were to consider any gap of 15 points or more to be policy relevant, then we would set the sample size such that gaps of 15 points or more would be found to be statistically significant. This means that such large gaps observed in our sample would represent a 'real' difference rather than being attributable to the result of random fluctuations.

Despite this explanation, the answer to our question still remains ambiguous, since international assessments have multiple analytical objectives, both internationally and nationally. As a result, international assessments have a slightly different perspective on this problem. They will generally set their sample size such that any national estimate will be reliable to within a fixed number of points on the achievement scale. This is generally stated as a confidence interval, whereby we can state with a known and high probability that the estimated mean achievement score will be within a fixed number of points of the true national achievement score. If we take TIMSS and PISA as examples, both set their expectations for national mean achievement scores to be within 10 points of the true national achievement score with 95 per cent confidence. Based on statistical theory, all of this implies that the major survey estimates, most notably achievement means, require sampling errors of 5 points.

The coefficient of intra-class correlation

Knowing the required sampling error is still not enough to determine the sample size in international assessments. Because these studies employ a multi-stage cluster sample design, the resulting sample of students is not as efficient as a simple random sample of students. We need to have some idea of the resulting loss of efficiency. This is measured by the coefficient of intraclass correlation (IC). The IC simply measures the disparity between schools. If schools tend to perform at comparable levels, then the IC will be low. If school perform at widely varying levels of performance, then the IC will be high. In the end, countries with a high IC will require a larger sample of schools than countries with a low IC. *Figure 8.3* illustrates the impact of the IC on the sample size. This table is taken from the PIRLS 2006 School Sampling Manual (Foy and Joncas, 2004). The figure also illustrates the impact of the minimum cluster size on the sample size. This factor will be discussed later.

PIRLS 2006 has set minimum sample size requirements for schools (150 schools) and students (4,500 students). Therefore, these values are set as default values in *Figure 8.3* whenever the theoretical sample size calculations would lead us to accept smaller sample sizes. Nonetheless, we can clearly see how the IC affects the sample size. For any given minimum cluster size, the required sample size increases as the IC increases.

The minimum cluster size (MCS)

The minimum cluster size also affects the sample size. The minimum cluster size (MCS) is in effect the student sample size within sampled schools. In the case of PISA, the minimum cluster size is usually set at 35. In the case of TIMSS and PIRLS, where classrooms are sampled, the minimum cluster size is usually the average class size in any given country. Thus, *Figure 8.3* offers a range of minimum cluster sizes to accommodate variations in average class sizes around the world.

Figure 8.3   Sample design table for PIRLS 2006

Minimum cluster size		Intraclass correlation								
		0.1	0.2	0.3	0.4	0.5	0.6	0.7	0.8	0.9
15	a	300	300	300	300	300	300	301	339	376
	n	4 500	4 500	4 500	4 500	4 500	4 500	4 515	5 085	5 640
20	a	225	225	225	225	225	258	296	334	372
	n	4 500	4 500	4 500	4 500	4 500	5 160	5 920	6 680	7 440
25	a	180	180	180	180	216	254	293	331	370
	n	4 500	4 500	4 500	4 500	5 400	6 350	7 325	8 725	9 250
30	a	150	150	150	175	213	252	291	329	368
	n	4 500	4 500	4 500	5 250	6 390	7 560	8 730	9 870	11 040
35	a	150	150	150	173	211	250	289	328	367
	n	5 250	5 250	5 250	6 055	7 385	8 750	10 115	11 480	12 845
40	a	150	150	150	171	210	249	288	327	366
	n	6 000	6 000	6 000	6 840	8 400	9 960	11 520	13 080	14 640
45	a	150	150	150	170	209	248	287	326	365
	n	6 750	6 750	6 750	7 650	9 405	11 160	12 915	14 670	16 425
50	a	150	150	150	169	208	247	286	326	365
	n	7 500	7 500	7 500	8 450	10 400	12 350	14 300	16 300	18 250
55	a	150	150	150	168	207	247	286	325	364
	n	8 250	8 250	8 250	9 240	11 385	13 585	15 730	17 875	20 020
60	a	150	150	150	167	207	246	285	325	364
	n	9 000	9 000	9 000	10 020	12 420	14 760	17 100	19 500	21 840

a = number of sampled schools
n = number of sampled students in target grade

From *Figure 8.3*, we can see how the minimum cluster size affects the sample size. For any given IC greater than 0.3, the sample size increases as the MCS increases. From closer scrutiny, one will observe that the student sample size does not simply increase because the MCS increases, but also because larger cluster sizes actually increase the clustering effect, thereby requiring larger sample sizes.

Sampling weights

The calculation of sampling weights is an important component of any sample design, yet in many educational research surveys it is often overlooked, or even ignored. Sampling weights are assigned to each sampling unit, more specifically the participating students. Their purpose is to maintain the 'relative balance' among sampling units in order to make proper inferences about the whole target population. As a simple example, if we sample 100 students from a population of 1,000 students, then each sampled student is assigned a weight of ten, indicating that one out of every ten students was sampled, or more to the point, that each sampled student is meant to 'represent ten students in the population'.

Sampled students are only rarely assigned equal sampling weights, as in the example above. For example, the need to produce reliable estimates for subgroups of a population can bring us to apply different sampling rates by subgroups. For example, we might want to compare the achievement level of students in public schools to that of students in private schools. Although we may find that 80 per cent of students attend public schools, we would want to allocate equal sample sizes to both subgroups.

Consequently, our sample would consist of 50 per cent of students attending public schools. Without sampling weights, our sample would mislead us into thinking there was a 50/50 split between both groups. More to the point, any difference in achievement levels between the two subgroups would lead us to estimate the overall achievement level incorrectly, by over-emphasizing the contribution of students in private schools. The sampling weights would restore the proper balance between both subgroups, giving larger weights to the students in public schools, in order to estimate the overall achievement level properly.

Selection probabilities

Sampling weights are computed based on the selection probabilities that were applied to select the sampling units. In its simplest terms, the sampling weight of a sampling unit is equal to the inverse of its sample selection probability. Because international assessments rely on multi-stage sample designs, the calculation of sampling weights is a more involved process. The sampling weights need to account for the selection probabilities at all sampling stages. The sampling weights will thus have possibly three components: a school weight component, possibly a classroom weight component, and a student weight component.

The school weight component is equal to the inverse of the school sample selection probability. Since international assessments use probabilities proportional to size, larger schools get larger selection probabilities and consequently smaller school weight components, and smaller schools get smaller selection probabilities, and hence large school weight components.

The classroom weight component is equal to the inverse of the classroom selection probability within a sampled school. This component is relevant only in studies that have a grade-based target population and have classrooms as sampling units. Generally, classrooms within a school are selected with equal probabilities. For example, if we sample one classroom from a school with four eighth grade classrooms, then each classroom has a selection probability of 0.25 and the sampled classroom will have a class weight component of 4.

The student weight component is equal to the inverse of the student selection probability, either within a sampled school in a two-stage sample design, or within a sampled classroom in a three-stage sample design. In either case, students are sampled with equal probabilities. If we take PISA for example, where the student sample usually consists of 35 15-year-old students in each sampled school, then students from a school with 100 age-eligible students will have a selection probability of 0.35, and the sampled students will get a student sampling weight of 2.85715 ($100 \div 35$). If we take PIRLS for example, where only one classroom is usually sampled per sampled school, and all students in that classroom are sampled, then all students in the sampled classroom have a selection probability of 1 and a students sampling weight of 1. If we were to sub-sample students from a sampled classroom, say 30 students from a classroom of 50 students, then all students in that sampled classroom have a selection probability of 0.6 and the sub-sampled students have a students weight component of 1.66667 ($50 \div 30$).

The product of these different weight components constitutes the theoretical overall student-level sampling weight.

Non-response adjustments

If all sampled schools, classrooms, and students were to participate, then the theoretical sampling weight would be appropriate. This, however, is rarely the case since there is usually bound to be some non-response

175

taking place at some level. Our theoretical sampling weights need to be adjusted to account for any non-response among sampling units.

Non-response adjustments can occur at each sampling stage. The school non-response adjustment corrects the school weight component to take into account any school-level non-response. This is usually done at the explicit stratum level. In its simplest form, the school-level non-response adjustment recalibrates the school selection probabilities based on the observed sample of schools, as opposed to the expected sample of schools. For example, if we had expected to sample 100 schools, but only observed 80 participating schools, then the simplest form of the school non-response adjustment will be 1.25 (100 ÷ 80). The school non-response adjustment can be more complex, using the observed and expected weighted school-level student sample sizes.

The classroom non-response adjustment corrects the classroom weight component to take into account any classroom-level non-response. It is computed in an analogous fashion as the school non-response adjustment. When sampling only one classroom per school, however, if the one sampled classroom in a school does not participate, then this constitutes school-level non-response and is accounted for in the school non-response adjustment.

Classroom non-response can be particularly problematic since we could suspect that a sampled classroom that does not participate might consist of low-achieving students. A classroom non-response adjustment computed at the school-level could potentially introduce a non-negligible amount of non-response bias. As a result, TIMSS and PIRLS compute their classroom non-response adjustment at the explicit stratum level to attenuate the effects of any non-response bias.

The student non-response adjustment corrects the student weight component to take into account any student-level non-response. It is again computed in an analogous fashion as the school non-response adjustment, simply re-calibrating the student selection probabilities based on the observed student sample rather than the expected student sample. The student non-response adjustment is computed either at the school-level in two-stage sample designs, or at the classroom-level in three-stage sample designs.

When the theoretical sampling weights are corrected for all non-response adjustments, the result is the final sampling weights. These are the sampling weights that must be used in all analyses in order to properly derive survey estimates. Conceptually, the final sampling weights consist of up to six components, based on the selection probabilities and non-response adjustments at all sampling stages. The exact derivation of these components can be different, depending on the specific sample designs employed by international assessments, but they are the essential building blocks for the derivation of any sampling weights.

It is important to note that the underlying assumption behind non-response adjustments is that non-response is a purely random phenomenon, not related to achievement. Although this is usually difficult to verify, we often suspect that non-response is indeed related in some way to achievement, especially school and classroom non-response. It is therefore very important to maintain high response rates in order to minimize the potential for non-response bias.

Weight trimming

The sample designs used in international assessments can conceivably produce what are termed self-weighting samples. In theory, this means that the final sampling weights are equal for all participating students in a national sample. In practice, however, this is rarely the case for a variety of reasons, thus the necessity to compute sampling weights. Sampling weights will vary when we apply different sampling weights by strata, particularly when reliable sub-national estimates are wanted. Sampling weights can also vary because of different non-response rates between explicit strata. For example, private schools may be less inclined to participate. Sampling weights can also fluctuate because of unexpected events arising either from unreliable information on the school sampling frame, or actual physical changes in the student and school populations. The usual culprit here is inaccuracies in the school measure of size.

We are very likely to find that any given school's MOS will have changed between the time we sampled it from the school sampling frame and the time we actually go to the school to carry out the assessment. These changes are to be expected since the MOS on the school sampling frame will usually be based on enrolment data from a school census conducted the previous school year. However, we would expect these changes to be rather small, and indeed they are in many cases. However, we do find from time to time that a school's MOS has changed dramatically, either being much smaller or much larger than expected. This can occur for legitimate reasons, such as re-structuring of a particular school's function, but can also occur when the school sampling frame is out of date.

The result of this process is the likelihood of finding that some sampling weights become extremely large, resulting in larger sampling errors and possibly wild fluctuations in some estimates. Extremely small weights can also occur, but their consequences are usually not as dramatic. In order to reduce the effect of extremely large sampling weights on sample estimates and their sampling errors, international assessments at times apply a weight trimming function.

The purpose of weight trimming is to reduce extremely large sampling weights to more reasonable levels and thereby reduce their influence on estimates and their sampling errors. The challenge in 'weight trimming' is in striking a balance between eliminating the negative effects of extremely large weights without unduly and artificially reducing the sampling errors. This is usually done by setting a relatively high limit for acceptable sampling weights in the hope that it will catch most of the outliers, but very few of the legitimate sampling weights. For example, PISA trims sampling weights that are greater than four times the median sampling weight.

Types of sampling weights

The sampling weights we have described so far could be termed 'population weights' since adding them up at the national level produces an estimate of the whole target population. These sampling weights are certainly appropriate for producing unbiased and reliable estimates of population characteristics. They may not be appropriate, however, for some particular types of statistical analyses.

The users of more sophisticated statistical analyses, such as factor analyses, hierarchical linear models, and the like, may encounter difficulties with population weights. As a rule, these statistical models will assume that the population weights are meant to represent the sample size. Thus, they will severely overestimate the degrees of freedom, and underestimate variances. These difficulties can be partially overcome by computing standardized weights. Standardized weights are a simple transformation of the population weights whereby the standardized weights will add up to the national sample size. With standardized weights, statistical analyses will produce more appropriate degrees of freedom, but will still tend to underestimate variances. Although the use of standardized weights is advisable for these complex statistical models, researchers and analysts must remain careful when using sampling errors.

Population weights and standardized weights may not be appropriate when making cross-national comparisons. The issue is on what basis are countries to be compared? Should countries be compared based on their population size, their sample size, or should they be compared 'equally' (that is, as if the same size sample was used in each country)?

Comparing countries with the population weights will make larger countries in terms of population dominate the comparison. Comparing countries with the standardized weights will make larger countries with larger samples dominate the comparison. If all countries are meant to be compared on an equal footing, then a third set of sampling weights is required, which we will call 'uniform weights'. Uniform weights are derived in a similar fashion as the standardized weights, but instead they are re-calibrated to sum up to a constant size for each country. For example, TIMSS and PIRLS compute what they call 'senate weights', which add up to 500 in each country.

Sampling errors

The sampling error of any survey estimate is a measure of its dispersion among all the possible samples that could have been drawn given the sample design and sample size used. Luckily, we do not need to select all of these samples to measure the sampling errors of our survey estimates. Statistics and sampling theory give us the tools to compute sampling errors from the one sample we have selected.

Sampling errors are used to construct confidence intervals centered on our estimates. We can then be assured with a known and high probability that our confidence intervals contain the true population estimate. For example, the 95 per cent confidence interval for a mean student achievement score is given by the following equation:

$$[\ \overline{X} - 1.96 \cdot se(\ \overline{X}),\ \overline{X} + 1.96 \cdot se(\ \overline{X})]$$

For example, if we were to estimate a national mean student achievement score of 538 points with a sampling error of 4.7, then its 95 per cent confidence interval would be:

$$[528.8, 547.2]$$

We would then be in a position to state there was a 95 per cent chance that the population value of the average student achievement was somewhere in that interval.

Clustering effects

Clustering has an effect on the sampling errors. Larger coefficients of intraclass correlations produce larger sampling errors. Sampling larger clusters also produces larger sampling errors. In *Figure 8.3*, we can observe the effect that clustering has on the determination of sample size. The effect that clustering can have on the sampling error, for a given sample size, can be observed from the following equation:

$$se(\overline{X}) = 100 \sqrt{\frac{1 + IC\,(m-1)}{n - m}}$$

This equation is an approximation of the theoretical formulation of the sampling error for multi-stage sample designs (Cochran, 1977). The quantity 100 is taken from the standard deviation that is fixed for most international assessments. The *IC* is the coefficient of intraclass correlation; *m* is the minimum cluster size (that is, the within-school sample of students); and *n* is the school sample size. The data presented in *Figure 8.4* are derived from this equation.

Figure 8.4   Sampling errors

Sample size	Coefficient of intraclass correlation									
	0.0	0.1	0.2	0.3	0.4	0.5	0.6	0.7	0.8	0.9
n = 300 m = 20	1.3	2.2	2.8	3.3	3.8	4.2	4.5	4.9	5.2	5.5
n = 200 m = 30	1.3	2.5	3.4	4.0	4.6	5.1	5.5	6.0	6.4	6.7
n = 150 m = 40	1.3	2.9	3.8	4.6	5.3	5.8	6.4	6.9	7.3	7.8

We can clearly see that the sampling error increases as the IC increases, recalling that the IC is a measure of disparity between schools. In addition, as the minimum cluster size increases, from 20 to 30 to 40, so does the sampling error, the rate of increase getting bigger as the IC increases. As a point of reference, the sampling error of 1.3 computed for an IC of zero is in effect the sampling error that standard software packages would normally compute. Such sampling errors can be serious underestimations of the true sampling errors. The resulting estimates of confidence intervals become much smaller and could likely lead policy analysts to make seriously flawed inferences from the data.

Estimation methods

For simple sample designs, sampling errors can be easily computed from straightforward equations, and this is what most statistical software packages do. Because international assessments use complex multi-stage cluster sample designs, the computation of sampling errors is no longer a straightforward affair. In fact, we would actually be challenged to come up with the exact equations needed to compute sampling errors because of the complex sample design and the PPS systematic sampling method. Furthermore, the clustered nature of the samples makes these samples less efficient and result in larger sampling errors.

As a result, international assessments rely on 'sample replication techniques' to derive the sampling errors empirically. These methods are often referred to as bootstrap or jackknife methods, and they have been demonstrated to have sound statistical properties, provided they are applied correctly (Wolter, 1985). The usual methods used by international assessments are either (a) the balanced repeated replication (BRR) method – such as in PISA, or (b) the jack-knife repeated replication (JRR) method – such as in TIMSS and PIRLS. The general principle of all of these sample replication methods is to draw multiple sub-samples from the full sample and derive appropriate sampling errors in accordance with the underlying theory supporting these methods. The methods are described in the technical reports of these international assessments (Martin *et al.*, 2000, 2003; Adams and Wu, 2002).

Both the BRR and the JRR methods define variance strata, or zones, which are usually pairs of schools. The pairing of schools respects the order in which the schools were sampled using the PPS systematic sampling method. In each zone, one school is randomly defined as the zero-replicate. They then produce as many sets of replicate sampling weights as there are zones.

For the JRR method, the first set of replicate sampling weights is computed by setting the sampling weights of the students in the zero-replicate school of the first zone to zero and doubling the sampling weights of the students in the other school in the first zone. The sampling weights of the students in all other zones remain unchanged. The second set of replicate sampling weights is computed in a similar manner, but this time dealing with the second zone. The procedure is repeated for all zones.

The BRR method employs a different approach in defining its replicate weights. It uses what are called Hadamard matrices to determine, in a complex and balanced way, which zero-replicates in which zone will get zero weights, or double weights. The result is also a set of replicate sampling weights, much like for the JRR method.

For both methods, the replicate sampling weights are used to derive replicated survey estimates, as many as there are sets of replicate weights. The variation among the replicated estimates is a measure of the sampling variance, from which we can derive the sampling errors.

Imputation errors

More and more, international assessments administer rotated test instruments since their pool of assessment items is too large to be administered in its entirety to each sampled student. As a result, they have come to rely on item response theory to derive student achievement scores. Item response models pool the results from all rotated test instruments to impute student scores for the entire assessment. Since each student responds only to a subset of the assessment items, there is an uncertainty associated with these imputations. As a result, each student is given multiple imputations, called plausible values, to derive reliable estimates of student performance on the assessment as a whole. The variability among the plausible values provides a measure of the imputation error. This imputation error must be combined with the sampling error in order to provide a standard error that incorporates both sources of variation.

Item response models are generally described in the technical reports of international assessments. They also describe how imputation errors are computed and combined with sampling errors to produce overall standard errors. The imputation error is usually relatively small when compared to the sampling error. Based on TIMSS 1999 and PIRLS 2001 data, the imputation error can account for 2 per cent to 30 per cent of the overall standard error. This obviously increases the size of confidence intervals, and should be taken into consideration when computing the required sample size. The sample sizes presented in *Figure 8.3* were all computed taking into account the anticipated imputation error.

Conclusion

Answering the questions 'Who should be measured?' and 'How should they be selected?' is a complicated endeavour in the context of international comparative assessments. We must first define the target population of students to be measured in a manner relevant to our research and policy objectives. The biggest challenge lies in making our population definition one that can be implemented uniformly and consistently across all participating countries. This is crucial if the survey results are to be comparable.

Relying on sound sampling methods seems an obvious statement. However, in the context of international comparative assessments, one must guard against national deviations from the standard procedures. These deviations might compromise or jeopardize the quality and comparability of the samples. Perhaps the biggest challenge lies in determining a suitable sample size. Many factors come into play, and many areas of expertise need to be consulted to resolve this riddle. Researchers and policy analysts need to contribute to this effort by providing the sampling experts the context in which the survey results will be primarily used. The sampling experts must also provide the researchers and the policy analysts sufficient guidance to formulate their requirements and their impact adequately on both the sample size and the sample design.

Sampling weights and standard errors are indispensable in any sample survey, but are sometimes overlooked. Sampling weights are necessary to maintain the proper balance between sampling units. Without them, survey estimates could be seriously 'flawed'.

Standard errors are required to know the reliability of the survey estimates and make proper inferences about any observed differences. Without standard errors, we will never know if observed differences are real, or simply the result of random fluctuations due to sampling. Standard errors must also be calculated properly. Relying on standard statistical software packages tends to underestimate seriously the true standard errors, leading data users to conclude that some observed differences are statistically significant, when in fact they may not be.

References

Adams, R.; Wu, M. 2002. *PISA 2000 technical report*. Paris: OECD.

Beaton, A.E.; Mullis, I.V.S.; Martin, M.O.; Gonzalez, E.J.; Kelly, D.L.;

Smith, T.A. 1996*a*. *Mathematics achievement in the middle school years: TIMSS*. Chestnut Hill, MA: International Study Center, Boston College.

Beaton, A.E.; Mullis, I.V.S.; Martin, M.O.; Gonzalez, E.J.; Kelly, D.L.; Smith, T.A. 1996*b*. *Mathematics achievement in the primary school years: TIMSS*. Chestnut Hill, MA: International Study Center, Boston College.

Beaton, A.E.; Mullis, I.V.S.; Martin, M.O.; Gonzalez, E.J.; Kelly, D.L.; Smith, T.A. 1996*c*. *Science achievement in the middle school years: TIMSS*. Chestnut Hill, MA: International Study Center, Boston College.

Beaton, A.E.; Mullis, I.V.S.; Martin, M.O.; Gonzalez, E.J.; Kelly, D.L.; Smith, T.A. 1996*d*. *Science achievement in the primary school years: TIMSS*. Chestnut Hill, MA: International Study Center, Boston College.

Cochran, W.G. 1977. *Sampling techniques.* 3rd ed. New York: John Wiley & Sons.

Foy, P. 1998. Sampling issues in international assessments. *International Journal of Educational Research, 29*, 555-568.

Foy, P.; Joncas, M. 2001. *TIMSS 2003 school sampling manual* (Version 1). Ottawa: Statistics Canada.

Foy, P.; Joncas, M. 2004. *PIRLS 2006 school sampling manual* (Version 2). Ottawa: Statistics Canada..

Lapointe, A.; Mead, N. A.; Phillips, G. W. 1989. *A world of differences: an international assessment of mathematics and science.* Princeton NJ: Educational Testing Service.

Martin, M.O.; Gregory, K.D.; Stemler, S.E. 2000. *TIMSS 1999 technical report*. Chestnut Hill, MA: International Study Center, Lynch School of Education, Boston College.

Martin, M.O.; Mullis, I.V.S.; Kennedy, A.M. 2003. *PIRLS 2001 technical report*. Chestnut Hill, MA: International Study Center, Lynch School of Education, Boston College.

Wolter, K.M. 1985. *Introduction to variance estimation. New York: Springer-Verlag.*

Chapter 9
What are the national costs
for a cross-national study?

Maria Teresa Siniscalco

Introduction

The total national costs of a cross-national study of the quality of education consist of two components: (a) the international costs, (that is, the national contribution to the costs for running the study at the international level); and (b) the national costs (that is, the costs for implementing the study within the country).

The international costs for a country vary greatly, depending on the study and on the international organization involved. Country fees for PISA (Programme for International Student Assessment) (Adams and Wu, 2002) which is organized by the Organisation for Economic Co-operation and Development (OECD), range from about 50,000 euros to about 600,000 euros per year, depending on the size of the country's economy. The participation fee for the TIMSS Project, organized by the International Association for the Evaluation of Educational Achievement (IEA) in 2003, was US$40,000 per study population for three years, and US$60,000 per two study populations.

The levels of these fees can often depend on the presence of additional funding, from other external sources. Country fees are the only source of funding for PISA, however, a number of IEA studies have received financial support from the United States Department of Education, the World Bank, and other agencies such as the United Nations Development Programme (UNDP). In the IEA studies, United States Government funds were mostly dedicated for preparing the framework and data collection instruments, and for conducting more complex analyses of the results, while World Bank and UNDP funds were used for supporting less affluent countries.

This article focuses on the costs and logistics related to the national implementation of a cross-national study of the quality of education – from the initial design of the data collection instruments up to the dissemination of the results, taking as a point of reference the OECD's PISA project.

The article has been presented in three main sections: human resource needs, phases of the work, and some 'real-life' experiences drawn from Italian participation in the PISA project. A final section summarizes overall 'visible' costs.

Costs and logistics issues are affected by the characteristics of the organization implementing the study within a country. This may be a government body (for example, a ministry of education), a government-funded institution (for example, a public university or a government funded research institution), or an independent institution (for example, a private university, an independent research institution, a consortium of groups, or another independent organization). If a study is organized around a government funded institution, there is likely to be a larger proportion of hidden costs (that is costs that are covered within existing budgets), while if the study is carried out within a non-government funded institution, most of the costs will be 'visible', that is they will be translated into actual monetary expenditures over and above existing budgets.

Human resources

In considering the human resources required for the implementation of a cross-national study of the quality of education within a country, choices must be made concerning the desired degree of direct management of tasks and operations at the national centre. This may range from the direct management of all tasks and operations at the national centre to subcontracting most of the work to external agencies. Between these two extremes, intermediate options imply the direct management of crucial tasks together with the subcontracting of some components to external providers. Within the latter scenario, the human resources needed for the implementation of the study at the national level include: (a) permanent staff at the national centre; (b) temporary resources at the national centre; (c) staff supplied by external providers; and (d) a national advisory committee and various groups of experts.

Permanent staff at the national centre

As part of the establishment of a national centre for the study, each participating country needs to appoint a person who takes responsibility for the implementation of the project within the country. In many cross-national studies, this person is referred to as the national research co-ordinator (NRC) or national project manager (NPM). He or she will work with a team whose size depends on the amount of work that will be directly managed at the national centre and the scope of the research associated with the particular study.

■ National project manager (NPM)

In most cases, the position of the NPM will be full time, but can be part time if there is adequate support via other project staff and statistical assistants.

A person appointed to the NPM position should have a relevant university degree and experience in planning, organizing and conducting large-scale surveys. Preferably, the person should have worked in an education system and gained some experience in educational assessment.

The stresses and challenges of the NPM position require skills in managing a team of project staff, the capacity to work on multiple tasks simultaneously, and a high level of oral and written communication skills. Sufficient knowledge and personal confidence is also required to represent the country at international meetings where aspects of the project will be discussed.

In general, the NPM will need to undertake (or delegate and take responsibility for) a wide range of tasks: including organizing and chairing meetings with experts; participating in international NPM meetings; communicating the country position on a range of aspects of the project, both to the international centre and during NPM meetings; managing the operational implementation of the study at the national level; and preparing national reports of results.

From the operational point of view, the NPM should be 'conversant' (though not necessarily an 'expert') in instrument construction (test and questionnaire), in sampling, and in data preparation and analysis. He/she requires sufficient knowledge in these areas to be able to interact with the study's 'experts', to set realistic deadlines, and to organize and supervise the work.

■ Staff at the national centre

In addition to the NPM, the national centre team should include at least two appropriately trained professional staff helping the NPM, and at least one person providing secretarial and administrative support.

The size of the team at the national centre may vary greatly across countries, even within the same study, depending on the available resources as well as on the scope the study is given at the country level. For example, a decision to increase a sample size within a country in order to obtain stable estimates for many strata could result in a major increase in staff numbers in order to address field work and data management requirements.

When selecting staff for the national centre, NPMs should make sure that technical competencies needed for implementing the study are covered – with particular attention being paid to the areas of sampling and data analysis.

Temporary staff at the national centre

The workload involved in a large-scale survey typically alternates between times where three to four staff members can manage the required work to times when a larger team, perhaps ten to twenty people, is necessary in order to address the required tasks. Extra staff will be needed, for instance, for contacting sampled schools before the main data collection, as well as for marking open-ended questions and for data entry.

The need for extra staff on a temporary basis will pose no problems if the national centre is located within a larger institution that has flexibility in allocating personnel. If this is not the case, then there will be a need to be able to issue staff contracts of a limited duration and for specific tasks.

In the PISA survey, a minimum sample size of 4,500 assessed students had to be selected from a minimum of 150 schools. Enough people were required for contacting sampled schools in order to obtain lists of students in the target population that could be used for within-school sampling. According to the PISA standard marking design, the marking of open-ended test items (taking into account that several literacy domains were assessed and that multiple marking was required for a sub-sample of students) required a marking team of 24 people.

One way to address the need for extra personnel at given times is to employ university students whose field of study is relevant for the required task (for example, mathematics students for marking open-ended numeracy questions).

Staff supplied by external providers

In PISA 2003, there were 25 countries that subcontracted some part of the work to external providers, while the other 15 countries managed all work at their national centre. Printing and data entry were the tasks most frequently given to external providers, followed by marking and translating the instruments. The cost of subcontracting specific tasks to external agencies must be taken into account when costs are budgeted.

National advisory committee

In a cross-national study of education systems, it is generally recommended to establish a national advisory committee in each country. This committee should be made up of persons who are leaders in areas such as survey research, and education management. The committee should also include representatives from the ministry of education, other government ministries, teachers' associations, and relevant university departments.

The committee should meet regularly to offer advice on project implementation, and to assure that national views are represented. The costs of operating such a committee will include travel and per diem expenditures for the participants and, if required, an honorarium.

International meetings

In a study such as PISA, international meetings of NPMs are held on two or three occasions each year. These meetings are convened for three main purposes: (a) to provide a forum for country representatives to review, comment on, and ratify proposals put by the international study centre relating to research questions, instruments, proposed indicators, and draft reports of results; (b) to provide training for NPMs and national centre staff on operational procedures and coding and entry of data; and (c) to brief NPMs on planned data analyses and report preparation at the international level.

The project budget should include funds to cover the NPM's travel and per diem costs for participating in international meetings, and should also take into account that other staff from the national centre may have to attend at least some of the international meetings during the study when specific training is provided, for example, coding open-ended items or questionnaire questions, data analysis, etc.

Material resources

A new project implies office space, telephone, office supplies, computers, and associated materials (such as paper, printing consumables, and the necessary office and statistical software). At different stages of the project, there will be a need for extra storage and working space – especially during the preparation of data collection instruments for dispatch to schools, and during the return and scoring of tests and questionnaires.

Phases of the work and operations

Most large-scale studies of the quality of education consist of four main phases: (a) the development of survey instruments; (b) the field trial; (c) the main study; and (d) data analyses and the preparation of the national report.

Development of survey instruments

The first phase of a study includes the definition of the research questions (which provide the conceptual underpinning of the assessment) and the use of these questions to provide a framework for the development of assessment instruments. The definition of the research questions is the first task of an NPM, and usually involves high-level discussion with heads of divisions in the ministry as well as with knowledgeable academics. Without this step there will be doubt about the relevance of the survey among the senior decision-makers – which will almost certainly ensure that the results will not be used for policy purposes.

Although it is normal to have groups of experts appointed at the international level working on the conceptual framework of the study and the assessment instruments, a truly cross-national study requires the maximization of contributions from all participating countries in the discussion of the conceptual framework, the specification of research questions, and the construction of assessment instruments.

At the national level, this implies that countries will have to organize meetings with representative groups of curriculum specialists, subject-area experts, and test developers in order to address the following tasks: (a) to undertake either (i) a content analysis of the curriculum of the country (assuming here that the study aims to measure what the students have learned) or (ii) define what is required for performing successfully on given outcomes (for example, the PISA project aimed at measuring how well 15-year-old students were 'prepared to meet the challenges of today's societies'); (b) to develop test items to supply to an international pool; and (c) to review test items (and questionnaires) provided by the international centre – including both the items prepared by the international test developers and those supplied by participating countries.

The cost of these groups, including travel expenses and fees, will vary depending on whether the experts are internal personnel of the ministry or external personnel (for example, teachers and test developers). Other costs may be required to translate the national test items before submitting them to the international centre.

The field trial

The second phase of a cross-national survey is the field trial, which is used to trial test the data collection instruments and the field procedures. This is an essential part of a good cross-national study because it is at this phase that problems in instruments and procedures are identified and corrected. The main field trial tasks are listed below: (a) translating instruments and field operation manuals; (b) selecting a field trial judgement sample, obtaining school co-operation, and selecting students or classes within schools; (c) appointing and training school co-ordinators and test administrators; (d) preparing, printing, packaging and shipping assessment materials; (e) scheduling and monitoring the data collection; and (f) editing, marking, entering and cleaning data.

The field trial data from all participating countries will then be analysed by the international centre in order to provide the countries with frequency distributions, item analysis statistics, and frequencies and constructed indices based on questionnaire items.

In the field trial, where a limited number of schools and students are sampled, most of these operations are less complex than in the main study. The exception here is the translation of the data collection instruments, because most of this work takes place during the preparation of field trial instruments. The translation work for the main study is confined to additions, revisions and improvements made to test questionnaire items and the data collection materials.

■ Translating instruments and manuals

The research results generated by a cross-national study of the quality of education need to be based on valid translations of all data collection instruments. Any weakness in the translation process will introduce biases that are likely to distort international comparisons.

The translation process must therefore follow systematic and vigorous procedures. A 'back translation' procedure is the most frequently used approach to ensure linguistic equivalence in international surveys. It requires translating the source version of the test (often in the English language) into the national language, then translating it back and comparing it with the source language to identify possible discrepancies. However, this procedure does not protect from mistakes due to a too literal transposition of the original version, which are not revealed by back-translating the passage.

A better procedure, which guards against excessively literal translations, is the 'double translation' procedure employed by TIMSS-R; this requires translating the source version twice by two independent translators and then reconciling the two national language versions.

PISA used the 'double translation' procedure applied to two different languages, English and French, (for which equivalent versions had been developed) in order to overcome the limit of both back translation and double translation from a single language. After two independent translators translated the source materials into the target language, a third professional reconciled these two translations into a single national version.

Irrespective of the procedure followed, a team of translators has to be appointed for the translation work. Two translators are required in the case of back translation, and two translators and a reconciler in the case of double translation. If the volume of test material is significant and it covers several subject areas (for example, mathematics and science), it may be necessary to entrust the translation tasks to parallel teams of translators, who would work independently for different subject-matters areas.

The translators responsible for this work must have a perfect command of both the source language and the target language, a solid command of the subject areas covered by the test (which is quite important in the case of mathematics and science), and an in-depth knowledge of the school system of the country so that they can work on the school, teacher and student questionnaires.

▣ Sampling for the field trial

The sample for the field trial is based on a 'convenience sample' of schools chosen by each country. Although not a probability sample, schools must be picked so that they include representation from the main stratification variables, such as: school type, geographical location, and socio-economic level. The within-school sampling for the field trial employs the same procedures as those for the main study (which have been described later in this article).

▣ Appointing and training school co-ordinators
and test administrators

It is necessary to appoint a school co-ordinator within each sampled school who is responsible for co-ordinating all project-related activities in the school. These activities include duties such as: the preparation of a complete list of all students or classes eligible for testing, establishing the date and time for the data collection in co-ordination with the NPM and the test administrators; informing all relevant people (school, staff, students, and parents), and securing parental permission for the data collection. School co-ordinators are typically school staff – however, different countries have different policies with respect to the payment of school co-ordinators and these policies impact upon the cost of this component of the study.

The national centre will have to appoint a team of test administrators for conducting the assessment in each sampled school. Test administrators are responsible for administering the tests fairly, impartially and uniformly in accordance with international specified standards and procedures. They should therefore be familiar with schools and how they operate, as well as with standardized testing procedures. As for school co-ordinators, different countries will have different policies concerning the payment of test administrators.

Test administrators may have different profiles in different countries. In some countries, they are part of the institution that is responsible for the study (for example, school inspectors within a ministry or national centre staff). In other cases they may come from 'outside' (for example, external contractor staff). If test administrators are teachers in the sampled school, it is usually required that they are not the instructor in the tested subjects of any students in the sessions that they will administer. In some countries, the same person can take the role of both test administrator and school co-ordinator.

Before the beginning of testing in each country, national centres should train the test administrators. Training should include an overview of the goals and design of the study, and a thorough review of the test administration procedures (as presented in the test administration manual) – especially the script to be followed during the administration.

The costs for the training of test administrators include travel expenses (either for test administrators to come to the training venues, or for national centre staff to go to 'decentralized' training venues) and per diems, when needed.

▪ Printing, packaging and shipping assessment materials

Sufficient staff and time must be planned for the finalization of data collection instruments prior to their printing. The 'print-ready' materials must include final revisions made at both the international and national level, and they must also look identical to the international versions, in terms of layout and formatting.

The NPM must ensure that test security is not compromised in the process of printing, packaging and shipping assessment materials. Carelessness at this stage could damage the validity of a whole data collection. Printing costs will vary depending on whether the printing is subcontracted to a printing company or it is done at the national centre. Given the relatively small sample of the field trial, and the possibility that multiple test booklets and multiple versions of the questionnaires have to be prepared, it may be more convenient to photocopy the field trial instruments rather than engage a professional printing company.

If the instruments have to be pre-labelled with school and student unique identification codes, then the time and the cost for this operation (which is usually carried out at the same time as the packaging) must be taken into account. Enough space must be available for packaging.

Costs, time constraints, and reliability must be considered when choosing the means (for example, normal mail or courier) for shipping the packages to the schools and from the schools back to the national centre after the assessment.

▓ Scheduling and monitoring test administration

School co-ordinators, in consultation with the national centre and the test administrators should establish the testing date and time. Each school co-ordinator must immediately inform both the NPM and test administrator of any test date or time change.

NPMs should monitor the field trial test administration. This can be done by having school quality monitors visiting a sub-sample of schools (on an 'un-announced surprise' basis), in order to ensure that procedures are fully and completely implemented and obtain information on aspects of the test administrators training that need to be improved. All school co-ordinators and test administrators should be informed that they 'could be visited'.

The national centre should organize a training session for school quality monitors if they are not part of the national centre staff. The training should cover an overview of the purpose, and design the study and a presentation of the test administration procedures in order to prepare them to conduct on-site quality monitoring in the schools and to report on the school visit. The cost of school quality monitoring will include travel and per diem expenses and fees if these people are not part of the national centre staff.

▓ Marking open-ended items

The tests may consist of different item formats, including closed items (that is, multiple choice or closed constructed response items) and open-ended items that require the students to write a more or less extended answer.

The assessment materials returned from the schools to the national centre can go directly to the data entry if the tests have been constructed only from closed items. However, the answers to open-ended items have to be evaluated and marked (scored). This is a complex and time-consuming operation that is based on comprehensive marking rules and criteria – which should include examples of acceptable and not acceptable responses that are not listed in marking guides provided to NPMs by the study international centre. In order to ensure that students' responses are scored uniformly from marker to marker (both within and across countries) it is necessary to employ 'quality control' procedures by applying multiple marking for sub-samples of student responses across all countries.

NPMs will need to recruit enough people to carry out the marking and multiple marking of open-ended items. In some countries, pools of experienced markers from other projects may be available to assist. In others, suitable people will need to be found. All people who mark the test items will have to undergo training, regardless of whether they have had related experience on other projects.

In recruiting markers, it will be important to obtain people who can commit their time to the project for the duration of the marking. It is also advisable to recruit markers who might be available for the main study. The number of markers required will depend on the number of domains assessed, on the deadlines for submitting the data, and on the recommended marking design, including the possible need for multiple marking.

The marking design of the PISA 2003 field trial involved eight markers, marking across the three domains of mathematics, science and problem solving. Since marking was to take place over an estimated period of two weeks, it was recommended that at least two back-up markers were trained and included in at least some of the marking sessions. Two of the markers were designated as team leaders, having the role to assist with the overall organization of the marking, resolve queries about the marking guide and monitor the quality of the marking. Team leaders had to be thoroughly familiar with both the test items and the marking guide ahead of the main training. The markers did not need high-level academic qualifications, but they had to have a good understanding of mid-secondary school level mathematics and science – given that the assessment concerned 15-year-old students. They were also expected to understand secondary level students and ways that students at this level express themselves. Teachers on leave, recently retired teachers, senior teacher trainees, and mathematics and science undergraduate or graduate students were all potentially suitable markers.

When planning for the marking team and budgeting the costs for this operation it should be borne in mind that markers should work for no more than 6 hours per day on actual marking, with some additional time for breaks.

The selected markers should be trained by national centre staff who have previously received marking training at an international training course. As part of the initial training, markers should be asked to respond to all the test items in the domain(s) that they would be marking. This is extremely important because it enables the markers to become familiar with the content of the data collection instruments and the test items, and it provides them with some insight into the kinds of problems that students might have in responding to some of the items. The markers should also be requested to read the marking guides in advance of the sessions, and should participate in a marking training workshop.

■ Entering and cleaning data

Data entry software is usually provided by the international study centre. This software contains the database structures for all data-collection instruments. The user can modify these database structures in order to adapt the database to the national version of the instruments. The software usually performs validation checks as data are entered. A separate data entry manual usually describes the operational functions of the data entry software. A person with data entry experience needs several days of training in order to enter data from the different instruments using the data entry software.

Data entry costs depend on the amount of data and type of instruments. In the PISA project instruments, a data entry person with some training was able to enter about 100-120 questionnaires, or 80-100 test booklets (whose answers take usually more time to be entered), in a 4-hour working day. This meant that in order to enter the data for an average PISA sample of 5,500 students, about 110 days had to be planned for, corresponding to 3.6 persons working 4 hours per day for 6 weeks. However, it is only by trial and error that one ends up with a good team. It is therefore important to assign each person entering data a personal 'identification number', in order to be able to identify unreliable data enterers, and replace them or, in some cases, ask them to re-enter data.

A data manager will need to be appointed within the national centre or within an external agency in order to take responsibility for data entry operations. The data manager will also have to implement data entry quality monitoring procedures. This can be done, for example, by double entering a sample of the data (for example, 5 per cent) and checking for the degree of inconsistency.

In the PISA project, it was necessary to run the checking procedures included in the data entry software and to correct any data errors detected before submitting the data to the international centre. Subsequently, NPMs were required to designate a data manager to work actively with the international centre during the international data cleaning process.

Responses to requests for information by the processing centre were to be provided within a short delay, by checking the problematic data with the responses on the original paper instruments and, in some cases, by going back to schools.

The main study

The third phase of a cross-national study of the quality of education is the main study data collection. At the national level the main study is comprised of the following operations: (a) revising the field operations on the basis of the field trial experience; (b) finalizing the assessment instruments based on field trial statistics; (c) preparing the sampling frame and extracting a probability sample of schools; (d) contacting sampled schools and obtaining participation; (e) appointing and training school co-ordinators and test administrators; (f) selecting students or classes within schools; (g) printing instruments, packaging and shipping assessment materials; (h) scheduling and monitoring data collection; (i) marking open-ended questions; and (j) entering and cleaning data.

Many of the operations listed above happen in overlapping periods and in most cases are more demanding than in the field trial, because of the larger sample size. For this reason, it may be necessary to increase the number of staff at the national centre –from the beginning of the main study up to the moment when the national data are submitted to the international centre, with a corresponding increase in the allocated budget.

■ Revising the field operations

A number of things may need to be revised from an organizational point of view, based on the field trial experience. These can include activities such as organizing a more extensive training for test administrators, and increasing efforts for obtaining school and student participation. These extra tasks will need to be examined with respect to cost implications.

■ Preparing the main study materials

The preparation of the assessment materials for the main study is a delicate and time-consuming operation. Mistakes made during this phase of the research could ruin the whole data collection. This work includes the revision of the main study translation of the retained test items and questionnaires based on: (a) the field trial statistical analyses; (b) the changes made by the international centre; and (c) the preparation and layout of the final instruments in print-ready format. Whatever revisions are made, the NPM needs to ensure that the layout of the national version is as close as possible to the source version.

In a study such as PISA, with multiple assessment domains and a rigorous mechanism for verifying the quality of the translations, the preparation of the national version of the instruments for the main study, requires the work of one full time experienced staff member at the national centre for about three months. On top of this, several experts may be involved in the process at different stages, thus increasing the number of people and costs involved.

   ▦   Preparing the sampling

Unless the NPM has advanced training and experience in the field of sampling (and even if the international centre provides close support), it is recommended that the sampling be undertaken in consultation with a national sampling expert. The main tasks include the preparation of the sampling frame according to the desired stratification design, the preparation of all sampling information required by the international centre, the extraction of the sample of schools, and the preparation of a sampling report.

   ▦   Achieving co-operation from sampled schools

Procedures for securing school co-operation will vary from country to country. In some countries, participation is not a problem. All selected schools are expected to participate. In other countries, it is very difficult to get schools to participate. The reasons for these difficulties vary – from concerns about too much testing and loss of instructional time, to the burden that the data collection places on students and teachers. In order to improve co-operation the following suggestions were given to countries that participated in the PISA project.

• *Develop informational materials.* These materials should address the particular concerns of the school system within the country. Although international materials provide useful information and examples, each national centre needs to develop a strategy for addressing the special needs and concerns of its own system.
• *Develop a strategy to notify appropriate authorities.* In many systems, there is an established hierarchy of authority that should be contacted in a defined order. Letters, informational materials, telephone calls and personal visits are all useful ways for contacting the appropriate authorities. Some of these approaches may be more effective than

others with different levels of authority. It is important to develop a plan or strategy that defines how contacts will be made and what information will be provided to each of the different levels.

- *Secure permission.* In some systems, it is not enough to notify the appropriate authorities. Permission must also be obtained. This may include permission from one governmental level to contact another, as well as permission from a governing board to contact individual schools. Obtaining permission can be time-consuming. It is important to begin the process of securing co-operation early enough so that all necessary permissions may be obtained.
- *Decide whether to use incentives.* Some studies have tried a variety of incentives, including the following: cash payments, instructional materials, study reports, certificates of appreciation, posters and banners. NPMs should decide whether incentives can or should be used in their countries.
- *Identify a school co-ordinator.* An important part of securing the co-operation of the selected school is to identify someone within the school who will act as the school co-ordinator. The school co-ordinator acts as the liaison between the school and the project – and therefore is a key person for ensuring that the data collection is undertaken in an environment that respects the needs of all stakeholders.
- *Share approaches that work.* Sharing information about approaches that work is an important part of participating in a cross-national study. Countries should be encouraged to submit information to the international centre. Example letters, informational materials, and general descriptions of successful approaches will be of interest to international centre staff and other NPMs as plans for the main study are developed.

The costs involved in the operation of contacting schools and maximizing their participation in the study may vary greatly depending on the procedures followed. In general, it will not be enough to contact schools by means of a letter or fax. One or more telephone calls will be necessary to present the project to the school principal and to contact the school co-ordinator. It will be necessary to telephone the schools as many times as necessary in order to talk to the school principal. In some cases, the telephoning work required in order to reach the target participation rates may be considerable.

▦   Selecting students within schools

Once a school has agreed to participate in the study, it must send a list of eligible classes or eligible students within the school. A within-school sample of classes or students will then be drawn, usually by means of a special computer programme. However, unless schools send electronic lists of students, it will be necessary to prepare student tracking forms listing all the students included in the sample. The preparation of the student tracking form will imply further communication with the school (usually with the school co-ordinator) in order to obtain all the needed information. Particular attention must be paid to identifying those students who can be included in the assessment and those who cannot. In *Box 2* the criteria used in PISA for excluding students from the assessment because of their 'special education' needs have been presented.

Box 2.   PISA 2003 criteria for within-school exclusions

Students with special education needs who cannot be assessed

The intent of the PISA project is to be as inclusive as possible. However, some students with limited proficiency in the language of the assessment or those who have a severe physical, mental or emotional disability may not be able to participate under these conditions. The numbers to the left are codes to be entered in Column 9 of the Student Tracking Form to identify students with special education needs who will not be included in PISA because of special education needs.

0 = Included

1 = Not included: functional disability. (Student has a moderate to severe permanent physical disability such that he/she cannot perform in the PISA testing situation.)

2 = Not included: intellectual disability. (Student has a mental or emotional disability and is cognitively disadvantaged to a degree that he/she cannot perform in the PISA testing situation. This includes students who are emotionally or mentally unable to follow even the general instructions of the assessment.)

3 = Not included: limited assessment language proficiency. (The student is unable to read or speak any of the languages of the assessment in the country and would be unable to overcome the language barrier in the testing situation.)

4 = Other. (Defined by the NPM and checked by the international centre.)

The allowable amount of within-school exclusions for the PISA project was limited to 2.5 per cent of the total population of enrolled 15 year-olds. The allowable school-level exclusion rate was less than 0.5

per cent of the total population of enrolled 15 year-olds, while another 2 per cent of the students could be excluded by excluding schools if they provided instruction only to students who were in one of the within-school exclusion categories listed in *Box 2*. The national defined population was therefore required to cover 95 per cent or more of the national desired population, with the total rate of exclusion limited to no more than 5 per cent.

◼ Printing, packaging and shipping assessment instruments

Given the amount of materials to be printed for the main study, the most convenient option is often that of subcontracting this operation to a professional printer. As for the field trial, there are two primary concerns to be considered by NPMs in making plans for printing, packaging and shipping the main study materials. The first is that the test items be secure at all times. The second is that instruments that are pre-labelled with student identification codes should be assigned to the correct students.

There may be several different ways to print materials and to prepare them for shipment and distribution, each having advantages and disadvantages with regard to cost, burden and efficiency. If the assessment materials include both cognitive material and questionnaires, it is usually strongly recommended that they be printed in separate booklets, especially if cognitive materials include open-ended items requiring marking. This will avoid double handling of booklets, and subsequent delays during data entry (as the questionnaires can be data-entered while the cognitive material is being marked).

If test material and questionnaires are printed together, the possibility of students returning to the test material during the questionnaire session exists. To avoid this possibility, a mechanism for sealing the cognitive section of the booklet at the end of the cognitive testing session should be considered. If this is not possible, then a specific instruction should be added to the test administration manual: that the test administrator should monitor that students are not returning to the cognitive section of the booklet during the questionnaire session.

If the cognitive material and questionnaires are printed separately, then care should be taken to make sure that the students receive the correctly identified booklets so that these can be matched to the corresponding questionnaires without resulting in errors during data entry. If the questionnaire is to be administered in a separate session, then the test booklets and questionnaire should be printed separately to help protect the security of the test items.

Another decision that NPMs will need to make is how to package the assessment materials in order to protect the security of the test items. To protect item security further, the test booklets for a school could be packaged in a secure bundle – sealed either in plastic or in some other form of packaging. If the packaging is transparent and has not been wrapped too tightly, test administrators will be able to check easily in advance if the correct number of booklets is in the package, without opening it. Similarly, the booklets could be sealed in envelopes, one for each student in the assessment.

The three scenarios described below were considered acceptable approaches to packaging and shipping the PISA 2003 assessment materials, which included a student questionnaire and thirteen test booklets assigned to students according to a rotation design.

- Country A shipped all assessment materials to the schools and used school staff (not teachers of the students in the assessment) to conduct the testing sessions. The national centre printed the test booklets and student questionnaire separately. The national centre assigned materials to students before packaging for shipment to the schools. They assigned each student listed on the student tracking form a test booklet and a student questionnaire, labelled these materials and then sealed them in envelopes also labelled with the students' names and identification numbers.
- Country B also shipped materials directly to the schools but used test administrators employed by the national centre. Because of concerns about when the administration of the questionnaires would take place, Country B printed and packaged the test booklets and questionnaires in separately bound bundles. The order of the booklets in each bundle was pre-recorded on the student tracking form. To protect student confidentiality after the assessment had been completed, Country B provided envelopes labelled with the students' names and identification numbers for students to put their assessment booklets into, and seal once the assessment was over.
- Country C used test administrators employed by the national centre and shipped the materials to these test administrators. Since the student questionnaire was administered during the same session as the test items, Country C printed everything in one booklet.

Bundles of the required number of booklets were sealed in plastic, so that the number of booklets could be checked without opening the packages. The test administrators opened the bundle assigned to a school immediately prior to the session and labelled the booklets with the students' names and ID numbers from the student tracking form, according to the assignment of booklets pre-recorded on the tracking form by national centre staff.

Procedures for the receipt of materials back at the national centre vary from country to country, but in general, it is recommended that a database of schools be prepared and updated regularly to monitor shipping and receipt of materials to and from schools, and the progress of materials through the various processing steps at the national centre. This phase may again require telephone contacts with the schools, in order to ensure that all materials are completed and returned in a timely fashion.

■ Marking open-ended questions

The selection and training of markers for the main study does not differ from the field trial. However, more markers will be required for the main study than for the field trial and this may pose problems, as it may be difficult to find enough markers who meet the required criteria and are available for the required time. One possible solution is that of recruiting graduate or undergraduate students, rather than teachers, and organizing the marking work so that different subgroups may choose different working hours that suit them better.

For PISA 2003, a marking design was recommended involving 24 markers, made up of 16 markers across the 3 domains of mathematics, science and problem-solving, plus 8 reading markers – taking into account that at least 4 markers were required in any single domain. Because the marking had to take place over an estimated period of 6 weeks, it was recommended that at least 4 back-up markers be trained and included in some of the marking sessions.

In order to contain the costs of marking, it may be desirable to establish payments to markers based on the completion of the work within a given period, rather than paying markers by the day or hour. This approach permits the NPM to budget a precise amount of money, and does not allow the cost of marking to increase unexpectedly if there is a need to re-mark some of the answers already marked. Re-marking can be required if team leaders find systematic errors in the work of one or more markers.

■ Entering and cleaning main study data

General requirements and factors of cost for data entry and cleaning are the same as those described in the corresponding field trial section. However, the organizational and cost implications for data for the main study must also be considered.

As in the field trial, after submitting the main study data, NPMs must designate a data manager who will respond rapidly to requests for information by the international centre in order to avoid unresolved problems. This process may last from one to three months – depending on the quality of the submitted data and on the organization of the work at the international centre. This phase of the data cleaning can be very time-consuming, as it involves solving as many inconsistencies as possible within the data, in order to avoid data loss.

Data analysis and report preparation

Once the data are cleaned, the international centre and the national centres will calculate the sampling weights, so that the data collected on the sample can be used to estimate population parameters with a degree of uncertainty, expressed by estimated standard errors.

The data are then analysed with the aim of preparing the international report and the national reports. If the research questions have been clearly specified at the beginning of the study, then the national centre will have prepared its dummy tables and already planned the data analyses.

Costs in this phase will include those for covering the position of a skilled data analyst. The NPM will usually be involved in drafting the national report, with the co-operation of other project staff or experts and in communication with the national committee.

Lessons learned

This section of the article presents a discussion of some of the 'lessons learned' from Italy's participation in the PISA cross-national study of the quality of education.

Communication

One of the keys to the success of a study is that good relationships and effective communications should be established and maintained throughout the study between the ministry of education and the staff and leadership at the national centre who have the scientific and technical responsibility for implementation.

This will ensure a good working atmosphere, and will improve the probability that the results will be fully and correctly used. A lack of communication often prevents key decisions being taken in a co-operative way – impairing the dissemination and exploitation of results.

It is important to select carefully the person within the ministry who will act as the 'political' reference point for the project. This person needs to be someone who is convinced of the utility of such a study, has some knowledge and experience in the field of assessment, and feels committed to the success of the study and the dissemination of its results.

Sampling

While the international centre provides the definition of the target population and the specification of the sampling design (including the required standards for exclusion accuracy and response rates), each country has to define its own stratification design.

In Italy the stratification design became rather complex in PISA 2003 due to the decision of 6 of the 20 regions to participate with samples that were sufficiently large to provide stable regional estimates. The Italian stratification design therefore had to employ 'over-sampling' in 6 regions and at the same time give due attention to other within-region stratification variables: type of programme (academic, technical and vocational programmes) and school type (public/private). These complexities required extensive negotiation and clarification between the national centre and the international centre in order to find an acceptable stratification design.

Translating the instruments

Translating and adapting instruments requires in-depth knowledge in the areas of assessment and the characteristics of the education system. In addition, enough time needs to be allocated for checking the materials. The Italian national centre invested a great deal of time and effort in the finalization of the translation for the PISA project and therefore had only a few minor problems signalled by the international agency responsible for translation verifications.

Contacting the schools

In order to encourage Italian sampled schools to participate in PISA 2003, they were sent a letter signed by both a senior staff members of the ministry and by the director of the national institute of evaluation where the PISA national centre was established.

For the PISA project in 2003, the Italian sample consisted of 500 schools. It was therefore necessary to appoint a sufficient number of persons to contact the schools by telephone. Several phone calls were required in order to ensure the participation of each school. All 'difficult cases', were notified to the NPM who contacted directly the school principal in order to explain the importance of the research, and thereby gain the principal's support. In some cases, schools accepted to participate on condition that the national centre provided the test administrator (whereas, normally, the role of both school co-ordinator and test administrator was given to teachers in the school).

Italian sample schools were given a guarantee that they would receive feedback after the release of the international report. This feedback included the results of the school compared with those of other similar schools.

Test administrator training

It is extremely important that test administrators be well trained. In Italy this was made a necessary condition for being paid. Despite this training, some of them experienced difficulties during the assessment (based on the report of the school quality monitors send by the international centre) because of an insufficient mastery of the required procedures.

Student response rates

In order to ensure that the required student response rates were reached for Italy's participation in PISA, it was suggested to hold follow-up sessions if more than 15 per cent of the students in a school were absent.

In Italy, many students were on strike (because of the war in Iraq) during the test administration. It was therefore necessary to ask school co-ordinators to follow-up on absent students even if only 10 per cent of the students (for example, 3 students within a cluster of 35) were absent. This implied again calling a large number of schools after having received the first return packages. Telephone expenditures before, during and after the test administration are one of the hidden costs of these types of studies.

'High-risk' areas

It is important that enough competent staff, who were involved in the main study, be available after its completion in order to cope with possible problems arising from the stages concerned with data cleaning, weighting and marking reliability studies. The international centre may ask for further information or documentation in order to be able to confirm the quality of the collected data, and in some extremes cases it may ask the national centre to re-do given operations, such as marking open-ended items, if this proves to be unreliable.

Sampling

Many things can go wrong with sampling. The quality of the sample depends, among other things, on the precision of the sampling frame. If, for example, the number of students enrolled in the target population within the school is not available, then proxies must be used. In the case of Italy, for example, the number of students in the modal grade (from this list) was used in PISA 2003 as an approximate estimate for the number of enrolled 15 year-olds. Weighting adjustments can be used to make compensations for a lack of precision in the sampling frame.

Test administration

If test administrators do not master the required procedures, do not respect them or are not committed to the work, this may reflect negatively on the quality of the collected data. One area of major concern here is ensuring that the data collection proceeds exactly as specified in the field manuals.

In Italy, a number of minor deviations were recorded by the quality control monitors when they visited about 10 per cent of the sampled schools. In particular, some test administrators made some minor additions or deletions to the 'script'. In addition, one quality control monitor observed that some test administrators felt insecure when applying the procedures. However, no major deviation was observed that could have invalidated the test administration in a school.

Conclusion

The major cross-national studies of the quality of education organized by IEA and the OECD are co-ordinated by high-level professionals whose tasks include delivering procedural manuals, explanatory documents and training programmes, which make it relatively 'easy' for national centres to implement the research.

However, it must be emphasized that such complex studies cannot proceed successfully unless national centres are fully involved in both the design of the logistical procedures and their improvement through active participation in all aspects of planning the research, conducting the field tests, and implementing and managing the main study.

Therefore, it is very important that national centres, and NPMs in particular, be genuinely involved as active partners in all the aspects of the research. They should not feel as if they are just 'executing' a piece of work in order to collect data for the international centre. Active participation by NPMs both improves the research and provides professional development for the NPMs as they 'learn by doing' the conceptual and technical sides of the study.

References

Adams, R.; Wu, M. 2002. *PISA technical report*. Paris: OECD.

Part III
Managing the impact of cross-national studies
of the quality of education

Chapter 10
How can countries move from cross-national research results to dissemination, and then to policy reform?
(Case studies from Kenya and Namibia)

Juliana Nzomo and Demus Makuwa

Introduction

The governments of Kenya and Namibia attached great importance to the declarations of 1990 Jomtien World Conference on Education and the 2000 Dakar World Education Forum. These declarations emphasized the need to achieve 'Education for All' by 2015 through increased participation in education and the need for all nations to strive 'to improve all aspects of the quality of education and ensure excellence so that recognized and measurable learning outcomes are achieved by all'.

The governments of both countries responded, in part, to these declarations by deciding to become active members of the Southern and Eastern Africa Consortium for Monitoring Education Quality (SACMEQ). The SACMEQ network of fifteen ministries of Education is dedicated to building the capacity of educational researchers and planners to monitor and evaluate the quality of their own basic education systems.

The quality indicators generated through the SACMEQ surveys have supplemented the annual education statistics collected by the ministries of education in both countries. Kenya implemented the SACMEQ I and II projects in 1998 and 2000, while Namibia did so in 1995 and 2000. In SACMEQ I, the reading achievement of Grade 6 pupils was tested, and in SACMEQ II, reading and mathematics were tested for both pupils and their teachers. In both SACMEQ projects, information was also collected through the administration of questionnaires given to pupils, their teachers and their school heads.

Namibia and Kenya took part in the two SACMEQ projects in order to measure the conditions of schooling and the quality of education in terms of benchmark inputs to education, the educational achievements of pupils, and a range of equity issues related to social background, school location and gender.

They also wanted some measures of the conditions of schooling and the quality of primary education in comparison with other neighbouring countries in the region as well as to assess the magnitude of changes between 1995 and 2000.

Which research results did ministries of education find to be important and/or controversial?

Disparities in provision

In both Kenya and Namibia, the results of the two surveys showed major regional disparities in the provision of materials, availability and quality of classroom facilities and resources, levels of absenteeism, grade repetition, and parental participation in their children's education and school management.

In Namibia, the immense disparities among regions became very controversial. The disparities seemed to be congruent with the racial and ethnic patterns created under the apartheid system. Differences were also noted among socio-economic groups, and between urban and rural communities. While the Namibian Government had shown great commitment to education, by allocating to it an annual average expenditure of about 9 per cent of GDP, some stakeholders argued that the government had not done enough to redress the disparities of the colonial past. Others questioned the contents of post-independence education 'reforms' – especially those concerned with automatic promotion, learner-centred education, competence-based continuous assessment, and the introduction of English as a medium of instruction in schools. There was widespread concern that the government had not adequately prepared teachers for these changes.

Teacher gender

In Kenya, the fact that the SACMEQ research results on gender equity were consistent with the Ministry of Education's own annual statistics provided some level of confidence and acceptability in the results. However, the results raised great concern with regard to the persistently low female representation in education in the North Eastern Province. It was also noted that the percentages of female reading teachers in North

Eastern Province were only 28 per cent and 33 per cent in 1998 and 2000, respectively. Even worse, only 11 per cent of mathematics teachers were female.

While the low enrolment of girls in this province could be explained to some extent by cultural factors, the low representation of female teachers at the Grade 6 level was seen as a factor that contributed towards poor levels of participation by girls.

The situation was different in Namibia where around 60 per cent of Grade 6 teachers were female in 1995, and around 50 per cent of teachers were female in 2000. In the Kavango region, there was a considerable increase in the representation of female teachers – from 5 per cent in 1995 to nearly 38 per cent in 2000. Nationally, both boys and girls who were taught by female teachers obtained higher average achievement scores than those taught by male teachers.

Absenteeism

In Kenya the two survey results indicated that pupils were absent for an average of 2 days in a month. In Namibia, the national average was 1.5 days per month, with considerable variations evident between regions. Over the course of a year, these figures represent a substantial number of 'lost days', and this raised great concern among policy-makers in both countries. The percentage of pupils absent due to illness and non-payment of school levies was significant and prompted discussion and debate in both countries.

In Kenya's North Eastern Province, the percentage of children that had been absent from school due to illness ranged between 25 to 51 per cent, and in the Coast Province it ranged between 18 and 37 per cent. In Namibia, the number of pupils who were absent from school due to illness ranged from 26 per cent in Caprivi to nearly 36 per cent in Oshikoto and other northern regions.

Although the findings on toilet facilities were not initially taken seriously by education officials in Kenya, it was later observed that the lack or inadequacy of toilet facilities contributed to absenteeism for girls at the higher levels of primary education. The major problem areas were North Eastern Province where, on average, one toilet was shared among 92 pupils, and in the Coast, Nyanza, and Nairobi provinces where, on average, 60 to 70 pupils shared one toilet.

Grade repetition

The issue of grade repetition was particularly controversial in Namibia and Kenya, because, in both countries, official government policies encouraged automatic promotion for primary education.

Kenya's Nairobi province had the lowest percentage of Grade 6 pupils repeating (3 per cent), while Western and Rift Valley Provinces the figures were both over 15 per cent. In Namibia, the SACMEQ II results showed that a very large 54 per cent of Grade 6 pupils had repeated a grade. This was only a slight decline from 1995 when 59 per cent of the pupils had repeated a grade.

Extra-tuition

The SACMEQ research results on the provision of extra lessons given to pupils outside school hours was another area of controversy – especially in Kenya where education policy does not permit teachers to be involved in 'tuition'. Numerous circulars have gone to Kenyan schools reminding teachers that extra tuition should not be practised, and providing guidelines on remedial teaching for 'slow learners'. Despite this, the results indicated that the proportion of pupils who received extra tuition had gone up between 1998 and 2000 from around 70 per cent to around 90 per cent of Grade 6 pupils. The findings also indicated that over 50 per cent of the pupils paid for the extra tuition, and the highest percentage of paid tuition was recorded in Nairobi where around 75 per cent of pupils were involved.

Linkages between resources and achievement levels

SACMEQ I and II research findings indicated a deficiency in the provision of textbooks as well as an overall lack of basic supplies, with notable variations among provinces. Kenya's Western and North Eastern provinces had the lowest percentage of pupils having their own textbooks for reading and mathematics. Pupils in these provinces also lacked exercise books, notebooks, and pencils. These resource shortages were reflected in pupil reading levels, where these two provinces ranked lowest, and Nairobi, with the highest resource levels ranked highest. A similar trend was observed in Namibia.

Focus on examination results

The performance of Kenya's Grade 6 pupils on the SACMEQ reading and mathematics tests were not consistent with the results of the national examination at the upper end of primary school. These discrepancies generated widespread debate among Kenyan educationalists concerning the performance 'standards' that were supposed to be established by Kenya's examination system. It was surprising to note that Grade 6 pupils in certain Kenyan districts with highly ranked examination performance could hardly read. Discussions with teachers in those schools often resulted in the rather optimistic claim that there was no cause for alarm at that level because " ... we still have plenty of time to work on them before the national examinations". While this explanation deserved further examination, it was clear that the SACMEQ research results indicated that 'all was not well' in some Kenyan schools.

Launching new programmes in response to SACMEQ research results

In Namibia, the problems highlighted in the SACMEQ I Project and the debate that ensued led to the introduction of a number of interventions (such as the English Language Teacher Development Programme (ELTDP), the expansion of the Basic Education Teachers' Diploma (BETD), the introduction of the Efficiency Programme, the Management Policy Co-ordinating Committee (MPCC)), and also encouraged the government to establish the Presidential Commission of Inquiry on Education and Training.

Further consultations within the ministry and with stakeholders culminated in the production of a 5-year strategic plan (2001-2006) of the Ministry of Basic Education, Sport and Culture (MBESC). The plan's goals and objectives were derived from a combination of SACMEQ I results, EMIS annual statistics, national debates and the results of the Presidential Commission on Education and Training.

From the results of the SACMEQ II Project in Namibia, it could be seen that even if there had been major improvements in the allocation of resources to schools, between 1995 and 2000 there were still disparities among regions in terms of inputs to schools and learner achievement. This raised concern that even if there were some successes in providing 'formal access' to education (more schools/classrooms, more teachers, and more resources), the key issue of 'access to the same quality of education' was still a problem.

Achievement levels of pupils and teachers

From the SACMEQ research results, it may be seen that there has been a decline in the percentage of Namibia's Grade 6 pupils achieving higher competency levels in literacy.

In Namibia, the situation was worse in mathematics because of the poor performance of both Grade 6 pupils and their teachers. In mathematics, around 77 per cent of the Namibia's Grade 6 pupils were performing at a level that could not be said to be numerate. In seven regions (Caprivi, Kavango, Ohangwena, Omaheke, Omusati, Oshikoto and Oshana), the numbers of 'non-numerate' Grade 6 pupils ranged from around 80 to 90 per cent.

In comparison with the other thirteen countries that took part in the study, Namibian Grade 6 learners were the poorest in mathematics. While the average mathematics test score for Namibian teachers was quite good, only 20 per cent of the teachers in four of the seven regions mentioned above reached the highest mastery level. These results were not only shocking to the government and the public, but have become very controversial within the Ministry of the Education, with different people blaming teachers, the curriculum, school managers, advisory teachers, school inspectors, and other education authorities.

It was found that in the regions of Namibia where the majority of Grade 6 pupils had low literacy and numeracy levels, the highest level of academic education for about 30 per cent of the teachers was primary education. Most of these teachers were not trained to teach mathematics or English, and their own competence levels in these subjects were low. These results were indeed a great surprise, given all the interventions that had been made between 1990 and 2000, such as the training of new teachers and upgrading of older ones.

Research dissemination strategies used by the ministries of education

Kenya

Following the SACMEQ Assembly of Ministers meeting in Paris in October 1999, the Minister for Education in Kenya convened the first

research results dissemination forum on SACMEQ I for senior management
and high-level policy-makers in December 2000. The outcome of that
meeting was the establishment of a team with representation from
different ministry departments (including planning, teacher education,
inspectorate and curriculum development). The sharing of SACMEQ
research results continued at regional level as part of a series of Education
for All (EFA) consultative meetings held in each province in Kenya in
2001. At these meetings, the findings of SACMEQ I were disseminated
and debated. These exchanges provided useful suggestions on quality
issues that needed to be addressed within the EFA framework. Shortly
after these two dissemination activities, the SACMEQ I research findings
were presented to the President's Commission of Inquiry into the Kenyan
education system.

In 2002, the World Bank's Education Sector Analysis for Kenya
made extensive use of the findings of the SACMEQ I project for the
development of proposals aimed at addressing deficiencies in Kenya's
education system. The Education Sector Review led to the development
of the Education Sector Strategic Plan, which was published with World
Bank support. Further use was made of SACMEQ research results in the
field of financial planning when the Ministry of Education used SACMEQ
research findings in the development of the Public Expenditure Review
and Medium Term Expenditure Framework.

The SACMEQ research results have also been shared at lower
decision-making levels of the education system. For example, in January
2001, UNESCO Nairobi convened a forum for provincial directors of
education in Mombasa to discuss issues affecting education in their
provinces. SACMEQ research findings were discussed at the forum and
there was general agreement that it was useful to know the performance
of pupils in their provinces compared to others. Other examples occurred:
(a) a meeting of district education officers held in Nakuru in 2003, when a
member of the SACMEQ research team was invited to make a presentation,
'The Use of Education Indicators for Policy Development'; and (b) when
the SACMEQ research team made a presentation, 'Internal Efficiency and
Education Quality', at the first National Education Conference, held in
Nairobi during November 2003.

Namibia

In Namibia, the results of the SACMEQ I project were disseminated in two important publications. The first was published by the International Institute for Educational Planning in early 1998, and the other was published soon after by the Ministry of Education in a book entitled *Inside reforms: policy programming considerations in Namibia's basic education reform.*

The results of SACMEQ research were discussed by managers within the Ministry of Education and at planning workshops involving all educational planners. The results also informed national debates during the hearings of the Presidential Commission. Given the experiences of the SACMEQ I project, a different approach on education has been adopted for the dissemination of the results of SACMEQ II – in order to ensure stakeholder contributions to the policy suggestions, thus developing ownership and increasing the chances of policy suggestion implementation.

The preliminary results of SACMEQ II were first presented to the Ministry of Education's Executive Management Team in June 2003. This was followed by other presentations to the Minister of Education, regional educational planners, and all directors of education who were members of the ministry's Management Policy Co-ordinating Committee. These preliminary dissemination meetings were aimed at sharing the main highlights of the research findings.

A draft SACMEQ II National Research Report was presented to the Education Management Team towards the end of 2003 for their information and comments. The draft report was also shared with all directors of education in the ministry. The SACMEQ National Research Committee embarked on national wide dissemination seminars covering all of the thirteen educational regions, starting in mid-February 2004. The dissemination seminars were completed during the second half of April. These seminars targeted the following people: regional management teams, school inspectors and advisory teachers, representatives of regional education, school board members, teacher trade unions, local traditional authorities, local business community, regional councillors and local political leaders, and other stakeholders in education who were invited by regional directors of education.

Feedback from the dissemination

Kenya

The feedback received from the dissemination programme conducted in Kenya showed that the SACMEQ research results had the power to precipitate important (and occasionally heated) debates. Some examples are presented below.

Kenyan teachers were criticized for sending children home for unjustified reasons, including levies and uniform. They were also blamed for high rates of absenteeism and high rates of repetition, particularly at the upper primary level.

The SACMEQ I research results indicated that a large proportion of children in primary school were over-aged, and SACMEQ II research results confirmed that the average age of Grade 6 pupils had risen from 165.9 months to 168.4 months. The issue of over-age pupils was partly attributed to repetition, and it was believed that some of the over-aged pupils end up dropping out.

The government was blamed for the poor terms and conditions for teachers, and the 'boom' that had occurred in the provision of private tuition by teachers was seen as being due to a lack of motivation by teachers. The government was also criticized for the negative impact of cost-sharing policies that impacted heavily upon poor families, because they could not provide the necessary resources for their children's education.

The SACMEQ research results also illustrated that parental participation in the management of schools and in their children's schooling was either lacking or quite low. Although the concept of parent-teacher associations existed in theory, it was not effectively practised.

Namibia

The SACMEQ research results generated a great deal of 'heat' when they were first released. The literacy and numeracy levels of Namibia's Grade 6 pupils were shown to be very low when compared with other countries – and people tended to look for someone to blame. For example, Namibia's regional education offices blamed teachers for incompetence and lack of commitment. The teacher unions were also accused of demanding higher salaries for their members without addressing their professional deficiencies.

In response, the teacher union representatives blamed the ministry's staffing norms and education authorities for 'forcing teachers to teach subjects that they were not trained to teach and at grade levels they were not trained to teach'. The teacher unions claimed that these problems were coupled with inadequate resources and very little professional support, especially in rural schools. Inspectors and advisory teachers were not very helpful. In some cases, regional education authorities tolerated inefficient and ineffective school principals. In some regions, it was reported that teachers did not teach from the prescribed syllabus with the knowledge of some school principals. It was also argued that there was very little demand by managers at various levels in the ministry for accountability for work done by their subordinates.

The SACMEQ research results showed that parental involvement in education was a major problem, especially among low socio-economic groups in rural areas, where the majority of parents were not literate in English – the language taught at school. In the Caprivi region, one School Board Member was under the wrong impression that teachers could summon parents to school only if there was a disciplinary problem, and not to discuss the academic progress of the learner.

When discussing the poor achievement levels of Namibia's Grade 6 pupils, one teacher union representative blamed the ministry's policy of 'automatic promotion'. He argued that pupils were promoted from one grade level to a higher one without fully acquiring the basic competencies associated with the lower grade. However, other ministry staff suggested that grade repetition was not the answer – and that the problems occurred because teachers were not applying 'compensatory teaching' methods for slower learners as expected of them.

Education authorities in the northern regions reported prolonged periods of teacher absence from school due to HIV/AIDS related illnesses. Learners often went without a teacher during such periods, and thus missed a lot of schoolwork.

Language experts in three regions have suggested that the poor pupil reading levels illustrated by the SACMEQ research results arose because the wrong teaching methods were being used. They were very critical of new teaching methodologies that were based on 'look and say' reading techniques, as opposed to the 'old' discarded method that emphasized 'phonetics'.

Policy and practice reforms based on research results

The whole focus of the SACMEQ research programme has been on delivering information that can be used as basis for policy analysis and policy development. In the following discussion, some examples have been provided of how the SACMEQ research results entered the policy arena in Kenya and Namibia.

Kenya

■ Resource benchmarks

SACMEQ I results highlighted the absence of comprehensive and up-to-date standards or norms for resource inputs. Where these existed, there were disparities between official standards reflected in government documents and practice on the ground. This prompted the ministry to develop a comprehensive set of acceptable standards to be followed by schools to ensure efficiency and effectiveness in the system.

■ Curriculum review

SACMEQ research results and other education sector reviews have prompted the need for continuous curriculum review. The Kenya Institute of Education (KIE) has been involved in the review and rationalization of the curriculum with a view to making it affordable to parents as well as ensuring quality and relevance. The number of subjects taught at primary school level was reduced from thirteen to seven, and the number of examinable subjects from seven to five.

■ Achievement levels and textbooks

SACMEQ findings on lower-than-expected levels of achievement and the undersupply of textbooks to schools have prompted the government, in collaboration with other key stakeholders and development partners, to vigorously implement a school-based teacher development programme. Donors have also come in to support the provision of textbooks to all public primary schools.

■ Quality monitoring systems

The ministry has recognized and appreciated the importance of SACMEQ research results in informing policy and, to that effect, has (a) introduced a ministry of education budget line under 'education quality monitoring and evaluation', and (b) started to use the SACMEQ research results as baseline data by providing these data to other surveys undertaken within the framework of the free primary education programme.

Namibia

- Efficiency programme

In Namibia, the ministry used the results of the SACMEQ I in designing an efficiency programme and the creation of the Management Policy Co-ordination Committee (MPCC) in order to work towards achieving more equity in the education system, and improve the quality of education.

- Use in presidential commission

The *Presidential commission report* (1999) used the results of the SACMEQ I project, among others, to recommend new approaches to making financial allocations to education regions. This work was subsequently absorbed into the ministry's strategic plan with the purpose of developing: "fair, transparent and equitable systems for allocating all financial resources to the ministry's education units based on real needs and equity".

Minimal achievement targets

Because of the low competence levels achieved by a large percentage of Namibian Grade 6 pupils in the SACMEQ research, another objective of the ministry's strategic plan is to "ensure that all learners completing Grades 4, 7, 10 and 12, respectively, have achieved basic competencies in the required subjects of the curriculum by 2005" and to "improve teaching and learning of English, mathematics, science and skills related subjects by 2006". On the basis of the preliminary results of SACMEQ II, one education region has already formulated its own 'minimum quality standards' in the form of a checklist of all the things that the teacher should do in the classroom, and actions expected of the principal in the school and the inspectors and advisory teachers. In another region, regional authorities have been conducting meetings with stakeholders, especially school board members, on how they could help the school to achieve better results.

The Inspectorate

The poor conditions of schooling and the low pupil achievement levels highlighted by the SACMEQ research results formed the basis for the presidential commission's recommendation for the establishment of a 'national inspectorate' to monitor the quality of education in the country based on national standards. The national standards have already been formulated and the national inspectorate is expected to be operational from 2005.

Support to the poor regions

The SACMEQ research results showed that the northern education regions of Namibia had the most important problems with respect to provision of adequate educational inputs and achieving acceptable pupil learning outputs. With the assistance of development partners, these regions have now been targeted for multi-level assistance starting with teachers and expanding to the regional education officers. Schools have been divided into inspection circuits, and into clusters for administrative and support services. In this way, a cluster of schools can share resources, good practice, and expertise in a manner that benefits struggling schools. Schools in these regions are being assisted with the formulation of school development plans with the participation of local communities.

The status and use of SACMEQ research

SACMEQ research results have played an important role by informing dialogue and decisions related to the Namibian education system. As a result, SACMEQ's research programme is regarded as strategic to the development of the system. Namibian educational researchers and post-graduate students have also found the data generated by SACMEQ to be an immense resource. A number of them have used the data as a basis for more in-depth research and dissertations. Three of the issues that have proved to be most popular as areas of such research are regional differences in achievement, gender-based differences in achievement, and parental involvement in education.

Conclusion

The SACMEQ research results have clearly made an impact on a very wide range of educational policy and practice areas in both Kenya and Namibia. However, it is possible to summarize these inputs in the form of two 'policy messages' with slightly different emphases.

In Kenya, the main message was that first-class educational policy research on the quality of education (as is conducted by the SACMEQ consortium) brings added value and substance to national policy reviews and new policy formulation. Two other related messages were that the establishment of successful educational monitoring systems requires: (a) the institutionalization of the monitoring systems within the ministry's policy and planning functions; and (b) the dissemination of research results about the quality of education should be undertaken as a multi-level process that involves all stakeholder groups.

In Namibia, the main message was that in order to establish a linkage between educational policy research and 'action' there needs to be broad participation by Ministry of Education staff at all decision-making levels. That is, decision-makers are more likely to show interest and take action based on research that addresses policy questions that they have helped to elaborate. The policy-action linkage can be further strengthened if decision-makers are also: (a) informed well in advance of the research and its intended benefits to the ministry; and (b) given clear information about the role that they are expected to play with respect to the implementation of the research.

References

Angula, N.A. 1994. "Civil society, research and policy formulation in Namibia". In: W.C. Snyder Jr (Ed.), *Exploring the complexities of education: Notes on research design and statistics*, pp. 1-12. Windhoek: Gamsberg Macmillan Publishers.

Beaton, A.E.; Postlethwaite, N.T.; Ross, K.N.; Spearritt, D.; Wolf, R.M. 1999. *The benefits and limitations of international achievement studies.* Paris: IIEP-UNESCO.

Cohen, C. 1994. *Administering education in Namibia: The colonial period to the present.* Windhoek: Scientific Society of Namibia.

English Language Teacher Development Project (ELTDP). 1999. *Research into the English language proficiency of teachers/student teachers and basic education principals' and teachers' perception of the use of English in Namibian schools.* Windhoek: Ministry of Basic Education and Culture.

Government of the Republic of Namibia (GRN). 1999. *Presidential commission on education, culture and training report. Vol. 1.* Windhoek: Gamsberg Macmillan Publishers.

Government of the Republic of Namibia (GRN). 2001. *Education for All (EFA) national plan of action 2001-2015.* Windhoek: Ministry of Basic Education, Sport and Culture.

Maja, B.I. 1997. "Access to learning: The enabling conditions for successful learning environments". In: N. Bak (Ed.), *Going for the gap: Reconstituting the educational realm,* p. 1. Cape Town: Juta.

Makuwa, D.K. 2003. "Looking beyond educational indicators: An analysis of differences in learner results of a standardized English language comprehension test administered in Katima Mulilo and Rundu educational regions of Namibia". Unpublished Doctoral Dissertation. University of the Western Cape, South Africa.

Ministry of Basic Education and Culture. 1995-2001. *Annual EMIS education statistics.* Windhoek: Ministry of Basic Education and Culture, Namibia.

Ministry of Basic Education and Culture. 1998. *Language policy for Namibian schools, Grades 5-10.* Windhoek: National Institute for Educational Development (NIED).

Ministry of Basic Education and Culture. 2001. *Requirements for promotion in Grades 1-9 and 11.* Directorate of Educational Programmes Implementation (EPI). Circular No. ED 10/2001. Windhoek: Directorate of Educational Programmes Implementation (EPI).

Ministry of Basic Education and Culture. 2001. *Strategic plan, 2001-2006.* Windhoek: Directorate of Planning and Development.

Ministry of Basic Education, Sport and Culture and Ministry of Higher Education, Training and Employment Creation. 2003. *National policy on HIV/AIDS for the education sector.* Windhoek: Ministry of Basic Education Sport and Culture.

Ministry of Education and Culture. 1993. *Towards Education for All: A development brief for education, culture and training.* Windhoek: Gamsberg Macmillan.

Namibia Economic Policy Research Unit (NEPRU). 1999. "Improving public education". In: *The Namibian Economy: A NEPRU Viewpoint* (25), October.

National Planning Commission. 2002. *2001 Population and housing census, preliminary report.* Windhoek: Census Office.

Reimers, F.; McGinn N. 1997. Informed dialogue: Using research to shape education policy around the world. Wesport, WA: Praeger Publishers.

Ross, K.N. 1995. "From educational research to educational policy: An example from Zimbabwe". *International Journal of Educational Research, 23(4), 303-403.*

Ross, K.N.; Postlethwaite, T.N. 1992. *Indicators of the quality of education: A summary of a national study of primary schools in Zimbabwe*. Paris: IIEP-UNESCO.

Sherbourne, R. 2002. "A secondary consideration? Public spending on education since 1990". Briefing Paper No.11. Windhoek, Namibia: Institute for Public Policy Research. June.

Snyder Jr, W.C.; Voigts, F.G.G. 1998. *Inside reform: Policy and programming considerations in Namibia's basic education reform.* Windhoek: Gamsberg Macmillan.

Voigts, F. 1998. *The quality of education: Some policy suggestions based on a survey of schools.* Paris: IIEP-UNESCO.

Chapter 11
How can countries use cross-national research results to address 'the big policy issues'?
(Case studies from Francophone Africa)

Jean Marc Bernard and Katharina Michaelowa

Introduction

The 'Programme d'analyse des systèmes éducatifs de la CONFEMEN' (Programme on the Analysis of the CONFEMEN Education Systems), more widely known as PASEC, was launched at the 1991 Conference of Francophone Education Ministers (CONFEMEN), and carried out its first country evaluation during 1992 in Djibouti. Since then, fifteen individual country evaluations have been carried out in francophone Sub-Saharan Africa, including panel studies following primary students from 2nd to 6th grade within a given country. These evaluations were initially implemented by various research teams from the North. However, from 1995 onwards implementation was assured by national PASEC teams under the guidance and overall responsibility of the CONFEMEN Secretariat in Dakar. This development ensured a higher degree of comparability across individual country studies, and the building up of an international database including data for students, teachers and schools. It also included a strong involvement of national PASEC teams with the objective of capacity building for future assessments of the quality of education.

The primary objective of PASEC evaluations has not been the comparison of student achievement across countries, but rather the analysis of key factors that can explain variations in educational quality. Given the tight budget constraints limiting educational expenditure in most Sub-Saharan African countries, PASEC has attempted to derive a hierarchy of potential educational interventions in terms of their efficiency. Educational outcomes have been measured in terms of enhanced student achievement based on test results of 2nd and 5th graders in mathematics and French. The regular administration of a pre-test to all students in the sample at the beginning of the academic year controls for prior performance so that the estimated impact of policy variables measured during a particular year can be correctly attributed to students' learning within the same period.

Created at the initiative of education ministers with the clear objective to inform educational decision-making, the translation of PASEC results into actual education policy has not been automatic. This article will discuss specific procedures and measures adopted in order to improve the chances that PASEC results are actually taken into account by policy-makers and other target groups within the education sector. In addition, the article will illustrate to what extent PASEC has already contributed to concrete educational policy reform.

As the interaction of different participants in PASEC evaluations plays an important role in this context, the article starts with a description of the typical process of a PASEC evaluation, from the formulation of the evaluation proposal and its implementation on the ground, to the dissemination of results and the promotion of further analyses. This is followed by a discussion of the advantages and disadvantages of this approach through the presentation of country case studies from Senegal, Guinea and Togo. Finally, some conclusions are provided in terms of necessary institutional conditions for the successful translation of PASEC results into concrete educational policy.

The management of a typical PASEC evaluation

At each biennial CONFEMEN meeting at ministerial level, a decision is taken about the number and orientation of future PASEC evaluations. This is the starting point for the elaboration of evaluation proposals by CONFEMEN member countries. Alongside their general expressions of interest, countries can suggest specific thematic orientations, which may be integrated through the adaptation of student, teacher and/or school director questionnaires. Country proposals are selected by the PASEC Scientific Board in co-operation with the PASEC technical advisers based at the CONFEMEN secretariat.

Once a country proposal has been selected, the national CONFEMEN representative is responsible for the creation of an interdisciplinary group of experts, within the ministry of education, which takes over the actual implementation of the PASEC evaluation. This national PASEC team benefits from several training sessions provided by the PASEC technical advisers, and is responsible for the management of funds. In co-operation with the PASEC advisers, it develops the questionnaires, trains the test administrators sent to the schools, manages the data entry, and participates in the analysis and the drafting of the national report. Once a first draft of this report is available, it is discussed in the PASEC scientific board and finalized by the PASEC technical advisers – again in co-operation with the relevant national PASEC team.

Concrete policy recommendations to be added to the national analytical report are formulated at a national 'dissemination seminar' to which the national PASEC team invites the relevant decision-makers at the ministry of education, and representatives of different stakeholder groups (teachers, teacher unions, inspectors, parents, and donor agencies). For several days, the national PASEC team and the PASEC technical advisers present their results, encourage discussions, and seek final policy conclusions. The media are also invited to this seminar so that policy outcomes are immediately reflected in press articles and often on the radio and television. As the results are of interest not only for the evaluated country itself, a separate press release is sent from the CONFEMEN secretariat to news agencies in other member countries. Moreover, flyers under the joint responsibility of the CONFEMEN and the national education ministry are prepared with the main results. Finally, selected results are presented at the next ministerial meeting of the CONFEMEN.

When the evaluation process is completed, data are made available to external researchers for further analysis. The CONFEMEN secretariat actively promotes the use of these data through co-operation with various universities and research institutions, the co-supervision of Masters degree theses, internship programmes, etc. Currently, at least twenty researchers work on studies based on the PASEC database. Exchanges between researchers and the PASEC technical advisers at the secretariat have already led to a refinement of the econometric analyses carried out for the draft of CONFEMEN country reports, as well as to a complementary household survey for Senegal carried out by Cornell University and the Laboratory of Applied Economics of the French National Initiative of Agronomy Research (INRA) – which will enable a deeper understanding of some of the issues raised by the initial PASEC evaluation.

The CONFEMEN intends to encourage national ministries to institutionalize the evaluation of their education systems and to maintain their national PASEC team as a small evaluation unit within the education ministry. PASEC technical advisers organize an annual training session at which at least one member of each national team is invited to participate.

Country case studies

Several country case studies for PASEC evaluations have been presented below. These case studies shed some light on major policy topics assessed by PASEC evaluations, and show the extent to which PASEC results have been relevant for educational reform.

The selected case studies cover the most recent PASEC country evaluations. The case studies commence with discussions of the Senegal six-year panel, and this is followed by an examination of PASEC assessments in Togo and Guinea. Finally, some complementary information will be provided from other country evaluations.

Senegal

The PASEC panel study in Senegal started in 1995 with a representative sample of students at the beginning of the 2nd grade. These students were followed until the year 2000 where those who did not repeat any class completed their primary education. At the end of each academic year, the students were tested in mathematics and French to obtain information about their progress over time. Moreover, the general PASEC questionnaires for teachers, school directors, and students were administered for complementary information in the 2nd grade, and, in a somewhat reduced version, in subsequent years.

The main objective of the panel analysis was to gain some insights into the effects of grade repetition, an extremely common practice in francophone sub-Saharan Africa. In 2000, average primary education repetition rates in francophone sub-Saharan Africa were 20 per cent against 10 per cent in anglophone Africa, and 2 per cent in OECD countries (UIS, 2003; MINEDAF, 2002). At the political level, during the early 1990s, it was felt that reducing grade repetition might foster the objective of universal primary education. First, the limited number of places available would not be blocked by the same students over several years, and second, reducing repetition might reduce early dropout. However, this gain in enrolment was expected to occur in association with reduced learning levels. That is, a quality-quantity trade-off was anticipated. The PASEC panel evaluation was expected to provide appropriate information to examine the validity of this proposed trade-off.

From the presentation of the initial results for the first three grade levels at the CONFEMEN ministerial meeting in 1998 (CONFEMEN, 1999) until the final publication in 2004 (CONFEMEN/MEN, 2004), the outcomes of the analysis have been consistent and clear. On average, a primary student who repeats a grade does not do significantly better than another student who does not repeat, provided that family background and school environment are corrected for, and if students start from the same performance level at the beginning of the year of analysis.

Grouping students into equal-sized groups of good, intermediate and weak students, according to their achievement on PASEC tests at the national level, shows that the effect of repetition is insignificant for the weaker students, and detrimental for the better students. Moreover, it turns out that while most repeaters belong to the third of weak students, more than one quarter of repeaters belong to the intermediate or even to the best students. The results thereby provide evidence for substantial ill-targeting. Finally, the hypothesis of repetition leading to higher dropout also finds some empirical support from the panel analyses.

Overall, PASEC results clearly indicated that a policy of reduced repetition will not have any negative impact on education quality, and that it is definitely one of the most efficient ways to facilitate enhanced enrolment and to avoid early dropout in Senegal.

These results were presented to stakeholders in the education system at a dissemination seminar, and separately to the Minister of Education and to his Cabinet. While repetition had been legally limited to 10 per cent at the beginning of the 1980s, a new ministerial decision reaffirmed it in 2003, after PASEC results had been presented. Moreover, the ministry decided to prohibit repetition between Grades 1 and 2, Grades 3 and 4, and Grades 5 and 6. However, it is important to note here that repetition cannot simply be reduced by decree, as enforcement may be very difficult if the decision-makers at the school level do not agree.

In fact, teachers, school directors, inspectors and even parents, all seemed to be convinced that repetition helped weak students to acquire the skills required for further learning in higher grades. A survey among Senegalese primary teachers in the 1999 PASEC sample indicated that 77 per cent considered that grade repetition was an efficient, or even very efficient, mechanism for fostering student learning.

A major problem seems to be that teachers' views about grade repetition are typically based on a comparison between the performance of an individual student and the performance of the class as a whole. Now grade repetition leads to a comparison with a different peer group (with a lower ability level) and, compared to this new peer group, the student's performance will appear higher than it actually is.

PASEC tried to inform the policy debate with its analytical results and to provide sound arguments to convince the different stakeholders concerned. In Senegal, the print and electronic media showed a high level of interest in following the debate. About ten different press articles were written on the topic, not only in French but also in various local languages. To engage a more direct debate with stakeholders, participants in the dissemination seminar proposed similar regional seminars involving the relevant decision-makers. It was pointed out that one highly relevant target group (after inspectors) should also be the 'pedagogical counsellors' who are responsible for teacher training in Senegal.

As an exceptionally rich database, the panel data for Senegal have also attracted considerable attention from external researchers. Most notably, a co-operation with INRA (France) and Cornell University (United States) started in 2002 with the objective of supplementing the existing data with a complementary household survey. Research based on the augmented dataset will provide additional insights into the linkages between social background and repetition, as well as between repetition and early dropout.

It should be noted that similar exercises have been carried out in Côte d'Ivoire and Burkina Faso. For Côte d'Ivoire, (where repetition rates were as high as 22 per cent) the research results were almost identical to those discussed above. However, given the general political instability in Cote d'Ivoire, the management and usage of PASEC results was considerably less effective. In Burkina Faso, PASEC results have not yet been fully analysed, and a dissemination seminar was not organized because data collection had to be undertaken in several stages, due to a lack of funding. Nevertheless, taking (provisional) results for the three countries together enabled PASEC to present a consistent picture at the CONFEMEN ministerial meetings in 2000 and 2002 – thereby promoting reduced grade repetition as a general objective for countries in francophone Sub-Saharan Africa. PASEC has planned to publish a book on the combined results for all three countries.

Togo and Guinea

In both Togo and Guinea, PASEC evaluations were carried out with a special thematic focus on teacher training and non-civil-servant teacher contracts. These issues were put forward by the two ministries of education because prior reforms in teacher employment policies called for an assessment of their impact on education quality.

While Togo had started to hire teachers on a non-civil-servant contractual basis from 1983 onwards, this process only started in Guinea in 1998. In Guinea, teachers received brief pedagogical training of six to nine months' duration – much shorter than the traditional training programmes of two to three years that had previously been in place. In Togo, they did not receive any initial training at all.

In Guinea, the new teachers were recruited with at least upper secondary educational attainment (*baccalauréat*, BAC); in Togo, while the formal requirement was the same, lower secondary attainment (BEPC) was considered sufficient in practice. In both countries, the main objective of the policy reform was to reduce costs in order to be able to meet the schools' rising demand for new teachers.

At the same time, there was some concern that these reforms might have a negative impact on students' learning: (a) it was feared that hiring teachers on a contractual basis – implying considerably lower salaries and less job security – might have a detrimental impact on their motivation and thereby, indirectly, on students' performance in their class; (b) it was considered that pedagogical training of less than one year might be too brief to effectively prepare the future teachers for their work in class; and (c) in the case of Togo, it was felt that teachers with only BEPC might not have sufficient mastery of the subject-matter that they were supposed to teach. Overall, it was anticipated that the reforms would reduce the cost of hiring more teachers, but at the price of considerably reduced education quality.

The PASEC results show that this is actually not the case. In general, PASEC results indicated that the new teachers employed on a contractual basis are by no means doing worse than their colleagues. In some cases and contexts, they seem to do even better (CONFEMEN, 2004; CONFEMEN, 2003). This can be explained as follows:

First, while reducing the duration of teachers' pedagogical training, its content was reformed so that the reduction in duration could be compensated for by increasing its relevance and quality. In the context of the new World Bank initiated teacher training programme in Guinea (Formation Initiale des Maîtres de Guinée, FIMG), for instance, a strong emphasis was placed on practical teaching experience under the guidance of senior teachers. This may have been an effective innovation in the training programme.

Second, teachers' own educational attainment beyond BEPC has frequently been shown to be of rather limited relevance for primary teachers' performance (CONFEMEN, 1999). This may be related to the quality of the education that teachers themselves receive, or to the low relevance of the academic knowledge acquired for practical teaching in class. The PASEC research results for other countries showed, for instance, that there was no significant correlation between teachers' educational attainment above or below the BAC, and their ability to point out the mistakes in a dictation correctly (Michaelowa, 2003). Moreover, there is some evidence that teachers with educational attainment beyond the BAC may be less motivated on the job (Michaelowa, 2002).

Third, non-civil-servant contracts may create an incentive for teachers to work hard in order to retain their current post, or to move to a permanent position later in their career.

To a certain extent, such arguments were welcomed by politicians because they provided justifications for policy reforms carried out under the pressure of budgetary constraints. At the same time, there is a lack of understanding why standard requirements for teachers in industrialized countries (such as the BAC) should be inefficient and therefore undesirable in the African countries concerned. Finally, there is considerable discontent among teachers. The teachers employed under the new conditions argue that they are underpaid and required to put up with unstable working conditions while doing the same work as other teachers. The older teachers complain that the new arrangement might undermine esteem for the teaching profession as a whole.

Given the nature of the reforms, dialogue with the different stakeholders was particularly important. Unfortunately, in both Togo and Guinea, teacher unions did not attend the dissemination seminar due to a dispute concerning daily allowances. Their exclusion from discussions was rather unfortunate as they were the stakeholder group that was most opposed to the policy reforms.

Teachers, ministry officials, inspectors, and school directors present at the seminar agreed upon the necessity of high-quality pedagogical training for teachers. The flyer with PASEC research results for Togo, jointly edited by the CONFEMEN Secretariat and the Togolese Ministry of Education, strongly argued for lower entrance requirements to the teaching profession in terms of educational attainment (only BEPC), but compulsory pedagogical training period for all new teachers.

In terms of actual policy developments, PASEC results have encouraged the Togolese authorities to retain the BEPC as the minimum academic entrance requirement for primary teachers. It remains to be seen, however, whether initial pedagogical training for all teachers will be ensured in the future. In Guinea, the idea is to continue the training programme initiated within the framework of the FIMG pilot project by the World Bank. As Guinea belongs to the group of countries included in the 'fast track' initiative, donor funding for future teacher training should be available. This shows that the implementation of PASEC results also depends upon the linkage of PASEC activities with the activities of other international organizations and bilateral donors. Generally, as countries tend to focus their efforts on important internationally supported programmes such as 'Education for All' and the 'Poverty Reduction Strategy Paper' (PRSP) processes, the interest for PASEC results within the national ministries of education is highly correlated with their perceived usefulness for the preparation and implementation of these wider international programmes.

Just like the issue of high repetition rates discussed in the context of Senegal, the issues of engaging teachers on non-civil-servant contracts and of adequate teacher training are also relevant for many other francophone African countries currently introducing policy reforms in these areas. To bring PASEC results to the attention of decision-makers in these other countries, analytical outcomes were presented at the CONFEMEN ministerial meeting in Ouagadougou in 2002, and a press release was sent by the CONFEMEN Secretariat to the relevant media in all Member States. It should be noted, however, that countries currently experiment with many different types of new teacher contracts and training programmes. Results for one country may not necessarily hold for another country, and therefore case-by-case analysis seems to be necessary. Currently, PASEC evaluations with a similar thematic orientation are going on for Mali and Niger, and it will be interesting to compare the results. An ongoing World

Bank survey of teachers in Senegal, Mali, Burkina Faso and Niger will add additional complementary information.

Further examples

While Senegal, Guinea and Togo have been discussed in detail, it may be worthwhile mentioning a few developments in other countries as well. In Madagascar, for instance, PASEC results had shown in 1997/98 that continuous teacher training had a negative effect on student achievement. This result came as a surprise and prompted a discussion as to why this might be the case. It turned out that continuous teacher training was primarily held during class hours resulting in reduced teaching. This practice has been changed since then.

In Cameroon, as a result of the first PASEC assessment, the ministry created a special evaluation unit to ensure the institutionalization of educational evaluation. Generally, it seems that successful follow-up of PASEC evaluations depends a lot on the stability of the national PASEC team. If there is no fixed group of people involved in educational assessment within a ministry of education, exchange of experiences becomes difficult, and the information about what actually happened as a result of the initial PASEC analysis becomes very difficult to obtain. Moreover, if the national PASEC team is not in a position to supervise and support the implementation of results, it is hardly probable that anything will happen.

If members of the team keep changing, the capacity of a follow-up at the national level is very low. In such a situation, the continuous training modules offered by the PASEC technical advisers become rather inefficient and the cross-national network of experts built up through regular workshops with representatives of all national PASEC teams also becomes less effective. In some country cases, such as the Central African Republic or Côte d'Ivoire, the stability of the PASEC team, the implementation of PASEC results, and the interest in educational policy have all been greatly affected by violent conflict and political unrest.

Conclusion

The above discussion shows the difficulties in managing the results of an international evaluation programme such as PASEC. While many provisions are in place to ensure adequate discussion and implementation of results, actual policy outcomes are subject to the stability of the national

PASEC teams, general political stability, and the capacity to mobilize additional financial means to finance reforms. Experience has shown that PASEC outcomes attract most attention if they can be directly fed into national education sector strategies or poverty strategies – thereby raising the chances for donor funding. Moreover, it is vital that, right from the beginning, host countries of a PASEC evaluation have a genuine interest in the thematic orientation of results. Optimally, such as in Senegal, Togo and Guinea, PASEC should provide answers to strongly relevant national policy issues. In these cases, PASEC outcomes have generally been well received, and have led to policy developments that were consistent with PASEC results.

References

CONFEMEN. 1999. "Les facteurs de l'efficacité dans l'enseignement primaire: les résultats du programme PASEC sur neuf pays d'Afrique et de l'Océan indien". In: *Programme d'analyse des systèmes éducatifs de la CONFEMEN (PASEC), Dakar.*

CONFEMEN/MEN. 2003. *Le Programme de formation initiale des maîtres et la double vacation en Guinée.* Dakar: Ministère de l'Enseignement pré-universitaire et de l'Éducation civique de Guinée/CONFEMEN.

CONFEMEN/MEN. 2004. *Le redoublement: pratiques et conséquences dans l'enseignement primaire au Sénégal.* Dakar: Ministère de l'Éducation du Sénégal/CONFEMEN.

CONFEMEN/MEN du Togo. 2004. *Recrutement et formation des enseignants du premier degré au Togo: quelles priorités? – Les résultats de l'évaluation thématique du Programme d'analyse des Systèmes Educatifs de la CONFEMEN (PASEC) sur les enseignants du Togo.* Dakar: Ministère de l'Éducation nationale du Togo/CONFEMEN.

Michaelowa, K. 2002. *Teacher job satisfaction, student achievement, and the cost of primary education in francophone Sub-Saharan Africa.* HWWA Discussion Paper No. 188. Hamburg: HWWA (Hamburg Institute for International Economics).

Michaelowa, K. 2003. *Determinants of primary education quality: What can we learn from PASEC for francophone Sub-Saharan Africa?* Background paper for the ADEA study: The challenge of learning: improving the quality of basic education in Sub-Saharan Africa. Paris: ADEA.

MINEDAF. 2002. *Universal primary education – a goal for all. Statistical document MINEDAF VIII*. Paper presented at the Eighth Conference of Ministers of Education of African Member States (MINEDAF VIII), Dar-Es-Salaam, United Republic of Tanzania. December.

UIS. 2003. *Education statistics: statistical tables (EF)*. Retrieved 17 May 2004 from:
http://www.uis.unesco.org/ev.php?URL_ID=5187andURL_DO=DO_TOPICandURL_SECTION=201

Chapter 12

How can a country manage the impact of 'excellent' cross-national research results?
(A case study from Finland)

Pirjo Linnakylä

Introduction

Considerable added value can be gained from participation in cross-national studies of the quality of education – such as those conducted by the International Association for the Evaluation of Educational Achievement (IEA) and the Organisation for Economic Co-operation and Development (OECD). International assessments can reveal, more clearly than national assessments, the special characteristics of a national education system and its pedagogical culture. From close range it is often much more difficult to see where the strongest points are; where the best potential lies; and on the other hand, what is weak, stagnant or problematic.

Taking this into consideration one can be certain that cross-national research results always generate lively discussions and heated debates among researchers, various interest groups, and policy-makers, and they are more likely to have a strong impact on educational planning and pedagogical practice. This seems to be the case especially when assessment results turn out to be weaker than expected. As regards the IEA's Reading Literacy Study (Elley, 1992) this occurred in Denmark, and with regard to OECD's PISA study (Adams and Wu, 2002) this was especially true in Germany.

Tensions between national and international assessment results

It is indeed quite strange that when the results are excellent, as the Finnish results were in both the reading literacy study and the PISA study, they seem to raise less attention and discussion and have less policy relevance at the national level. At the same time that the international press was glorifying the Finnish success in PISA, in Finland the Ministry of Education and the Finnish press, were energetically downgrading the PISA research findings, and instead emphasizing Finnish students' weaknesses in reading and writing achievement that had been revealed in the national assessment conducted by Finland's National Board of Education in 2001. The ministry publicized the results of the two assessments at the very same time, but gave much less prominence to the PISA findings than to the national ones. This information strategy quite possibly had something to do with the new allocation of lesson hours for basic education, which the ministry had just approved in 2001, and related curricular plans, which increased the number of hours for mother tongue, mathematics and health education, in response to alleged shortcomings in these subject areas. The international results were clearly contradictory to the arguments presented in favour of these policy reforms.

There was a particularly striking disparity between the international results and the national assessment findings. The latter claimed that young people's reading literacy, both in terms of performance and engagement in reading activities, had declined dramatically, and that there was significant variation among schools, among regions and among socio-economic groups as a result of the devolution of educational decision-making powers. Firm political decisions to redress the situation had already been taken: the aim was to recentralize decision-making powers, make curricula more uniform (particularly in the core subject areas), lessen the ratio of elective subjects and courses, and define learning objectives and grading standards with greater precision. In the new Curriculum Framework published in 2002, the role of the core subject areas – mother tongue, mathematics, civics and health education – had been strengthened. In addition, criteria for 'good performance' had been added for the 2nd, 5th and 9th grades.

Variations in interest levels: the press and teacher unions

The press coverage of the initial PISA findings was limited in the beginning. The main newspapers did publish the international 'league tables' – which ranked the PISA countries on average student achievement scores. However, national assessment results received much wider coverage, so that in newspaper editorials, as well as on current-affairs television programmes, the media expressed deep concern for the shortcomings detected in Finnish teenagers' literacy skills.

The information presented in *Table 12.1* provides an objective analysis of the amount of press coverage that occurred for the PISA research results one month their release. It is clear from these figures that there was relatively little initial interest in the PISA results in Finland, and this was also the case with the IEA study a decade earlier.

The Ministry of Education was quite active in publicizing the IEA results, but the teachers' union was more cautious and afraid of losing resources for instruction. The teachers' union was particularly worried about increasing class sizes, since according to the IEA results, good learning achievement occurred in both larger and smaller classes.

Table 12.1   Press coverage in the PISA countries approximately one month after the release of research results

Country	Number of pages	Country	Number of pages
Germany	687	United States	36
Switzerland	149	Belgium	32
Canada	93	New Zealand	25
United Kingdom	88	Republic of Korea	21
Japan	84	Finland	8
Australia	54		

In the context of PISA, however, the teachers' union applauded the results and praised the good work of teachers. This might have something to do with the fact that the teachers' union were seeking public support for their demands for wage increases.

The teachers' union was in favour of keeping elective subjects in the curriculum. The PISA findings supported this viewpoint by showing that high achievement in core subject areas was possible in association with a relatively high degree of subject choice, and also more choice did not result in large between-school differences. However, the union news magazine, *Teacher*, never published the initial PISA results. This occurred much later after the foreign delegations and study tours started their stampedes into Finnish schools.

International attention raises interest levels in Finland

The international press kept praising the Finnish education system for the success shown by the PISA results (OECD, 2001, 2002). This even led to a new type of 'tourism' where hundreds of visitors, among them journalists, teachers, researchers and official delegations from different countries, came to explore the 'secret of Finnish success'. This vast and sustained international attention started to have repercussions within

Finland. Suddenly, the Finnish press began to wonder about the 'real' achievement level of Finnish students, and they also began to explore why such extraordinary attention was being given to the Finnish education system. The press even started to cite articles published abroad about Finnish success.

This all started to get too much for several Finnish professors who had completed their studies in Germany. They were shocked when the PISA results showed that German students were performing far below their Finnish counterparts – and they voiced their surprise and disapproval. They even suggested that there should be a ban on criticizing the school achievements of an old civilized country such as Germany.

The professors expressed their doubts about the validity of the tests, the equivalence of translations, and the comparability of data and analyses. Other researchers specialized in women's studies belittled the gender gap in favour of girls that was evident in the PISA results, and they brought forward research findings that highlighted discrimination against girls in daily school practices (Gordon and Lahelma, 2004). Further, a number of sociologists criticized the relevance of international assessments, challenged the role of the OECD in the field of educational evaluation, and expressed their concern that Finland should give more attention to national assessments focused on national education policy (Ball, 2004; Rinne *et al.*, 2004).

The continuing vast and relentless international attention, however, gradually began to impact upon the attitudes of senior staff in the Ministry of Education. They started to take the PISA findings seriously, although constantly reminding others that there was no reason to be enthusiastic about Finland's international results and that everybody should keep in mind the alarming national findings. Eventually, the 'good news' started to filter down to the school level – where it reinforced principals' and teachers' professional self-esteem, and increased parents' faith in the quality of Finnish education.

In public discussions, teachers and their associations began to explain Finland's excellent results in PISA by accentuating the significance of sound teacher training. The advocates of independent civic education underlined the importance of up-to-date library services and related leisure-time reading activities, while the people involved in the social services sector emphasized the social and cultural support given to families. Psychologists proposed explanations related to the clarity and transparency of Finnish orthography (Aro, 2004), whereas sociologists attributed the success to the Finnish traditional belief in education and strict school discipline (Simola, 2004).

International attention raises interest levels in other PISA countries

The Central European press was very active in publicizing comparative PISA results and glorifying the Finnish education system, perhaps, or very probably, because of below-average results in their own countries. It seems that, in the view of the media, 'poor results make the best news'. It also seems that resources for educational research and development are more readily available when achievement levels are low.

This happened, for example, in Denmark after the IEA Reading Literacy Study when the Danish Ministry of Education funded a further comparative study on pedagogical practices in order to discover why the high achieving Nordic countries (especially Sweden and Finland) performed better than Denmark, where performance levels were among the lowest. A central result of this study was the finding that teachers' and parents' expectations had a significant impact on students' achievement. In Finland and Sweden, teachers' expectations were also noted to be significantly higher than in Danish schools.

In the Danish education system, the same classroom teacher follows the same student group throughout the comprehensive school. As a result, the teacher gets to know the students well, but on the other hand, his/her expectations tend to be lower than in Finnish and Swedish schools where the teachers change after the primary grades, at the latest, resulting in (a) higher demands on students in the upper grades, and (b) avoidance of the danger of persistent subjective categorization of students by teachers. The Danish researchers' initial hypothesis that strict discipline and demanding tests were the driving forces behind Finnish students' good results received no support from the analyses (Sommer *et al.*, 1996).

German educational authorities also became interested in the Finnish basic education system, especially in the national curriculum, teachers' pre- and in-service education, students' learning standards, teaching and learning in heterogeneous groups, special needs education, and assessment practices. Furthermore, the German Federal Ministry of Education and Research funded a comparative study, 'Conditions of School Performance in Seven Countries', with the aim of understanding international variations in PISA results, and to find out which school system factors and educational cultures were associated with high performance in Canada, England, Finland, France, the Netherlands and Sweden – as compared with the performance in Germany (Döbert *et al.*, 2004; Linnakylä, 2004). As one result of this comparative study, German researchers and policy-makers moved towards the introduction of general competency-based standards for German schools, and commenced planning for a national assessment programme in order to monitor the development of learning outcomes (Klieme, 2004).

Important research findings for Finland

Gradually, the strengths and weaknesses of Finland's education system revealed by the PISA results came under further inspection and review by Finnish researchers. The results were presented in three national reports (Välijärvi *et al.*, 2001; Välijärvi and Linnakylä, 2002; Linnakylä *et al.*, 2004*a*). In addition, the Finnish PISA research team published – often because of the urgings of interested parties abroad and not because of the encouragement of the Finnish Ministry of Education – their own conclusions and explanatory discussions in English (Välijärvi and Linnakylä, 2002). In these publications, the researchers emphasized what they considered the most significant research result from PISA – that quality and equity do not have to compete with each other or be mutually exclusive, but rather they may be complementary as was clearly the case in Finland. The Nordic interpretation of the principle of equity, which favours the policy of equal access, equal opportunities to learn, and special support to the weak and vulnerable, was clearly encouraged by the PISA results. Carroll (1987) argued nearly two decades ago that any gains in terms of higher average levels of national literacy have been achieved because of improved performance among disadvantaged students. This view received support from the Finnish PISA results.

One of the most important PISA research findings in terms of policy relevance was that in Finland the gap between the high and low achievers was narrow – with the variance in student achievement being the second smallest after the Republic of Korea. In addition, Finland displayed a below OECD average impact of parents' socio-economic status on student performance, and the differences among schools in average student performance were among the smallest of all OECD countries. It was also particularly interesting for policy-makers that the lowest performing 10 per cent of Finnish schools scored almost 100 points above the respective

OECD average (Välijärvi and Malin, 2003), and that regional differences in the PISA results within the country were insignificant.

Altogether it was shown that in Finland it does not make much difference which region you live in and which school you go to because the opportunities for students to learn are about the same all over the country.

In guaranteeing gender equity, however, Finland was less successful – which was indicated in PISA by a gender gap in reading literacy that was widest in Finland. The gap in Finland was 51 score points – with the OECD average being 32 points. Compared to previous international reading literacy assessments, the gender gap seemed to have widened not only in Finland but also in other OECD countries. The gender difference, however, was not due to Finnish boys doing poorly but rather to Finnish girls performing exceptionally well.

It should be noted that Finnish boys scored better than boys in any other OECD country and even better than girls in many of the participating nations. However, the fact remains that in Finland the gender gap in reading literacy was exceptionally high. This same alarming finding has been made in national assessments as well.

Challenges for policy and practice reforms

Finland's greatest challenge as regards reading literacy development seems to relate to reducing the gender gap both in reading literacy performance and in engagement in reading activities outside school. Since engagement in reading activities proved to be the strongest determinant for good performance, the most critical questions are how to stimulate interest and engagement among boys, and how to help them find enjoyment in reading. The quest for finding answers to these questions has had significant implications for both policy and research. The National Board of Education has launched a national and a joint Nordic programme to enhance literacy skills of weak readers, particularly of boys. The national campaign 'Reading Finland' set the following objectives for the period 2002-2004, which were in line with the challenges flowing from the PISA results: (a) improved performance of the weakest fifth of students; (b) development of methods to make reading attractive to boys; (c) improved performance for reflective and critical literacy; (d) increased time spent by students in reading and writing both at school and in their leisure time; (e) improved conditions for school libraries, and enhanced co-operation between schools and community libraries; (f) increased efforts by all teachers to develop reading comprehension and writing skills; (g) improved competence for classroom teachers in mother tongue and literature instruction; (h) increased teachers knowledge of literature for children and young people; (i) expanded co-operation between school and students' homes in the field of reading and writing; and (j) enhanced instruction for immigrant students both in Finnish as the second language and in their first language.

As can be seen above, the ministry and the National Board of Education have taken measures to improve the language and literacy skills of immigrants. This is partly a consequence of the PISA results. Although the percentage of immigrants in the Finnish population is still quite low, the PISA results from other Nordic countries and Central Europe imply that there is good reason to address immigrant children's literacy skills development early enough in order to avoid problems arising from poor literacy skills and a consequent lack of motivation for further studies and opportunities for active citizenship.

Enhanced Nordic research collaboration

Outside the ministry, there are several further studies in progress on PISA, both nationally and as Nordic collaboration projects. Nordic collaboration, which already had started in the context of the IEA Reading Literacy Study, has been active in the PISA context as well, and focused particularly on deepening the understanding of differences and similarities in school cultures and also on joint pedagogical efforts to improve the literacy performance of students at risk from disadvantaged backgrounds.

Even the Scientific Academy of Finland has supported various studies on the Finnish PISA data. This research has been concerned with exploring factors that impact on equity in the assessment and achievement of reading literacy. For instance, one prospective doctoral thesis has focused on the equivalence of international test translations, and another one on the 'authenticity' of reading tests in the Finnish cultural context. There has also been thesis work on exploring the differences between schools by means of multi-level modelling.

Nordic collaboration among the PISA researchers has resulted in a flow of further studies. In 2003, the researchers published *Northern Lights on PISA* (Lie *et al.*, 2003), which focused on equity with a special emphasis on gender. One secondary study reported in the book suggested that the most critical affective factors behind the wide gender gap in the Nordic countries were engagement in reading, reading fiction frequently, strong self-esteem in learning to read, and student efforts and perseverance. Controlling for these factors simultaneously, it was possible to construct an 'imaginary' situation where boys and girls were 'evenly engaged' in reading during school and leisure time, where boys' self-concept was as strong as that of girls, and where boys and girls showed equal effort and perseverance with regard to reading. In this imaginary situation, the gender gap either disappeared, as in Denmark, or at least diminished significantly, as was the case for all other Nordic countries. In Denmark, the difference after controlling for the crucial factors even turned slightly in favour of boys. These research findings emphasized the importance of linking the cognitive and affective elements of learning.

The PISA results suggested that Nordic countries could learn more about gender equity from other countries, particularly with regard to boys' reflective and evaluative reading. In Australia, Ireland, New Zealand, and the United States there were smaller gender gaps than for most of the Nordic countries in reflective and evaluative reading, which was the domain where all the Nordic countries faced a challenge.

Nordic collaboration among researchers has included a special issue of the *Scandinavian Journal of Educational Research*, entitled 'Nordic PISA 2000 in a Socio-cultural Perspective' (Lie and Linnakylä, 2003). The articles in this special issue focus on socio-economic and cultural capital associated with learning outcomes in the domains of reading and science literacy. In articles focusing on reading literacy, emphasis is placed on the determinants of low-achievement among both minority and majority students as well as on students' multiliteracy profiles (Hvistendahl and Roe, 2004; Linnakylä *et al.*, 2004*a*; Leino *et al.*, 2004).

Even though Finnish students' reading literacy performance, in the light of PISA 2000, proved excellent on average, there is still room for improvement. Yet, such improvements presuppose increasing sensitivity to, and catering for, the individual needs of students. In PISA, for example, 7 per cent of Finnish students were found to have severe difficulties. By international standards, the proportion is small, but if each student is entitled and supposed to reach adequate learning standards and related success, the struggle to minimize low achievement has to continue. Finnish and Swedish researchers have joined forces to analyse further which factors increase the risk of low literacy achievement (Linnakylä *et al.*, 2004*b*). The findings of this further study revealed no big surprises, but proved again that male gender, immigrant status, low socio-economic background, several siblings, low academic self-esteem, lack of engagement in reading, and a heavy use of computers – were all factors that were significantly associated with low reading literacy achievement in both Finland and Sweden, when the other factors were controlled for. In Sweden, the risk of low achievement was further increased by single-parent family status and lack of possessions related to classical culture. In Finland, the risk was further increased by rare cultural communication at home and skipping classes at school (Linnakylä *et al.*, 2004*a*).

Conclusion

The IEA and PISA research results show that the Finnish comprehensive school system is successful in providing the majority of its students with a solid foundation for further schooling. The results also predict an auspicious future for the small nation, whose cultural originality, economic success, and social cohesion are all premised on the performance of its education system. The Finnish PISA research findings show that an education system that accentuates equity can also reach high quality.

The pursuit of the Finnish tradition of equity will shortly be put to a severe test due to the increasing numbers of immigrant students and growing cultural heterogeneity. To tackle this issue, Finland will have to learn a great deal from countries that have had extensive experience in managing educational programmes for immigrant children.

Finnish people strongly believe in comprehensive basic education, where every child attends school free of charge for nine years from the age of 7 to the age of 16. The comprehensive school is, however, not only a system. It is also a matter of pedagogical philosophy and practice. It accentuates the fact that schools have to adjust to the needs of the child, and not vice-versa.

The pedagogy applied in Finnish schools has been designed to cope with heterogeneous student groups, and its purpose is to teach all children to learn and to work together, and ultimately through this to strengthen social cohesion in society. In this system, the teachers cannot exclude anybody or simply send a less able student to another school. Instead, in every school, students' interests and choices have to be taken into consideration when selecting course content, textbooks, learning strategies and assessment devices. Success in addressing this within-school diversity can only be achieved with small class sizes, a flexible school-based and teacher-planned curriculum, student-centred instruction, counselling, and special educational support for students with difficulties.

In Finnish culture, teaching is rated among the most important professions in society, and a lot of resources have been invested in teacher education. Teachers have also been trusted to do their best as true pedagogical experts vested with considerable independence in the classroom. Likewise, schools have enjoyed substantial autonomy in organizing their work within the flexible limits of a national curriculum framework. This autonomy will hopefully be sustained in the future since it makes the teaching profession more attractive, and it helps to attract the most able students into teacher training programmes. Creative, independent and responsible teachers who have strong internal motivation are, after all, the best guarantee for educating a new generation of creative, independent and socially responsible individuals.

The assessment system and evaluation culture however, are changing in Finland, partly because of PISA. The controversy about national and international assessment results, and the downgrading of international findings, have played some role in the re-organization of the national educational evaluation in Finland. Based on a Decree by the Council of State, the Ministry of Education appointed an independent body in spring 2003, the Education Evaluation Council, with responsibility for planning and co-ordinating all national and international assessments in Finland. The secretariat of the council is based at the University of Jyväskylä, which has long traditions in managing international comparative assessments of learning outcomes. Time will tell how this new body will succeed in its efforts to develop an evaluation programme that is independent of the administration, and where national and international assessments are reasonably in balance and co-ordinated to complement each other, yet avoiding excessive burdens and restrictions on schools' and teachers' work.

References

Adams, R.; Wu, M. 2002. *PISA 2000 technical report*. Paris: OECD

Aro, M. 2004. *Learning to read. The effect of orthography*. Jyväskylä studies in education, psychology and social research (publication No. 237). Jyväskylä, Finland: University of Jyväskylä.

Ball, S. 2004. Suorituskeskeisyys ja yksityistäminen jälkihyvinvointivaltion koulutuspolitiikassa [Performativity, privatisation and the educational policy of the post-welfare state]. *The Finnish Journal of Education Kasvatus*, 35(1), 6-20.

Carroll, J.B. 1987. "The national assessments in reading: are we misreading the findings?" In: *Phi Delta Kappa*, 68, 424-430.

Döbert, H.; Klieme, E.; Sroka, W. (Eds.). 2004. *Conditions of school performance in seven countries. A quest for understanding the international variation of PISA results.* Waxmann: Münster.

Elley, W. 1992. *How in the world do students read?* Hamburg: International Association for the Evaluation of Educational Achievement (IEA).

Gordon, T.; Lahelma, E. 2004. "Etnografinen katse koulutuspolitiikkaan [Ethnographic view to educational policy]". In: *The Finnish Journal of Education Kasvatus*, 35(1), 66-78.

Hvistendahl, R.; Roe, A. 2004. "Achievement, family background and motivation among students with an immigrant background in Norway". In: *Scandinavian Journal of Educational Research* (3).

Klieme, E. 2004. Zur Entwicklung nationaler Bildungsstandards. Grundpositionen einer Expertise. In Th. Fitzer (Hrsg.), *Bildungsstandards. Inernationale Erfahrungen – Schulentwicklung – Bildungsreform.* pp. 256-265. Bad Boll: Evangelische Akademie.

Leino, K.; Linnakylä, P.; Malin, A. 2004. "Finnish students' multiliteracy profiles". In: *Scandinavian Journal of Educational Research* (3).

Lie, S.; Linnakylä, P. (Eds.). 2003. "Nordic PISA 2000 in a socio-cultural perspective". In: *Scandinavian Journal of Educational Science* (3).

Lie, S.; Linnakylä, P.; Roe, A. 2003. *Northern lights on PISA. Unity and diversity in the Nordic countries in PISA 2000.* University of Oslo. Department of Teacher Education and School Development.

Linnakylä, P. 2004. "Finland". In: H. Döbert, E. Klieme and W. Sroka (Eds.), *Conditions of school performance in seven countries. A quest for understanding the international variation of PISA results.* pp. 150-218. Waxmann: Münster.

Linnakylä, P.; Sulkunen, S.; Arffman, I. 2004a. *Tulevaisuuden lukijat. Suomalaisia lukijaprofiileja. PISA 2000.* [Readers for future. Finnish students' reader profiles]. University of Jyväskylä: IER.

Linnakylä, P.; Malin, A.; Taube, K. 2004b. "Factors". In: *Scandinavian Journal of Educational Research* (3).

OECD. 2001. *Knowledge and Skills for Life. First results from PISA 2000.* Paris: OECD.

OECD. 2002. *Reading for Change. Performance and engagement across countries.* Paris: OECD.

Rinne, R.; Kallo, J.; Hokka, S. 2004. "Liian innokas mukautumaan? OECD:n koulutuspolitiikka ja Suomen vastauksia [Too eager to comply? Educational policies of the OECD and the Finnish response]". In: *The Finnish Journal of Education Kasvatus, 35*(4), 34-54.

Simola, H. 2004. "Kenraali Aadolf Ehrnrooth ja PISA:n ihme – koulutussosiologisia huomautuksia erääseen suomalaiseen menestystarinaan". In: *The Finnish Journal of Education Kasvatus, 35*(4), 91-98.

Sommer, M.; Lau, J.; Mejding, J. 1996. Nordlaes – en nordisk undersögelse af laesefaerdigheder i 1.-3. klasse. Copenhagen: Danmarks Paedagogiske Institut.

Swap, S. 1993. *Developing Home-School Partnerships.* New York: Teachers College Press.

Söderberg, S. 2001. "Attitudes and expectations in relation to school: Swedish findings and some international comparisons". In: *Schooling for tomorrow: what schools for the future.* Paris: OECD.

Välijärvi, J.; Linnakylä, P. 2002. (Eds.) *"Tulevaisuuden osaajat. PISA 2000* [Competent for future]". In: University of Jyväskylä: IER.

Välijärvi, J.; Linnakylä, P.; Kupari, P.; Reinikainen, P. 2001 *Suomen tulevaisuuden osaajat* [Competent for future in Finland]. University of Jyväskylä. IER.

Välijärvi, J.; Linnakylä, P.; Kupari, P.; Reinikainen, P.; Arffman, I. 2002. *The Finnish success in PISA – and some reasons behind it.* University of Jyväskylä: IER.

Chapter 13

How can a country manage the impact of 'poor' cross-national research results?

(A case study from Germany)

Jeanne Rubner

Introduction

Many German parents think of school as a necessary but rather unpleasant place. This attitude has had a long tradition, and goes some way towards explaining why German primary schools only operate in the morning – with children spending their afternoons at home. German parents also tend to see the world of education as having two distinct purposes: to form the personality and to deliver knowledge. The first purpose is seen as the preserve of parents – who are responsible for raising children, and the second is seen as the business of the school – which is expected to concentrate on the cognitive development of children.

For a very long time much of the German public has been under the impression that this 'separation of powers' has worked well. They assumed that German schools were better than those in other developed countries, and they were convinced that the German *Abitur* was superior in terms of content, balance, and intellectual challenge when compared to other European and American high-school diplomas.

These assumptions were shattered towards the end of 2001 when research results emerged from the Programme of International Student Assessment (PISA) (OECD, 2001) conducted by the Organisation for Economic Co-operation and Development (OECD). These results showed that 15-year-old German students performed relatively poorly when compared with 15 year-olds in other OECD countries. In fact, German 15-year-olds were ranked only 25th out of 32 countries in reading, and 21st in mathematics and science. An even more shocking result was that in Germany the correlation between the socioeconomic background of pupils and their educational achievement was extremely strong. This indicated that there were major differences in educational achievement between children from poor and rich families. Taken together these research results provided clear evidence that the German education system was far behind many other OECD countries in terms of both 'quality' and 'equity'.

Just as this gloomy news was being absorbed in Germany, further concerns emerged with respect to the connections between education and the labour market. In particular, it was pointed out that, compared with most OECD countries, German university graduates are very 'old' – with an average age of around 27 years. This has occurred because of a three-stage process: (a) German high school students do not graduate until they are, on average, around 19 years old; (b) they then have to complete a year of military service; and (c) finally, German university degrees take a relatively long time to complete. For many years, the German public were not very concerned with this issue – because they simply assumed that the German education system produced older but better graduates. However, the TIMSS and PISA research results, combined with an increase in workforce mobility within the European Union, have caused anxiety – with even highly-educated Germans being concerned about 'competition for jobs' in an increasingly globalized world.

Several years before the release of the PISA research results, the first TIMSS (Beaton *et al.*, 1996) study conducted by the International Association for the Evaluation of Educational Achievement (IEA) provided similar messages about the poor performance of the German education system. The German newspapers were 'shocked' to report that United States schools, which were widely considered as somewhat inferior, ranked at about the same level as those in Germany for mathematics and science.

Despite these earlier 'warning signals' about the quality of education in Germany, the TIMSS results did not generate a great deal of discussion and debate among the government, public and teachers. Some people have suggested that the reason for this was that TIMSS, unlike PISA, did not test in reading – which has always been regarded in Germany as central to the role of schooling, and an essential foundation for a cultivated society. Others thought that the limited reactions to the TIMSS results occurred because these results 'broke the ice' in terms of beginning a wave of government and public awareness about comparisons. The PISA results then capitalized on this increased awareness several years later. Still others thought that because PISA was sponsored by the OECD, it was better able to connect comparative educational performance with national economic performance – right at a time when political debates had emerged about a widespread public perception of a decline in Germany's competitive edge in new technologies and industrial manufacturing.

What results did the ministry find important and why?

Regional differences in achievement

It is important to bear in mind that compared with many other European countries, 'educational politics' is a complicated affair in Germany because there is one ministry of education for each of the 16 *Länder* (regions). Each *Land* is responsible for its schools, universities and cultural development. In recent years, there has been some progress in co-operation among the *Länder* with respect to the acceptance of each other's high-school diplomas. However, heated debates about education are still quite common – especially among *Länder* that are governed by different political parties.

One of the great surprises observed in the PISA research results was that the average 15-year-old student in several *Länder* was around one year ahead of the average 15-year-old student in other *Länder*. In fact, for a while, the differences in achievement levels between Bavaria and Nordrhein-Westfalen attracted more attention from ministries of education, parents, and newspapers than did the generally poor performance of Germany as a whole!

Duration of high school

The TIMMS research results raised questions about the structure and duration of upper secondary schooling in Germany. A debate was already under way on this matter when the TIMSS results were released – because the unification of East and West Germany had been accompanied by the *Länder* taking different approaches to the total length of schooling. For example, several of the 'new' *Länder* in East Germany had 12 grades of school – however, a number of these switched to 13 grades, in order to align themselves with many of the West German *Länder*.

These changes to the length of schooling were challenged by the TIMSS research results because it was demonstrated that gains in knowledge between Grades 12 and 13 in Germany were only noticed for the area of physics – and this was explained by scientists as being due to additional teaching of modern quantum physics which helped students to better understand certain physical concepts. However, it was the mathematics results – where no gain was noted between Grades 12 and 13 – that set off a public discussion about the length of high school.

Because of the TIMSS results, the 'Conservative' *Länder* immediately started plans to shorten the length of high school, whereas the 'Social Democratic' *Länder* were reluctant to follow. The issue was, and still is, highly controversial since teacher unions and most parents' organizations support the 13-grade option. Teachers have argued publicly that fewer years would reduce the amount of knowledge that pupils gain from school, and privately they have expressed concerns that a reduction in the length of schooling would be followed by a reduction in the number of teachers. In contrast, parents were worried that fewer years at school would put more pressure on their children, since it had been argued that any reform in this area should not result in reduced student achievement levels.

Comparisons with other countries

The TIMSS research results also showed that German students had performed poorly compared with several South East Asian countries. This signalled a search for explanations – which at times became a search for a 'silver bullet' that was expected to provide an immediate and successful pathway to educational reform. The most popular 'explanations' were associated with differences between Germany and South East Asian countries with respect to teaching methods, teacher training and school segregation.

■ Teaching methods

Video evidence from the TIMSS research indicated that German and Japanese mathematics teachers differed in their teaching approaches. This sparked off calls for German teachers to follow their Japanese counterparts by placing more emphasis on knowledge of mathematical concepts than on learning formulas by heart, and to encourage students to look for many ways of solving a problem rather than insisting on only one 'correct' solution.

■ Teacher training

Teacher unions did not want to be treated as scapegoats for educational problems, and they argued for more teacher training in both pedagogy and subject matter. Given the length of German university degrees, it was agreed that German teachers were well trained in their subject matter, and that the 'training problem' was associated with deficits on the pedagogical side. This was addressed in a variety of ways across the *Länder* – including changing the organization of university degrees to a Bachelor's/Master's structure that would provide training in subject-matter during the Bachelor's phase and pedagogy and psychology during the Master's phase.

  ▪ School segregation

After four years of elementary school, German children either continue elementary school until the ninth grade, or pursue middle school until tenth grade, or attend high school for eight or nine years – depending on their elementary school achievement levels. This segregation into different types of school has been an issue in Germany for many years. In the 1970s, there had been a move to install comprehensive school systems in *Länder* ruled by the Social Democratic Party. However, the idea of comprehensive schools was never really accepted across Germany because of a widely held assumption that a segregated system was better for children because they could learn more effectively when placed in homogeneous ability groups.

The PISA research results challenged these assumptions. Several countries with good performance in the PISA project had comprehensive school systems – with Finland and Sweden being the role models. The comprehensive schools in these countries have a philosophy of supporting every child as much as possible, and yet they still obtain excellent results. Many German politicians, researchers, government officers and representatives of teacher unions travelled to these two countries in an attempt to discover why student support and student performance were not mutually exclusive. In Germany, a vigorous debate on this issue took place at two different levels: between various *Länder* ministries of education and various stakeholder groups within the *Länder*.

  ▪ Social equity

The German Federal Government sees itself as the guardian of equal opportunity – and this mission has featured in the German Constitution. However, the PISA results suggested failures in this area. For example, German 15-year-olds in Bremen scored at levels similar to their counterparts in developing countries, while Bavarian 15-year-olds were closer to levels associated with the better-developed countries. Even more troubling was that the correlations between student socioeconomic background and their achievement levels were higher in Germany than in any other OECD country. This PISA research result prompted a great deal of speculation as to why German schools should have such a high level of social inequity. Educationalists pointed towards three main reasons for this situation.

First, there has been poor integration of migrant children into the German school system – and many of these children (especially from the Turkish community) have been unable to follow classroom lessons. Suggested reforms have included better language assessment methods and the provision of intensive language classes.

Second, German children start school much later than children in other countries, and most German children do not have access to pre-school education that includes formal teaching time. As a result, there have been discussions among the *Länder* ministries of education about the introduction of a formal curriculum in pre-school education that includes the requirement of meeting minimal education standards.

Third, Germany is one of the few industrialized countries in the world where children do not go to school in the afternoon. For example, school finishes on most days at 1:00 p.m. – with children being expected to go home for lunch and do their homework under their mother's supervision. Reforms in this area are still under discussion by the *Länder* ministries of education, and are being actively promoted by the German Federal Government.

What dialogue/reporting/target-groups did the ministry use, and why?

The German researchers involved in both the TIMSS and the PISA projects work at the Max Planck Institute for Educational Research in Berlin. These researchers, together with representatives of the Conference of the *Länder* Education Ministers, presented the results of the studies at press conferences. The results were published as books, and the researchers gave interviews. The researchers were careful not to make statements that could be misused for political purposes. However, some politicians and teacher unions resented this as a 'diplomatic' way of interpreting results. The *Länder* ministries of education concentrated their dissemination strategies on scientists, and took no specific actions to involve other groups directly.

When the TIMSS and PISA data were released, there was a rush to re-analyse them in the hope that the 'bad news' from these projects was due to some fault in the data analyses. For example, the TIMSS ranking of countries was put into question by scientists who argued that less able German pupils from vocational schools had been included in the testing, whereas in France and other countries only the more academically oriented high-school students had been included.

What ministry policy and practice reforms flowed from the results?

One of the most important impacts of the TIMSS and PISA projects in Germany has been the manner in which they have precipitated an acceptance that there was a need for widespread educational reform after many long years of misguided contentment and parochial self-centredness. This has placed Germany and its 16 ministries of education on the pathway to change – guided by the results of cross-national studies of the quality of education.

There were four main areas where concrete policy and practice reform occurred in Germany due to the availability and use of the TIMSS and PISA research results.

The establishment of 'standards' and other common measures

The *Länder* ministers of education have moved to establish agreed 'standards' in the form of educational goals for specified grade levels. That is, the ministers of education have finally accepted that there is some commonality across Germany with respect to 'what every student should learn'. The first 'standards' have already been published and they will be obligatory for all schools in all *Länder* at the start of the 2005/2006 school year. This outcome is indeed remarkable because, for many years, there had been no agreement at all across the *Länder* about curriculum content and sequence.

Meanwhile, the ministers have established an agency responsible for working out tests in order to supervise the standards. This agency is an institute at the Humboldt University in Berlin, and should be in full operation by the end of 2005.

A more symbolic act is the agreement between the federal government and the *Länder* to issue a common report on the educational system every other year. Up to now, because of shared responsibility, the *Länder* have more or less regularly published such reports on the school system, with the federal government issuing reports on professional education. In the future, they will put their reports in one book.

Full-day schooling

A federal programme has been planned, initially costing 4 billion euros, which will gradually move German students towards full-day schooling. Following extensive debate, all *Länder* have now signed their agreement with the federal proposal, and funding is expected to flow to the regions during 2005. By now, all *Länder* have started to use the federal money and it is widely accepted that Germany needs more full-day schools.

Length of secondary schooling

In many regions, high schools have changed, or will be changed, from a 13-grade to a 12-grade system. Even the rather conservative and traditional Social Democratic Nordrhein-Westfalen *Länder* has decided to shorten the length of high school – and it would not be too ambitious to predict that within ten years, all high-school students will receive their diploma after 12, and not 13 years.

School segregation

With each new round of PISA results (the last one being in December 2004), the discussion resumes about the structure of the German school system, mainly about the segregation of 10-year-old children into different types of schools. This early segregation is, according to many experts, one of the causes of social inequity, or at least reinforces it. Others deny that there is such a correlation and continue to believe in the benefit of different types of schools. The federal government has tried to push public discussion on an integrated school system, but the general opinion is not in favour of it. However, some *Länder*, such as Rheinland-Pfalz, have increased the number of integrated schools. Others, especially those in former Eastern Germany, have (after reunification) always only had two types of schools, and realize that it is also less costly than three or even four parallel types of schools – in particular in less populated areas. Due to a decline in birth rate, Germany might, in the long run, move towards a less differentiated system.

The final two years of schooling

Reform in this area is both limited and controversial. Bavaria and Baden-Württemberg *Länder* have taken a leadership role by deciding to make the existing arrangements more structured. Senior students were allowed to choose two main subjects and two secondary subjects, one of which was tested orally. In these two regions, this flexibility has been replaced by the requirement of choosing German, mathematics, one foreign language, and one scientific subject.

Conclusion

The most important overall impact of Germany's participation in cross-national studies of the quality of education has been a far-reaching re-consideration of the role of schooling within an increasingly globalized world. Long-established traditions have been questioned, new approaches to school management and school operations have been considered, new discussions have been held on effective educational strategies among *Länder* ministries of education, and the public has been drawn into the debate about the nature and importance of an effective education system. These pleasing outcomes are based on hard evidence drawn from the TIMSS and PISA research results.

References

Beaton, A.; Martin, M.; Mullis, I.; Gonzalez, E.; Smith, T.; Kelly, D. 1996. *Science achievement in the middle school years.* Boston: IEA, TIMSS International Study Center.

OECD. 2001. *Knowledge and skills for life: first results from PISA 2000.* Paris: OECD.

Chapter 14

How can international organizations work with the media to manage the results of cross-national studies?
(A case study from the OECD)

Andreas Schleicher

Introduction

The main objective of the Programme for International Student Assessment (PISA) that is conducted by the Organisation for Economic Co-operation and Development (OECD) is to work with the governments of the OECD countries in order to produce a small but critical mass of comparative policy-oriented benchmarks that focus on the quality of education delivered by school systems.

Many researchers who commence work in this area assume that, if they design and administer data collection instruments that deliver valid cross-national data, the research results will automatically be taken into consideration by policy-makers who will then facilitate the publication and use of the most important findings. Unfortunately, such linear connections between 'information', 'dissemination', and 'policy impact' is practically non-existent in the field of education. For this reason, researchers who wish to influence policy need to integrate strategies for the wide dissemination of research results into the design of cross-national studies.

Researchers who wish to optimize the impact of cross-national studies need to arrange for the distribution and use of research results in two phases. The first phase is to obtain and disseminate valid cross-national results and to analyse their policy implications. The second phase is concerned with raising awareness of the policy implications among the main stakeholders in a manner that motivates governments to respond with appropriate action. However, in order to strengthen the linkages between research results and action, there is also a need to understand fully how governments respond to cross-national research findings, and what leads them towards policy implementation. In addition, there is a need to give some thought to sustaining the impact of the research by implementing assessments on a regular basis within a coherent long-term framework.

What do we know about the quality of education?

Education is a field that is contested among many interest groups. There is considerable research evidence (OECD and UNESCO, 2003) to show that education is a key determinant of individual success, and also an important driving force behind the aggregate economic performance of nations. Therefore, both parents and governments are concerned about the quality of education that is delivered by their own school system. Teachers also have personal and professional interests in being focal points for assuring the delivery of high-quality education. Taken together, these interest groups cover a substantial percentage of the population of most countries of the world – and this is why the media has become aware of the importance of reporting the results of international comparisons of education outcomes.

However, what do we really know about the quality of education? What do teachers know about the work of their colleagues in the next classroom? What do schools know about how nearby schools address similar challenges? What do policy-makers really know about the effectiveness of their education systems? The answer to all of these questions in most countries is: 'Very little!'

Many education systems operate in the dark, making 'reform' decisions without having sound knowledge about the performance of their schools, and with limited understanding of the potential impact of policy changes. Such approaches are usually based on the belief that having good intentions is enough to obtain positive results. The problem here is that information-free decision-making can be dominated by traditions, ideologies and the views of influential individuals and/or pressure groups. Even worse, poor decisions can lead to long-term problems because of a lack of information about policy impacts. In such an environment, the media is free to speculate about education systems and to confuse the important stakeholders by publishing conflicting opinions that are provided by 'experts'.

Well-designed comparative studies of the performance of education systems can help to shed some light on this area – with the aim of moving towards informed decision-making. However, high-quality comparative studies often reveal important differences among education systems and this usually heightens media interest because many news 'stories' are driven by a thirst for information about contrasts such as: successes/ failures, improvements/declines, and differences/similarities.

Some policy implications of PISA

The media had a key role in raising awareness of the policy implications of the PISA research results because it was able to describe where each country's education system stood in relation to others, and also to suggest that the best performing education systems provided concrete evidence of 'what could be possible' for all systems.

Descriptions of student performance

When students receive marks in schools, their parents and the general public often wonder what these numbers actually mean, in terms of what students are actually able to do. The same problem can arise in cross-national studies of the quality of education if each country is simply assigned a 'score' that is equal to the average achievement for students in that country. National average scores provide no information about the underlying competencies of students.

In order to address this problem, the OECD has reported student performance in the PISA project thorough the construction of 'proficiency levels'. For example, the PISA data showed that around 10 per cent of 15-year-old students across the OECD countries reach a 'very high level of literacy'. That is, they are able to formulate their own hypotheses, they have quite sophisticated knowledge, and they can deal with concepts that are contrary to expectations.

In contrast, at the lower end of the performance spectrum there were also around 10 per cent of 15-year-old students across the OECD countries that had only basic knowledge and skills. These students were not able to use information creatively in order to extend their own knowledge.

The implications of skill deficit

At the very lowest performance level, there were around 5 per cent of 15-year-old students whose skills were so limited that they appeared to have 'lost connection' with the fundamental performance requirements of formal schooling. These students will certainly face very grim prospects in later life – especially with respect to their employment prospects.

Some people believe that skills deficits can be addressed and overcome through continuing education and training later in life. Unfortunately, evidence provided by the OECD Indicators Project (OECD and UNESCO, 2003) showed that this is not the case. The last thing that young adults with major skill deficits seem to have in mind is to return to a learning environment where they have only known failure. Furthermore, even if they find a job, their employers are unlikely to invest in their education and training. That is, the OECD research has shown that these unfortunate 15-year-old students have major skill deficits that are likely to disadvantage them throughout their whole lives.

Is there a 'quality' versus 'equity' trade-off?

The first reaction of the media when the results of cross-national studies are published is to rank countries in the form of 'league tables' in which countries are ranked from the country with the highest mean student achievement down to the lowest. Many people argue that such tables must be interpreted in association with context data. For example, average student achievement levels are known to be related to factors such as per capita gross domestic product (GDP), and the educational attainment and literacy rates of the adult population. However, governments aiming for improvements within a competitive marketplace in national economic development are often more interested in what their education systems deliver to whole cohorts of students – and not just the 'average student'.

In searching to improve the 'quality' of student achievement there is a need to keep a close eye on both average student achievement levels and 'equity' issues. The PISA project examined these two dimensions by constructing the graph presented in *Figure 14.1*. The horizontal axis represents average student achievement scores for OECD countries. These scores were scaled to an OECD an average of zero. The vertical axis represents the degree of social equity (measured by the strength of the relationship between student socioeconomic background and his/her educational achievement). These scores were also scaled to an OECD average of zero.

The countries in the top right-hand corner of the graph are in the very desirable position of having relatively higher student achievement ('high quality') and a relatively low relationship between socioeconomic background and educational achievement ('high equity'). The least desirable position for a country is to be in the bottom left corner – where both quality and equity are poor.

Figure 14.1 The quality and equity of education

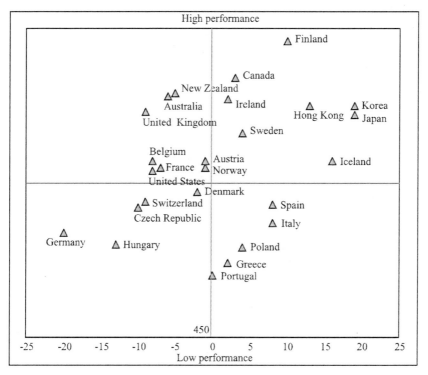

Source: OECD, 2001.

The countries in the top left-hand corner of *Figure 14.1* have high quality and lower equity.

Some people might argue that in these school systems, educational quality may drop if these countries tried to achieve a higher degree of equity in educational outcomes. They may also argue that the application of policies geared towards improving the quality of education in the lower performing countries in the bottom right-hand corner would risk losing equity. However, there are many countries, such as Canada, Finland, Hong Kong, Japan, Republic of Korea and Sweden, that do well on both dimensions. The performance of these countries provides concrete evidence that it is possible for countries to have both high quality and high equity.

In contrast, there are a number of countries (for example, Hungary, Germany, Czech Republic and Switzerland) where the average achievement levels of students are relatively low and there are substantial social inequalities with respect to student achievement.

The most important message that emerges from *Figure 14.1* is that there is no need for a trade-off between quality and equity – because there is evidence that some countries achieve both. That is, governments and ministries of education need to recognize that quality and equity need not be considered as competing policy objectives.

On what did the media focus?

Many of the early media reports about PISA simply documented the 'league table' results and their own country's standing within them. Much of this material focused on a 'winners and losers' discussion. However, as time passed, more serious attempts were made to draw out the lessons for policy that emerged from the results. Several of them have been presented below.

From inputs to outputs and the factors that influence outputs

One of the most important impacts of media reports of PISA results was to move public discussion about the quality of education systems away from a concentration on material and human resource inputs towards a more intensive examination of educational outputs and the factors that influence them.

PISA showed that students' engagement with their studies and their motivation to succeed were both strongly related to their learning outcomes. While direct cause-and-effect relationships have not yet been established, these results indicated that parents and schools needed to recognize that enthusiasm, enjoyment and involvement (as well as hard work) are factors that must be acknowledged as contributing towards positive learning outcomes.

PISA also developed policy messages in this area that had relevance for school-level administrators. It showed that a school environment characterized by high performance expectations, a readiness to invest effort, good teacher-student relations, and high teacher morale, was associated with better student learning outcomes.

Decentralization, assessment and accountability

PISA provided policy suggestions for the general operations of school systems. In particular, PISA indicated that beneficial impacts on student achievement were linked with countries that have progressively shifted the focus of education policy and practice away from centralized control over resources, structures and the content of education towards a much higher profile for school-based management. Beneficial impacts on learning were also noted for countries that had established clear educational objectives in association with systems for monitoring and assessing the achievement of these objectives. Central examinations and assessments can be important elements in such strategies; however, what is most crucial is that the assessment results are fed back into the school system in order to help students to learn better, teachers to teach better, and schools to be more effective.

Collecting data is not enough if this activity cannot be used to make schools function better. Many of the best performing countries such as Finland and Sweden set good examples. In both countries, there are national assessment systems that define frameworks within which teachers evaluate the performance of students and are accountable for their results. At the end of the year, it is the teachers' responsibility to work with students and parents in order to establish individualized student-based agendas for improving performance.

Autonomy and heterogeneity

If schools are to be accountable they also need an appropriate degree of autonomy in order to implement policies and strategies aimed at achieving performance targets. PISA showed that schools in many of the best-performing countries had a high degree of freedom with respect to the selection and appointment of teachers, teacher salary levels, the design and management of the learning environment, and the choice of subjects that were offered to students.

Some educationalists have argued that giving schools greater freedom will lead to greater differences among schools and thus to larger disparities in learning achievement. This is certainly a risk. However, several countries in PISA have shown that such outcomes can be avoided. For example, while Finland and Sweden give their schools a very high degree of autonomy, in these two countries the variance in student achievement that can be attributed to differences among schools is very small – somewhere around 10 per cent. That is, Swedish and Finnish parents can send their children to any school – and still expect similar learning outcomes.

In both, Finland and Sweden, more autonomy is combined with (a) a high degree of accountability demanded of schools with respect to their results, and (b) a heightened responsibility to address the needs of a diverse client base. In contrast, when German or French students fail to reach minimal performance targets, they often have to repeat the grade and thereby tend to receive 'more of the same'. Almost all of the countries that performed well in PISA showed that grade repetition did not have to be the automatic result of learning difficulties. In these countries it was the responsibility of the school to deal constructively with heterogeneity of performance, to find solutions for performance deficits without resorting to grade repetition or to student transfer to different educational streams or to moving students to different types of school that have lower performance expectations and requirements.

Foundations for lifelong learning

PISA provided a number of important clues about educational experiences that foster improved learning outcomes. Students who do well tend to be those most closely 'engaged' in their own learning. That is, they are able to plan what they need to know rather than waiting to be fed with information by the teacher. Developing the predisposition of students to engage with learning, and the capacity to do so effectively, is an aspect that needs to receive more attention in education systems because of the major payoffs that this has with respect to encouraging lifelong learning. Students who leave school with the autonomy to set their own learning goals (and with a sense that they can reach these goals) are potential learners for life.

Motivation and engagement can also influence whether students' will successfully pursue further educational or labour market opportunities. Education systems in many countries have a long way to go in order to reform their educational practices in these areas. A failure to deliver these reforms runs the risk that a significant number of students will develop negative attitudes towards learning and a lack of engagement with school. Not only are negative attitudes associated with poorer student performance, but students who are disaffected with learning at school will also be less likely to engage in learning activities outside school in later life.

Tracking, streaming and ability grouping

As the causes of differences in student performance differ, so too do the approaches chosen by different countries to address these. Some countries have non-selective school systems that seek to provide all students with the same opportunities for learning and require each school to cater for the full range of student performance. Other countries respond to diversity by forming groups of students of similar performance levels through selection, either within or among schools, with the aim of serving students according to their specific needs.

How do such policies affect student performance? The question is difficult to answer but PISA has suggested that both overall variation in student performance and performance differences among schools, tend to be greater in those countries with rigid selection practices at an early age between types of programme and school. PISA has also indicated that the effect of social clustering is greater in school systems with differentiated types of school than in systems in which the curriculum does not vary significantly among schools. Schools systems that 'track' students from an early age, (for example, Austria, Germany and Switzerland) also exhibit large performance differences among schools – which is what one would expect from highly selective systems. None of these school systems were among the best performing countries. That is, PISA research results illustrated that more integrated and flexible educational pathways, combined with individual support for students, tended to be conducive to better results and a more balanced distribution of educational opportunities.

These policy conclusions clearly underline the need to place learning and the learners at the centre, rather than programmes or institutions. All the most successful countries in PISA have taken steps to integrate education alternatives and move towards the individual promotion of students, starting with pre-school education, and to bring about increased flexibility in education pathways. The integrated and individual promotion of students in countries such as Finland, Japan, Canada, Republic of Korea and Sweden provide examples of how to achieve both high enrolment in education streams that lead to higher leaving qualifications and higher levels of performance. These countries achieved not only above-average overall performance, but also a significantly better exploitation of performance potential, especially for students from disadvantaged social backgrounds.

It should be noted that comprehensive school systems are not a guaranteed recipe for success. There were a number of comprehensive systems in PISA that performed poorly. What is required is a comprehensive approach to schooling in association with highly individualized support for students. In Finland and Sweden, up to 40 per cent of the curriculum is individual, and there is a lot of individual support for students, in different forms, which enables them to learn successfully. A concentration on individualized teaching enables school systems to compensate for differences in students' abilities and learning dispositions, and thus avoid and counter disadvantage while, at the same time, talent and excellence are fostered.

PISA has provided strong evidence showing that school systems often make bad judgements about student potential. As a result, students tend to be sorted by social background – rather than true ability. This leads to a waste of human potential, as has been highlighted by the performance in PISA of countries with highly selective school systems.

Conclusion

The reporting of PISA research results by the media was, as expected, initially focused on a 'league table' view in which countries were ranked and either congratulated or admonished for their rankings. Over time, a degree of maturity began to emerge as the media saw the deeper implications of the PISA results and their potential for guiding policy aimed at improving the quality of education.

Newspapers and the electronic media in many countries are now extending their coverage of PISA results to engage questions related to quality and equity trade-offs, the integration of decentralization and accountability, the linkages between autonomy and heterogeneity, and the management of different student ability groups. The PISA research results have provided a sound information base as a resource for conducting informed discussion of these vital areas of policy. This has challenged the comfortable domains of many 'educationalists' – whose views have often been derived from an overdependence on tradition and personal opinion.

The PISA researchers have therefore succeeded in lifting the quality of educational policy debate above the level of the 'league table' discourse by providing a wider audience of parents, students, and the general public with information tools that can be used to engage senior decision-makers in evidence-based discussion. However, more work remains to be done – especially in terms of seeking new ways (especially visual/graphical formats) of presenting information summaries that convey 'the meaning behind the PISA.

References

OECD. 2001. *Knowledge and skills for life. First results from PISA 2000.* Paris: OECD.

OECD; UNESCO. 2003. *Literacy skills for education in 21 countries: a technical report.* Stockholm: Almqvist and Wicksell.

Part IV
Conclusion

Chapter 15
The 'main messages'
arising from the Policy Forum

Kenneth N. Ross, Carola Donner-Reichle, Ingrid Jung,
Ulrike Wiegelmann, Ilona Jürgens Genevois, and Laura Paviot

Introduction

One of the key features of the worldwide discussion and debate about the need to achieve Educational for All (EFA) has been a broader interpretation of this challenge to ensure that increased participation in education is delivered in association with improvements in the conditions of schooling and student achievement levels. This intense focus on quality has been encouraged by the emerging belief that education systems can act as pathways to national economic development in an increasingly globalized and competitive world (Hanushek, 2005).

These trends, coupled with the enormous expenditures by governments on education, have precipitated demands for more information and accountability concerning the quality of education. Governments can only respond to these demands if they have trained personnel who are able to employ modern research methodologies to make valid comparisons of (a) the performance of single school systems across several time points ('Are we improving, or staying the same, or getting worse?'), (b) the relative performance of several school systems – particularly those that share similar socioeconomic conditions, and patterns of historical development ('Are we better, the same as, or worse than other countries like us?'), and (c) the performance of single *and* several school systems on particular topics within school subjects ('Are we doing well or poorly on topics X and Y within school subject Z, and how are other countries like ours performing on these topics?').

Most industrialized nations have already established systems for monitoring and evaluating the quality of education as part of the normal management operations of their ministries of education. A number of these systems have been developed as an integral part of the large-scale cross-national studies of the quality of education that have been organized by the Organisation for Economic Co-operation and Development (for example, the OECD's PISA Project) and the International Association for the Evaluation of Educational Achievement (for example, the IEA's TIMSS Project).

Major international meetings, such as the 1990 Jomtien World Conference on Education and the 2000 Dakar World Education Forum, have strengthened the interest of developing countries in establishing similar monitoring and evaluation mechanisms because the final declarations from these meetings have encouraged nations to achieve EFA in a manner that ensures that "measurable learning outcomes are achieved by all". In Africa, for example, a regional group of 14 countries - known as the Southern and Eastern Africa Consortium for Monitoring Educational Quality (SACMEQ) - has responded to these declarations by undertaking a series of cross-national studies of the quality of education.

UNESCO's International Institute for Educational Planning (IIEP) in France has worked for over a decade with African and Asian ministries of education in order to address the Jomtien and Dakar declarations by providing training programmes for educational planners and researchers in the area of quantitative research methods for monitoring and evaluating the quality of education. The Internationale Weiterbildung und Entwicklung (InWEnt) in Germany has also provided important capacity building opportunities in developing countries through the organization of training, exchange, and dialogue activities designed to improve the quality of educational instruction and to strengthen education sector management.

The Policy Forum and this book

Following discussions held among IIEP and InWEnt staff members in early 2004, it was agreed that the increased interest of developed and developing countries in participating in cross-national studies of the quality of education needed to be accompanied by efforts to ensure that they derived maximal policy benefits from such research.

On the basis of these discussions, the IIEP and InWEnt decided to arrange an International Policy Forum in Paris during June 2004 that would share global knowledge and national experiences concerning the topic of 'Cross-national studies of the quality of education: planning their design and managing their impact'.

The earlier chapters of this book have presented the papers that were delivered at this forum. This final chapter of the book has attempted to highlight the main messages for ministries of education arising from the Policy Forum's papers and discussions - and especially from the inputs received from Policy Forum participants during the 'Open space sessions' that concluded the forum.

The Open space sessions consisted of small discussion groups that provided facilitative settings within which the Policy Forum participants could reflect upon, critique, and synthesize the key issues that had emerged during the formal forum presentations. The participants were able to move freely among the discussion groups – and this 'floating membership' generated many lively, innovative, and useful exchanges. The leader of each discussion group summarized the participants' contributions, and this material was added to the Policy Forum papers as a further resource for the preparation of this book.

Five groups of 'Policy Forum messages'

The topics and many experiences that were covered by the Policy Forum's papers and associated Open space sessions covered a great deal of territory in the general field of cross-national studies of the quality of education. In some instances there was general agreement among the Policy Forum participants concerning the guidance that should be given to ministries of education about the decisions, actions, and methodologies that were most likely to result in beneficial policy impact for participating countries. In other cases the Policy Forum participants identified particular problems and/or complexities related to such studies – and these were used to develop suggestions about research management, dissemination approaches, and training strategies for addressing these challenges.

The Policy Forum's papers and Open space sessions covered many different topics and a diversity of experiences. In some cases the Policy Forum participants shared a common vision about the suggestions that should be made to ministries of education concerning the decisions, actions, and methodologies that were required in order to derive maximal policy benefits from participating in cross-national studies of the quality of education. In other cases the participants had concerns about particular features, complexities, or shortcomings of such studies – and these were used to develop suggestions about strategies for addressing these challenges.

All of these suggestions – which the Policy Forum participants described as **'Policy Forum messages'** – represented a rich resource for ministries of education to use as part of a continuing dialogue within their organizations, and also with, and among, other external partners.

A total of 18 Policy Forum messages were identified by the Policy Forum participants. Each of these were placed into one of the following five groups, and then presented in the form of a general discussion followed by **'Recommendations'** that suggested what ministries of education should be doing in order to respond to the message.

Group 1 messages:
planning the measurement design of cross-national studies

Most school systems are expected to provide effective instruction to students on a similar set of 'basic' school subjects such as the national language, mathematics, and science. For this reason, cross-national studies of the quality of education have tended to focus on the assessment of student performance in these 'mainstream' school subjects.

While the choice of what subject matter to measure has been quite similar across most cross-national studies, there have been major changes over the past 15 years in terms of the measurement techniques that have been used. The most prominent of these have been concerned with: different approaches to the construction of test frameworks, the use of advanced measurement technologies that permit researchers to assess students on a more comprehensive coverage of subject matter content, the linkage (or equating) of tests containing common anchor items, and a general trend away from numerical descriptions of student performance (in the traditional form of total test scores) towards descriptive hierarchical accounts of student competencies.

These developments have strengthened the validity and utility of research results derived from cross national studies – but they have also required participating countries to become involved in preliminary discussions and decisions about measurement issues that define the particular focus of what is measured and how it is measured.

There were five Policy Forum messages concerned with measurement issues: constructing test frameworks, monitoring school systems versus measuring change in individual students, testing teacher competencies, choosing between an international and a regional study, and monitoring the acquisition of sustainable development skills.

Message 1(a): Constructing test frameworks

A test framework provides a system of rules for defining 'what should be measured' by specifying clear guidelines that govern the construction of test items - in the same way that an architect's blueprint describes detailed specifications about 'what should be built' for the construction of a house. Ministries need to be involved in the main decisions pertaining to the preparation of test frameworks because, after they have been completed, the development and selection of test items becomes a tightly-constrained process with little room for manoeuvre.

The Policy Forum participants noted that the world's largest and most complex cross-national research programmes - the IEA's series of TIMSS studies and the OECD's series of PISA studies - had taken quite different approaches to the construction of the test frameworks that were used to guide the development of student tests.

For example, the TIMSS student mathematics tests used detailed international analyses of school curricula to prepare test frameworks defined by two dimensions: (i) a 'content' dimension with five categories: number, algebra, measurement, geometry, and data; and (ii) a 'cognitive' dimension with four categories: knowing facts and procedures, using concepts, solving routine problems, and reasoning (Mullis *et al.*, 2001).

In contrast, the PISA student mathematics tests employed test frameworks defined by three dimensions: (i) a 'content' dimension with four categories: quantity, space and shape, change and relationships, and uncertainty; (ii) a 'process' dimension (that was similar to the TIMSS 'cognitive' dimension) with three categories: reproduction of basic steps, connection of mathematical ideas with problems, and reflection (in terms of mathematical thinking and insights); and (iii) a 'situations' dimension with five categories: private life, school life, work and sports, local community, and scientific.

The TIMSS test framework was designed to provide a representation of the 'official' core curriculum covered in the majority of participating countries. In contrast, the PISA test framework was designed to produce tests that were (i) "forward looking, focusing on young people's ability to use their knowledge and skills to meet real-life challenges, rather than on the extent to which they have mastered a specific school curriculum", (ii) concerned with "things that 15-year-olds will need in their future lives", and (iii) directed towards "what students can do with what they learn at school, and not merely with whether they have learned it" (OECD, 2001: 14).

The Policy Forum participants noted that these subtle, but important, differences between the TIMSS and PISA test frameworks had implications for the way in which school systems could be called to account for the educational achievement of their students. For example, if governments placed the highest priority on explicit curricular goals then it could be argued that the TIMSS tests provided a fairer assessment of the quality of education delivered by school systems. On the other hand, if governments were more concerned with the capacity of school systems to provide students with the skills required to face 'real-life challenges' in their 'future lives', then it could be argued that the PISA tests were better suited to judging school system performance.

Recommendation 1(a): Ministries of Education need to be fully involved in all decisions concerning the design, construction, and application of test frameworks for cross-national studies of the quality of education – and to understand the implications of the selection of a particular test framework for making judgments about the performance of school systems.

Message 1(b): Monitoring school systems versus measuring change in individuals

The Policy Forum participants observed that at the very early stages of research design there was a need to decide whether a cross-national study would concentrate on a cross-sectional data collection (in which educational achievement data were collected from a sample of students at one time point), or a longitudinal data collection (in which educational achievement data were collected from the same sample of students at two or more time points).

A longitudinal approach to data collection is preferable (provided it is well-conducted) because it enables researchers to answer the same research questions as the cross-sectional approach – but it also offers greater possibilities for detailed examinations of those factors associated with the educational environment that contribute towards growth in student learning. However, it is important to note that a longitudinal data collection requires greater research complexity (because of the need to assess, and keep track of, the same group of students on at least two occasions, and then to connect these bodies of information at the data processing phase) and higher costs (because of the need to make at least two visits to the sample schools).

The Policy Forum participants pointed out the need to make a careful choice of timeframe for a longitudinal data collection. This choice depends upon whether the impact of a particular teacher is being studied (with data collections at two time points within one academic year), or the general impact of the school is being studied (with data collections at 'entry' to school and again after several years of schooling).

The former approach was used during the IEA Classroom Environment Study in the 1980s – but the results from this study suggested that teacher behaviours had limited impact on student achievement (Anderson *et al.*, 1989). Since the completion of this study, some powerful data analysis techniques have emerged (including Hierarchical Linear Modelling) that could offer better avenues for detecting school and teacher effects on student learning.

Recommendation 1(b): Ministries of Education should ask the research specialists who design cross-national studies of the quality of education to provide justifications for their choice of either cross-sectional or longitudinal data collections. If the latter approach is selected then further questions should be addressed to these specialists concerning: (i) whether the 'value added' by an educational environment is to be linked with an individual teacher (over a single academic year) or a collection of teachers (over several years), (ii) the magnitude of the additional (logistical, financial, and time) costs of multiple data collections, and (iii) the selection of the most appropriate data analysis techniques.

Message 1(c): Testing teacher competencies

The Policy Forum participants acknowledged that 'teacher training' represented the most critical aspect of educational policy concerning resource inputs to schooling - because in many countries the largest item of expenditure on school education was teacher salaries. They noted with some concern that governments, agencies, and donors have raised many important policy questions on this topic that had either been ignored or poorly-researched in cross-national studies of the quality of education. As a result there were major gaps in available knowledge about the most fundamental aspects of teacher training.

For example: (i) What is the optimal balance in teacher training programmes between time spent on developing subject matter knowledge and time spent on the development of pedagogical skills?, (ii) What is the 'added value' of teacher training - in terms of the differences in student performance when they are exposed to either trained or untrained teachers?, and (iii) Which of the following has most impact upon student performance: better teacher training, improved teacher recruitment procedures, or enhanced teacher incentive systems?

The participants agreed that these and other research questions concerning teacher training could not be examined in a systematic fashion without testing the subject matter knowledge of teachers. Unfortunately, the testing of teachers has been problematic in many countries because of strong opposition by teacher unions.

The SACMEQ research programme has provided an exception in this area. The SACMEQ National Research Coordinators were able to demonstrate to teachers and their unions that teacher test score data could be collected on a confidential basis, and then used in a productive manner for a range of research applications without making criticisms of teacher professionalism. The SACMEQ research used 'overlapped' student and teacher reading and mathematics tests (Andrich et al., in press) in order to score Grade 6 students and their teachers as if they had completed the same tests. These data permitted the identification of gaps in teacher subject matter knowledge, and this information was subsequently used to identify topics for inclusion in teacher in-service training programmes.

Recommendation 1(c): Ministries of Education involved in cross-national studies of the quality of education should: (i) encourage their national research teams to include high-priority research questions about teacher training in the initial research design, (ii) ensure that these studies address important gaps in available data about teachers, and (iii) negotiate with teacher unions in order to seek permission for the confidential testing of teachers, and for the responsible use of these data for research and training purposes.

Message 1(d): Choosing between an international study and a regional study

The Policy Forum participants observed that one of the important issues that faced ministries of education was whether to participate in an "international study" of the quality of education that included countries from around the world (such as TIMSS), or to participate in a 'regional study' that was restricted to nearby countries that have more similar levels of social and economic development (such as SACMEQ).

Prior to the 1990s, the test scaling procedures used in most cross-national studies required that students be given the same test booklet and asked to complete all test items. Modern Item Response Theory (IRT) approaches, which became more widely applied during the 1990s, have removed these constraints. Instead, researchers are now able to test in schools by giving students 'different but overlapped' test booklets (containing both unique and common (anchor) test items). Then, by using the 'magic' of IRT, students may be scored as if they had completed all test booklets. This revolutionary new approach has permitted an expansion in the coverage of tests by allowing much larger numbers of test items to be included in testing sessions without placing an undue burden on individual students.

The participants noted that another very important aspect of IRT was that it could be used to equate tests used in different studies by different groups of students. That is, as long as two different studies (that have been focused on the same type of student achievement) have employed 'different but overlapped' tests, then students from one study can be scored on the other study's test, and vice versa.

Luo *et al.* (in press) demonstrated this technique by equating the reading tests used in the 1990 IEA International Reading Literacy Study (Elley, 1992) and the reading tests used in the 2000 SACMEQ II Project (Ross *et al.*, in press). This permitted the students from the 30 developed countries that participated in the IEA study to be scored as if they had completed the reading test that had been given to students in 14 African countries during the SACMEQ II Project. That is, the technology offered by IRT made it possible for the 14 SACMEQ countries involved in a 'regional study' to make valid comparisons with other countries that had participated in a different "international study".

The developing countries involved in the SACMEQ studies preferred this approach to making cross-national comparisons because they were able to undertake valid worldwide quality comparisons and, at the same time, proceed with their own research programme under their own control and according to their own timetable. They were also free to employ student, teacher, and school questionnaires that were more closely aligned with their own policy priorities; and to ensure that their own research agendas were not dominated by more technically able research teams from the developed world.

The Policy Forum participants agreed that SACMEQ's use of IRT had demonstrated that one approach to encouraging all countries of the world to monitor the quality of their education systems would be to replace (or perhaps to supplement) international studies such as TIMSS and PISA with a connected set of "regional studies" based on suitable sets of anchor items. They also noted that the synergies that can emerge from the use of common test items across different studies suggested that there was a need to consider how an 'International Anchor Item Bank' might be developed and maintained.

UNESCO would appear to be well placed in terms of mandate and programme to take a leadership role in this area – perhaps by convening an initial meeting of the world's measurement experts to discuss the advantages and disadvantages of these proposals.

Recommendation 1(d): Ministries of Education should, in association with an appropriate international agency, convene a meeting of the world's measurement experts to discuss the advantages and disadvantages of proposals to: (i) undertake linked networks of 'regional' and 'international studies' of the quality of education, and (ii) establish an 'International Anchor Item Bank' that could be used to provide test items for making valid cross-national comparisons by using linked networks of regional and international studies.

Message 1(e): Monitoring the acquisition of sustainable development skills

The Policy Forum participants noted that the 2002 Johannesburg World Summit on Sustainable Development had connected the concept of 'sustainable development' with the educational objectives of both the Millennium Development Goals and the Dakar World Conference on Education for All. This Summit proposed that the period 2005-2014 should be known as the 'UN Decade of Education for Sustainable Development'. This was subsequently ratified by the United Nations General Assembly, with UNESCO nominated as the lead agency.

The participants agreed that in order to monitor progress towards implementing the UN Decade of Education for Sustainable Development there was a need to test the relevant competencies imparted to students by school systems. This would require the generation of an agreed list of learning objectives in the field of sustainable development which could then be employed to generate a test framework and associated test questions. Unfortunately, for most school systems, the available learning objectives in this area offer very little specific guidance for test construction because they tend to be described in vague terms (such as the "the skills required to satisfy the social, economic, and environmental needs of the present generation without compromising the needs and resources available for future generations").

Several Policy Forum participants pointed out that some school systems had made more progress than others in exploring options for specifying and developing educational programs for sustainable development, and it was agreed that full advantage should be taken of this successful work. The participants proposed that an international agency should be asked to convene a meeting of experts at which the more advanced countries could present and share their 'best practices' and teaching materials.

An alternative approach explored by the participants was to link notions of sustainable development with the even broader concept of 'life skills'. However, again, problems were noted with respect to identifying a universally accepted operational definition of 'life skills' that could be used to guide the construction of valid measures. Several participants pointed out that this difficulty had also been noted by the Interagency Working Group on Life Skills – which had concluded that "indicators that demonstrate progress in this field at the international level are difficult to identify" (UNESCO, 2004: 11). The following examples illustrate why there has been limited progress with the development of measurements and indicators in this field.

UNICEF (2005) has defined life skills in the form of a list of 28 psychosocial and interpersonal skills grouped under three main headings: communication/interpersonal, decision-making/critical thinking, and coping/self-management. The OECD perspective makes a clear distinction between life skills for work and life skills for life – but has also recognized the impossibility of agreeing on a list of all specific life skills (Werquin, 2004). The International Bureau of Education (IBE) derived its understanding of life skills from the Delors four pillars of learning (Singh, 2004) by defining life skills as "personal management and social skills which are necessary for adequate functioning on an independent basis in the areas of: learning to know, learning to do, learning to be, and learning to live together". The World Health Organization complicated matters even further by defining life skills as psychosocial competencies such as: dealing with conflict and authority, solving problems, making and keeping friends/relationships, co-operation, self-awareness, creative thinking, decision-making, critical thinking, dealing with stress, negotiation, clarification of values, resisting pressure, coping with disappointment, planning ahead, empathy, dealing with emotions, assertiveness, active listening, respect, tolerance, trust, sharing, sympathy, compassion, sociability, and self-esteem (WHO, 1999).

Recommendation 1(e): Ministries of Education should work towards the establishment of mechanisms for the cross-national monitoring of progress made by school systems towards the improvement of sustainable development competencies among their students – with the first steps being: (i) the organization of an international meeting at which the more advanced school systems could present and share their 'best practices' and teaching materials, (ii) the systematic development of an agreed international operational definition of 'sustainable development' that can be used to guide the specification of required student competencies and related test frameworks and test items, and (iii) an exploration of the possible linkage of these activities with a broader debate on the concept of 'life skills education'.

Group 2 messages: planning the sample designs for cross-national studies

Data collections for cross-national studies of the quality of education have usually been restricted to the study of a sample rather than a complete coverage of the population under study. Provided that scientific probability sampling procedures are used, the use of a sample rather than a population offers a number of advantages compared with a census: reduced costs associated with data collection and data analysis; greater speed in most aspects of data preparation for analysis; reduced logistical and personnel requirements; and greater accuracy in measurement due to more extensive control of fieldwork.

'Good' sample designs for cross-national studies of the quality of education are systematically constructed using established sampling procedures combined with a sound and practical knowledge of the ways in which populations of schools, classes, and students are administratively and geographically arranged.

There were three Policy Forum messages concerned with sampling issues: choosing between age-based and grade-based target populations; estimating required sample size; and understanding and using sampling weights and sampling errors.

Message 2(a): Choosing between age-based and grade-based target populations

The Policy Forum participants agreed that the main goal of cross-national studies of the quality of education was to make valid cross-national comparisons of the conditions of schooling and levels of student achievement that were deemed to be of interest to researchers, parents, the public, and governments. To address this goal required the identification of appropriate target populations – and in the field of educational research this meant that researchers must first decide whether to employ an age-based target population definition or a grade-based target population definition. This decision was usually made after taking the major research questions into account. However, making this decision can become quite complicated in cases where studies are driven by multiple national and cross-national policy interests.

The OECD's PISA Project has used an age-based target population definition focused on "all 15 year-old students in a national education system" (Adams and Wu, 2002). Age-based definitions appeal to economists because of their simplicity and straightforward interpretation. However, in the context of cross-national studies, age-based target populations can deliver very different outcomes compared with grade-based target populations because the resulting samples of students may be spread across several grade levels – depending on the degree to which school systems apply grade repetition and/or have flexible school entry policies.

Age-based samples make it difficult to develop explanatory models involving classroom characteristics and instructional practices – because the within-school samples of students will often be thinly spread across grade levels and classrooms. In addition, they also present problems with respect to the interpretation of basic summary statistics such as average teacher qualifications or percentages of students with access to a computer – because the deployment of human and material resources in a school system may be influenced by different administrative decisions operating at different grade levels.

In contrast, the IEA studies have tended to focus either on a specific grade or a specific set of grades. For example, in the IEA International Reading Literacy (IRL) Study one of the target populations was described as "all pupils in the grade level in which most 9 year olds are located at the eighth month of the school year" (Elley, 1992). Grade-based definitions appeal to educationalists because the whole sample of students within a given country will have been exposed to the same curriculum, and also because the required mechanical procedures for within-school sampling are easier to apply due to schools being organized administratively by grade level.

The problem with grade-based samples is that the average student age can vary a great deal across countries due to differences in school entry requirements and grade repetition policies. For example, in the IRL Study, the average age of Population A students (as defined above) in the Netherlands was 9.2 years, while in Portugal it was 10.4 years.

Recommendation 2(a): Ministries of Education should be aware of the advantages and disadvantages of employing either age-based or grade-based sample designs in cross-national studies of the quality of education, and should be fully informed about the impact of these different sampling approaches on: (i) the kinds of research and policy questions that can be addressed, and (ii) the interpretation of various summary statistics that describe student achievement and the conditions of schooling.

Message 2(b): Estimating required sample size

Cross-national studies of the quality of education usually employ complex sampling procedures that include the use of stratification, disproportionate selection of schools and students across strata, multiple stages of sample selection, and the selection of students in clusters or groups. These complexities – combined with the nature of the target population under study – can lead to very different sample size requirements across countries in order to achieve the same level of sampling accuracy.

An accurate estimate of the 'required sample size' ensures that the data collection for the national component of a cross-national study provides answers to the key research questions without wasting money on excessively large samples of schools and students. The main danger here is actually underestimating the required sample size – which can result in sampling errors that are so large that there is a high degree of uncertainty in trying to answer the key research questions.

The Policy Forum participants noted that some school systems had large variations between schools in average student achievement due to the residential segregation of socio-economic groups or because of the use of different school 'streams' for students with different achievement levels. In these kinds of school systems there was usually a need to select relatively larger samples of schools and students in order to reach a given level of sampling accuracy.

The degree of variation among schools was usually measured by the coefficient of intraclass correlation (rho) – and the value of this statistic can vary markedly across school systems that have participated in the same cross-national study. It was also important to note that this statistic varied according to grade level and school subject matter – and therefore care needed to be taken to ensure that estimates of rho were appropriate for the study that was being planned.

For example, in the SACMEQ II Project, the values of rho for Grade 6 student reading achievement ranged from around 0.25 in Botswana and Mauritius to 0.60 or more in Namibia and South Africa. This meant that, for a fixed number of 20 students selected in each school, the required total samples of schools to reach a given level of sampling accuracy in Namibia and South Africa were around two and half times larger than in Botswana and Mauritius (Ross, 2005).

It was agreed that ministries of education did not necessarily need to have a qualified sampling statistician in the research team that was undertaking the national work on a cross-national study of the quality of education. However, it was essential that the research team had a good grasp of fundamental sampling principles, and – if required – had access to a sampling statistician in order to clarify issues and to check the details of calculations.

Several Policy Forum participants pointed out that the calculations needed to make accurate decisions about the size of the required samples of schools and students for a cross-national study of the quality of education could be simplified through the use of 'sample design tables' (Ross, 2005), and specialized sample design software systems (such as the SAMDEM software developed by the IIEP in order to explore, at high speed, a wide variety of sampling options that take into account the size of the coefficient of intraclass correlation (Sylla *et al.*, 2005)).

Recommendation 2(b): Ministries of Education that are involved in cross-national studies of the quality of education should ensure that their research teams understand and can apply the basic rules of sampling that are used to estimate 'required sample size' – and that they have access to: (i) good national estimates of the coefficient of intraclass correlation for the appropriate grade levels and subject matter areas, (ii) a qualified sampling statistician (when required), and (iii) training in the use of research tools that facilitate the rapid exploration and testing of sample design options (such as 'sample design tables' and specialized sample design software systems).

Message 2(c): Understanding and using sampling weights and sampling errors

The Policy Forum participants discussed a number of issues related to the application of sampling weights and sampling errors to cross-national studies. These two statistics were considered to be *essential* for interpreting sample estimates of the quality of education.

The participants emphasized that in many studies the *calculation and checking* of these statistics was a complex task that would normally require assistance from an experienced sampling statistician. However, it was agreed that research teams involved in cross-national studies of the quality of education should be able to *understand and apply* (i) sampling weights *before* the main data analyses - during the data preparation phase of a study, and (ii) sampling errors *after* the main data analyses – during the report preparation phase of a study.

Sampling weights are required in order to account for unequal probabilities of sample selection. For example, where disproportionate sampling is applied across population strata by taking equal sized samples in education regions that differ a great deal in size, it is essential to avoid biases in sample estimates by increasing the sampling weights of students selected from large strata, and vice-versa for students selected from small strata. Sampling weights often need to be 'fine-tuned' in order to make adjustments for deficiencies in sampling frames and minor levels of non-response.

Sampling weights are usually calculated so that either the sum of the sample weights across the sample is equal to the population size ('population weights'), or the sum of the sample weights across the sample is equal to the achieved sample size ('standardized weights'). Both kinds of weights should be calculated and added to data files – because each has advantages in certain important circumstances. For example, population weights are useful if the research requires estimates of the actual number of students in the defined target population with a specific characteristic; whereas standardized weights are preferable if a research team is not accustomed to having a difference between the actual number of respondents in a survey and the 'weighted number of cases' reported by statistical software systems.

Sampling errors of survey estimates are required to provide measures of the confidence that we can have in the stability of sample estimates across all possible samples that could have been drawn using the same sample design. Fortunately, there are statistical procedures available that permit researchers to calculate this measure of confidence by using data from one sample to infer what would have been the case for all possible samples.

The main use of sampling errors is in the construction of confidence limits for sample estimates of population characteristics. For example, if we were to estimate a national mean student achievement score of 550 points with a sampling error of 5 score points, then we could be 95% confident that the true national student mean score was between 550 plus or minus 2 x 5 = 10 score points. That is, between 540 and 560 score points. These confidence intervals are essential if we wish to make valid and meaningful comparisons of (i) the national means of student scores for two different countries, and (ii) the national means of student scores for one country on two different occasions.

Recommendation 2(c): Ministries of Education involved in cross-national studies of the quality of education should ensure that their research teams are able to: (i) have access to an experienced sampling statistician for the *calculation and checking* of sampling weights and sampling errors, (ii) *understand and apply* sampling weights *before* the data analyses – during the data preparation phase of a study, and (b) *understand and apply* sampling errors *after* the data analyses – during the report preparation phase of a study.

Group 3 messages:
planning the logistical design of cross-national studies

The logistical design of a cross-national study of the quality of education within a country is concerned with the management of the human, material, and financial resources required for the successful implementation of the study. The Policy Forum participants observed that the logistical design for the same study may be quite different in different countries – depending on the nature of the national organizations that are responsible for undertaking the study.

The Policy Forum participants noted that at the heart of a successful within-country implementation of a cross-national study of the quality of education there were two essential ingredients: (a) a well-trained, experienced, and motivated research team led by an able and inspiring

National Research Coordinator; and (b) a detailed plan and timetable for the deployment of all resources and activities associated with the implementation of the research.

The organization responsible for a study could be a government body (for example, a ministry of education), a government-funded institution (for example, a public university), or an independent institution (for example, a private university, an independent research centre, or a consortium of private organizations). If the study is organized by a government body or a government-funded institution there is likely to be a higher proportion of 'hidden' costs that can be covered within existing budgets. Whereas if the study is carried out by an independent institution, then most of the costs will be 'visible' in that they will be translated into actual monetary expenditures over and above existing budgets.

There were two main Policy Forum Messages concerned with logistics issues: building and keeping an in-house research team and preparing detailed logistical plans.

Message 3(a): Building and keeping an in-house research team

The manner in which a ministry of education approaches the management of the national component of a cross-national study of the quality of education may vary a great deal. In some countries all of the work – right down to the provision of extra technical and clerical support – is sourced from within the ministry. In other situations, ministries will use varying degrees of out-sourcing to provide support for some or all of the tasks related to printing, field data collection, data entry, and data analyses.

The first approach is preferable because it gives the ministry full control over all aspects of the research, and it provides excellent 'hands-on' training for the ministry's educational planners and researchers. The second approach is acceptable if some, but not all, of the work is subcontracted.

The Policy Forum participants emphasized that whatever approach was adopted it was important that the within-house research team was well-trained, well-managed, and had access to suitable space, equipment, and working conditions. These working arrangements were more likely to encourage members of a research team to stay together for the duration of the study, and to continue on to other important studies where their training and experience could be used to good effect. Even where outsourcing of some components of the research was undertaken – it was necessary to have solid in-house skills available in order to provide a quality control mechanism for the external contractors.

The Policy Forum participants agreed that ministries needed to realize that the advanced skills required to undertake a cross-national study of the quality of education were 'marketable' in many other areas. Therefore a major investment in building a research team for a project that lasts several years needs to be buttressed by an appropriate reward structure that will help keep the research team motivated, and also encourage them to stay in the team, and to share their experience and training with others.

The participants noted that the reward structures for talented and serious researchers were not always based solely on financial issues. The best people in this field were also interested in publications, opportunities to meet and work with other like-minded professionals, and opportunities to travel and gain further training.

Recommendation 3(a): Ministries of Education involved in cross-national studies of the quality of education should establish the recruitment and reward system structures required to: (i) select and build a well-trained, experienced, and motivated research team, (ii) sustain this research team throughout the life of a multi-year cross-national study of the quality of education, (iii) encourage this research team to stay with the ministry so that full advantage can be taken of their research skills and their capacity to assist and train other staff.

Message 3(b): Preparing detailed logistical plans

The task of managing the day-to-day operations of the national component of a cross-national study of the quality of education is the responsibility of the National Research Coordinator (NRC) who is normally a senior staff member within the research and planning office of a ministry of education. Several Policy Forum participants who have previously acted as NRCs indicated that this role demanded advanced planning and leadership skills in order to cope with project work that changes dramatically in terms of topic, magnitude, personnel, and pressures as the study proceeds.

At different stages of the study, the NRC will need to have the support of specialists to guide work on test construction, sampling, and data analysis. At other stages, larger numbers of general support staff will be required to assist with managing the flow and processing of data collection materials, test administration, data entry, and data cleaning. Another group of people – often teachers – will be needed to mark open ended test questions, practical test items, and written material collected during language testing. Yet another group of people – often planners or researchers from within the ministry of education – will be needed to: coordinate the interface between the project work and the 'ministry's machinery' by contacting and briefing senior staff, train within-school project coordinators, obtain relevant permissions from school principals, and address general 'emergency and crisis work'.

These human resources need to be managed in association with adequate material resources – such as office space, office equipment, telephone/communications systems, computers, filing systems, open-space work areas (for packing, distributing, returning, marking, storing, and checking data collection instruments). At various phases of the project, office and working space will be an important issue, while at other times it may be that computers or communications or transport become priority areas.

All of the above tasks represent a very substantial planning challenge for NRCs. The Policy Forum participants agreed that the successful NRC needed to be able to develop, and work within, a meticulously planned schedule where every working week across a two to three year period was fully planned in association with landmarks and deadlines that must be satisfied in order for the study to be completed in a timely and scientific manner. It was noted that all of this work needed to be undertaken within a supportive administrative environment provided by the ministry of education's senior decision-makers.

Recommendation 3(b): Ministries of Education can only participate successfully in a cross-national study of the quality of education if they appoint suitably-qualified and experienced National Research Coordinators that have: (i) the capacity to plan and manage the long-term deployment of a wide range of human and material resources, (ii) the personal qualities that are required for sustained and inspiring leadership throughout the whole course of a two or three-year study, and (iii) the full support of senior decision–makers within the ministry of education.

Group 4 messages:
managing the impact of cross-national studies

Many countries that have participated in cross-national studies of the quality of education have generated a great deal of data and produced numerous publications containing research results. However, the existence of data and research results does not always imply either (a) the availability of clear evidence that can be used to guide policy, or (b) an environment that is conducive to transforming policy into concrete reforms.

The Policy Forum participants agreed that what was required in this situation was greater attention to be given to moving from data and research results, and then from the construction of evidence-based policy to its subsequent implementation. Some of the participants characterized this process as being synonymous with 'moving from talk to action'.

The participants noted that a much greater impact on policy could be achieved by giving due attention to four dimensions: 'what' research issues were selected for study and then reported; 'who' was involved in providing and receiving and managing the flow of communications about results; 'how' these results were communicated; and 'when' these results were communicated. It was emphasized that all dimensions needed to be addressed successfully – and that this often presented problems because they often demanded skills that fall outside the experience and interests of educational planners and researchers.

There were five main Policy Forum messages concerned with managing the impact of research results. These were aligned with the above four dimensions as follows: 'what': framing the important research questions; 'who': working with ministers and senior decision-makers; 'how': reporting research results and broadening participation in the discussion of research results; and 'when': avoiding time lags.

Message 4(a): Framing the important policy questions

At several stages during the Policy Forum the participants discussed options for establishing stronger linkages between research results, policy reforms, and action. It was agreed that the simple act of providing data and evidence to an educational decision-maker represented genuine communication only when the decision-maker was actively listening, and focusing on a related issue. Without these essential pre-conditions, educational planners and researchers may find themselves providing evidence to an audience that is only concerned about finding answers to other unconnected questions.

Communication breakdowns of this kind can never be improved by providing more information. They can only be addressed if educational planners and researchers move beyond a mechanistic approach to the transmission of data and evidence, and instead develop interactive dissemination strategies based on a dialogue with decision makers.

The purpose of this dialogue was *not* to examine the kinds of curiosity-driven questions that are central to the research programs of university professors. Rather, the purpose was to encourage educational planners and researchers to (i) listen to decision-makers who are demanding information according to their own priorities, (ii) 'grasp' how a problem is being interpreted and understood by decision-makers, and (iii) adopt a proactive stance by assisting decision-makers to frame their policy questions and concerns in technically sound ways that are amenable to research.

Several Policy Forum participants noted that the approach to research design adopted by the SACMEQ consortium offered an innovative approach to harmonizing research design with a ministry's high-priority policy concerns. This operated as a three-step process that was put into practice *before* work commenced on implementing a cross-national study of the quality of education.

The first step invited senior decision-makers in ministries of education to discuss their policy concerns and to arrange these according to priority. These policy concerns were then combined across countries to reach a set of 'general policy concerns'. In the second step the researchers used the general policy concerns to construct more detailed 'specific policy questions' which provided precise guidance concerning the information that needed to be collected. Finally 'dummy tables' (or blank tables) were prepared in discussion with decision-makers so as to provide templates for the presentation of research results.

These three steps were used to guide all stages of the SACMEQ research design process, which guaranteed that senior decision-makers had a central role in deciding what data should be collected and how it should be summarized and reported.

Recommendation 4(a): Ministries of Education should insist upon a 'pre-planning' component for cross-national studies of the quality of education in which: (i) the high priority policy concerns of senior decision-makers are used to provide a framework for research design, and (ii) senior decision-makers are consulted on all aspects of data summarization and research reporting *before* a study is implemented.

Message 4(b): Working with ministers and senior decision-makers

Several Policy Forum participants pointed out the need for educational planners and researchers to understand what ministers and senior decision-makers in ministries of education 'really thought' about cross-national studies of the quality of education. For these people, such studies carried risks because the research results might either enhance their public image or erode confidence in them as leaders.

The participants agreed that an essential requirement for working with ministers and senior decision-makers was that these people needed to have confidence in the technical skills and experience of their research teams – so that whatever statements or explanations they offered for research results could be checked for accuracy and consistency prior to their release. It should be emphasized here that, even if a ministry decided to outsource many (or most) of the tasks involved in participating in a cross-national study, there was still a need for a strong 'in-house' team to provide wise counsel at the stage when results were being published, discussed, and debated.

The participants discussed options for reducing anxieties about risks. They noted that it was essential for senior decision-makers to be active players in the conceptualization and evolution of cross-national studies – so as to enhance a sense of ownership of the results. The main issue here was to avoid 'surprises' at all stages of the research – especially at the reporting phase when there may be a mixture of both 'good news' and 'bad news' about the conditions of schooling and the quality of education.

Several participants reported that the ministers in their countries appreciated being informed about research findings well before they were circulated or published. The ministers wished to have time to develop a good grasp of the main issues arising from the research, and also sufficient time to consult with their advisors before they were called upon by the media or the parliament to 'explain' the results.

Recommendation 4(b): Ministries of Education should ensure that the research teams that they establish for a cross-national study of the quality of education: (i) have the skills and experience to inspire confidence among senior decision-makers, (ii) involve senior-decision makers in the evolution of the study so that they feel a sense of ownership, (iii) make certain that there are 'no surprises' for senior decision-makers concerning either good or bad results, and (iv) provide information and explanations about the research results to the minister for education well in advance of publication so that he/she can confidently present and defend the results to the media and the parliament.

Message 4(c): Reporting the research results

The Policy Forum participants considered that many educational planners and researchers were poor communicators of their research results. The main reason for this was that they had been trained over many years to read, respect, and reward the reporting of research in the language and style of traditional scholarly journals – which tended to be somewhat inaccessible outside the walls of research-oriented universities.

The participants agreed that, in order to reach broader audiences of stakeholders that have a more direct impact upon educational policy and practice, the results arising from many cross-national studies of the quality of education needed to be more skilfully and more thoughtfully disseminated by using attractive and user-friendly communication methods.

For example, greater attention needed to be given to breaking free of traditional academic reporting formats by employing: (i) journalists and publicity experts to re-write research results in more communicative formats, (ii) electronic media to deliver research results to the public, (iii) shorter and more accessible research reports – with technical material placed in appendices, and (iv) greater amounts of 'visual material' (for example, colourful graphs, charts, and pictures – instead of page after page of tabulated figures).

The Policy Forum participants also noted that the general 'tone and balance' of research reports needed to be addressed. In particular, they suggested a re-examination of the wide-spread 'academic writing style' of seizing upon problems, failures, limitations, inequities, and discrepancies – while tending to downplay efforts, improvements, contributions, hard work, and achievements. This problem was compounded by the media in some countries by a tendency to give 'headline treatment' to 'educational problems'.

The participants agreed that the sensitive reporting of controversial or 'harsh' research findings could still generate productive policy debate and reforms - provided that the research was reported in a balanced manner such that positive findings were presented with the same enthusiasm as negative findings. This approach also required care in presenting options for policy reform to ensure that these were realistic and affordable, and that they were put forward without seeking to blame individuals or groups for any shortcomings.

The reporting of research results also needed to acknowledge that an insightful choice of research topics could improve the reception that research reports received by ministries of education. For example, several of the OECD's PISA reports had targeted issues that were 'hot topics' in OECD countries (for example, the linkages between school autonomy and school performance; the importance of students becoming self-motivated learners; and the impacts of tracking, streaming, and ability grouping on student performance). These PISA research reports had therefore been able to 'grab the attention' of senior ministry of education decision-makers and the public.

Recommendation 4(c): Ministries of Education should expand their dissemination approaches when reporting the results of cross-national studies of the quality of education by: (i) moving away from the traditional style of academic journals towards more user-friendly alternatives that include: journalistic approaches to reporting, electronic media outlets, and attractive reporting formats that are short, visual, and colourful; (ii) providing more balanced accounts of both positive and negative research results; (iii) presenting realistic and affordable policy options that do not seek to allocate blame for perceived shortcomings; and (iv) taking due account of educational issues and concerns that are 'hot topics' for senior ministry of education decision-makers and the public.

Message 4(d): Broadening participation in the discussion of research results

The Policy Forum participants observed that the traditional approach to reporting and sharing research results from cross-national studies of the quality of education had often targeted professionals in ministries of education, universities, teacher colleges, and education-specific organizations and agencies. It was agreed that this narrow focus could be counter-productive because it ignored the fact that many other stakeholder groups played a major role with respect to both the acceptance and implementation of educational policy reforms.

These (often inadvertently) ignored groups included people from the media, religious organizations, the private sector, non-governmental organizations, parliaments, teachers' unions, parent groups, and schools. In many cases these people, especially parliamentarians and school principals, represented important 'gatekeepers' at critical stages of a research-policy-action cycle because they had a major role in decisions related to identifying, facilitating, and delivering the approvals, legislation, funding, and grass-roots support that were required to transform research results into formal policy and then into concrete actions.

The Policy Forum participants noted that it was particularly worrying that while laws about education systems were made in parliaments, very few educational planners and researchers had ever briefed or had discussions with individual parliamentarians or groups of parliamentarians (other than ministers of education) about the policy implications arising from cross-national studies of the quality of education. The participants considered that this situation required immediate attention, and they encouraged ministries of education to think carefully about how this problem might be addressed – especially in countries where the political culture was quite volatile and may neither encourage nor permit educational planners and researchers employed as public servants to make contact with parliamentarians.

The other very important, but also often forgotten, group was school principals. The Policy Forum participants noted that this group had become a very important target audience for research results because the worldwide trend towards greater decentralization of decision-making power in school systems had given school principals increased authority over many aspects of school organization.

It was agreed that school principals valued feedback from research studies in which their own schools participated – provided that comparative results concerning student achievement were reported alongside *both* the results for 'the average school' and the results for 'other schools that have similar student intakes to my school'.

Several Policy Forum participants proposed that communicating research results to certain stakeholder groups located in ministries of education might be more effective if this was conducted in an international setting. The aim here was to provide opportunities for countries to learn from each other by sharing national experiences. This could take the form of international conferences or workshops targeted towards groups with common interests and responsibilities within a ministry of education (for example, chief executive officers, permanent secretaries, and heads of curriculum and examination branches).

Recommendation 4(d): Ministries of Education should involve a greater diversity of stakeholder groups in discussions, debates, and meetings that provide information concerning the policy implications of cross-national studies of the quality of education – particularly parliamentarians and school principals

– but also people from the media, religious organizations, the private sector, non-governmental organizations, teachers' unions, parent groups, and senior management levels in ministries of education. The communication of research results to certain groups working in ministries of education might be more effective if this was undertaken in an international setting – with the aim of encouraging countries to learn from each other by sharing national experiences about the strategies used to transform research results into policy and action.

Message 4(e): Avoiding time lags

At several points during the Policy Forum the participants indicated that research results arising from cross-national studies of the quality of education were often very slow in arriving on the desks of senior ministry decision-makers. However, it was agreed that the speed at which research reports were completed depended a great deal on whether a cross-national study of the quality of education gave the highest priority to the production of educational indicators (such as the IEA's TIMSS studies and the OECD's PISA studies), or gave the highest priority to providing advanced training in technical skills required to monitor and evaluate the quality of education (such as the SACMEQ studies).

The OECD and (in recent years) the IEA have placed a very high priority on the timely delivery of cross-national educational indicators in the very first wave of research reports for each data collection. This has required the production of initial reports to be placed in the hands of a small centralized circle of individuals that have the skills and experience to deliver excellent reports quite soon after the completion of data collections.

In contrast, the SACMEQ studies have been designed to give highest priority to hands-on training for national research teams. The goal has been to ensure that SACMEQ National Research Coordinators understand and complete every step of the educational policy research process – including conceptualization, research design, instrument construction, sampling, data management, test scoring, data analyses, and reports – *no matter how long each of these steps takes to complete.*

The problem with SACMEQ's approach to conducting cross-national research has been that it delays the delivery of initial research reports. To illustrate, in the SACMEQ II Project the educational planners and researchers in several countries (Mozambique, Tanzania, Uganda, Zambia, and Zanzibar) took around two years to complete the data cleaning phases according to the standards that had been set down for the study. This delayed the completion of *all* SACMEQ research reports because data from all countries were required to complete the scaling and scoring of student test data.

Recommendation 4(e): Ministries of Education involved in cross-national studies of the quality of education should recognize that the speed with which cross-national research results are reported in a form that is suitable for use in policy review and development depends upon whether the highest priority is given to either the production and reporting of cross-national educational indicators or to the provision of 'hands-on' training to national research teams in all steps of the research process.

Group 5 messages:
capacity building needs and modalities

The complexity of the methodology required to design and implement cross-national educational policy research has increased dramatically over the past 50 years. In the late 1950s and early 1960s when the initial IEA research programmes were in full swing, the majority of the IEA's National Research Coordinators had no access to computers, and only a small number of the IEA's specialized central researchers had access to 'mainframe' computers (which were modest in power, difficult to use, and limited in their software applications).

This earlier research environment contrasts dramatically with today's conditions and expectations whereby educational planners and researchers (including those from developing countries) are required to use computers for (i) the layout of tests, questionnaires, and field manuals; (ii) the design and selection of samples of schools and students; (iii) data entry and data cleaning; (iv) test scoring and file building, (v) data analysis and tabulation; (vi) report preparation; (vii) the electronic archiving of research data and related tools, and (viii) a general vehicle for cross-national sharing of information and research resources.

The 'modern era' has also seen major advances in research methodologies. For example, today's research teams are able to conduct cross-national studies with the benefits of new educational measurement technologies (for example, Rasch scaling and its application to 'overlapped' tests) and new software systems (for example, computer programs for conducting sampling error calculations and powerful multi-level data analyses).

All of these technical advances have required today's National Research Coordinators and their research teams to have much higher levels of training and experience in computer-based quantitative educational policy research methods, and this has generated the need for expanded capacity building opportunities for educational planners and researchers – especially in the case of developing countries.

There were three Policy Forum messages concerned with training needs for participating in cross-national studies of the quality of education: training in advanced technical methodologies, training in information brokerage skills, and applying effective training modalities.

Message 5(a): Training in advanced technical methodologies

The Policy Forum participants noted that modern cross-national studies of the quality of education had become very complex – which had given rise to a temptation to give centralized groups of experts the responsibility for making most of the major decisions about technical issues. The participants noted that this situation increased the risk that some countries with less technical research teams might be excluded from important discussions and decisions about research design.

To illustrate, the technique of 'test score conditioning' has become widely used in cross-national studies of the quality of education. This technique 'adjusts' student scores to account for supplementary information provided about a student and his/her educational environment. Some observers have questioned this practice on the grounds that it seems unusual (and perhaps 'unfair') to adjust a student's test score downwards if the student achieves a very high score and is from a relatively disadvantaged home environment and a relatively poorly resourced school environment. Unfortunately, the technical procedures required to implement conditioning and the justifications for employing this procedure are quite complex. Therefore ministries of education can only make meaningful contributions to debate about whether or not to use conditioning if they have staff with a sound knowledge of Modern Item Response Theory (IRT).

There were many other important research design decisions from which ministries of education could be excluded if they lacked research teams with advanced technical training and experience in test construction and scaling, sampling, and the management and analysis of large-scale data collections.

Some of these decisions involve important choices among competing research design options such as whether: 'to apply either age-based sampling – or grade-based sampling', 'to employ either the same test for all students – or rotated test forms', 'to administer either a one hour test for 10-year-olds – or a two hour test', 'to base test blueprints either on official curriculum frameworks – or expert predictions of future skill needs', 'to use only multiple choice test questions – or other question formats such as open response and/or practical questions', 'to permit the replacement of sampled schools that decline to participate – or to use only schools that agree to participate", 'to score test items that were not reached as wrong – or to score them as missing responses", 'to only use forward translation of tests – or to use both forward and back translation", 'to present test scores in numerical scaled format – or to transform these into described scales that reflect levels of competence", and 'to trim extreme sampling weights – or to leave them as they are calculated".

Recommendation 5(a): Ministries of Education that wish to participate fully in the important technical discussions, debates, and decisions related to the fundamental design of cross-national studies of the quality of education should ensure that their research teams have been trained in the latest methodological developments concerned with: applied survey sampling; the development, scaling, and scoring of student achievement tests; and data analysis techniques for educational policy research.

Message 5(b): Training in information brokerage skills

Several Policy Forum participants pointed out that many ministries of education that had participated in cross-national studies often possessed large amounts of data and many "reports of research results – but had limited or no capacity to transform this 'raw material" into justifiable, feasible, and affordable agendas for policy and action."

It was agreed that this situation occurred because educational planners and researchers lacked the capacity to undertake two essential tasks in the field of educational policy research:

(i) to undertake *secondary data analyses* in a proactive fashion that focuses on emerging issues and the related policy concerns of senior decision-makers – and then uses the results of these analyses to prepare policy proposals that address these issues and concerns;

(ii) to undertake *research syntheses* of policy-oriented research literature and other information resources (such as official government reports and policy documents related to administration, staffing, resource allocation, curriculum, student performance, budgets, etc.) in a manner that provides a research-based framework for examining, developing, and implementing policy.

These two tasks require educational planners and researchers to have skills in dealing at very high technical and conceptual levels with: (i) the analysis of large and complex data archives, (ii) the transformation of data summaries into policy-related arguments, (iii) the anticipation of information requests and their potential linkages with available information, (iv) the extraction of themes and messages from extensive bodies of research literature in a way that provides guidance for concrete action, and (iv) the capacity to explore, reveal, and disseminate 'the meaning behind the data'.

The demonstration of these skills by educational planners and researchers suggests that they adopt the working style of an 'information broker' by operating in the zone between the policy concerns of senior decision-makers in ministries of education and the world's available information resources. The term broker seems an appropriate expression here because this work aims at keeping decision-makers 'ahead of the market' in a manner that seizes upon emerging trends and opportunities, but at the same time avoids undue risk.

Recommendation 5(b): Ministries of Education that wish to manage and capitalize on the policy potential of information that emerges from cross-national studies of the quality of education should ensure that their research teams have been trained in information brokerage skills that will permit them to undertake: (i) *secondary data analyses* for policy purposes, and (ii) *research syntheses* aimed at informing the examination, development, and implementation of policy.

Message 5(c): Applying effective training modalities

There was some concern expressed by the Policy Forum participants that participation in a cross-national study of the quality of education should provide 'learning-by-doing' capacity building opportunities for educational planners and researchers in the participating countries – so as to avoid the possibility of countries being treated as 'data collection agencies' for studies designed elsewhere.

The participants agreed that capacity building should not be treated in isolation – but rather 'embedded' within the execution of a 'real' cross-national study of the quality of education. That is, cross-national studies should provide educational planners and researchers with a 'learning-by-doing' experience focused on 'hands-on' training that is delivered in a manner that permits research teams from many different countries to work together, to share their experiences, and to learn from each other.

Recommendation 5(c): Ministries of education involved in cross-national studies of the quality of education should ensure that their research teams are provided with training in a 'learning-by-doing' mode that offers (i) 'hands-on' training in new research methodologies, and (ii) opportunities for working in a 'learning-by-doing' cooperative mode alongside counterparts from other countries.

Concluding comments

In an increasingly globalized and competitive world there is intense interest in delivering 'Education for All' in a manner that acknowledges the need for all students to be provided with a high quality of education concerning the general conditions of schooling and student achievement levels. This increased interest has been accompanied and encouraged by the establishment of a range of cross-national studies of the quality of education that have been used by ministries of education to monitor and evaluate the performance of school systems with respect to national educational standards and the educational performance of other school systems.

This book was prepared from the contributions made to a joint IIEP-InWEnt Policy Forum that was held at the IIEP in June 2004. The forum focussed on the actions that need to be taken by ministries of education if they wish to derive maximal policy benefits from their participation in cross-national studies of the quality of education. More than 50 participants from 20 countries attended the forum – including ministers of education, professors, researchers, planners, education ministry officials, and senior staff from the United Nations and other international and donor organizations.

The Policy Forum's papers, discussions, debates, and concluding Open Space Sessions covered a wide range of issues concerned with how to successfully plan and manage cross-national studies of the quality of education. This final chapter of the book reviewed all of these inputs to the Policy Forum and then summarized them in the form of **'Policy Forum Messages'** and associated **'Recommendations'** for action. For example, a number of recommendations were concerned with the steps that should be taken by ministries of education to facilitate, support, and improve the technical and logistical work of their research teams. Other recommendations identified a range of dissemination and training needs, while others suggested that ministries, agencies, and donors should organize settings whereby countries could work together and learn from each other.

The Policy Forum Messages and Recommendations represent a rich resource for further productive discussion and debate – both within ministries of education and among ministries and various external partners. The IIEP and InWEnt are therefore delighted to offer this book as a contribution towards expanding and strengthening opportunities for national and international exchanges that serve to build the capacities of countries to plan and manage the quality of education that is offered by their school systems.

References

Adams, R.; Wu, M. 2002. *PISA 2000 technical report.* Paris: OECD.

Anderson, L.W.; Ryan, D.W.; Shapiro, B.J. (Eds.) 1989. *The IEA classroom environment study.* Oxford, UK: Pergamon Press.

Andrich, D.; Luo, G.; Ross, K.; Saito, M.; Leite, S. (in press). *Scaling, scoring, and equating the SACMEQ reading and mathematics tests.* Paris: IIEP-UNESCO.

Elley, W. 1992. *How in the world do students read?* Hamburg: International Association for the Evaluation of educational Achievement.

Hanushek, E.A. 2005. Economic outcomes and school quality. *Education Policy Booklet Series: Number 4.* Paris: IIEP-UNESCO.

Luo, G.; Andrich, D.; Ross, K.; Saito, M.; Leite, S. (in press). *Equating the reading tests used in different cross-national studies of the quality of education.* Paris: IIEP-UNESCO.

Mullis, I.V.; Martin, M.; Smith, T.A.; Garden, R.A.; Gregory, K.D.; Gonzalez, E.J.; Chrotowski, S.J.; O'Connor, K.M. 2001. *TIMSS assessment frameworks and specifications 2003.* Chestnut Hill, MA: Boston College.

OECD. 2001. *Knowledge and skills for life: First results from PISA 2000.* Paris: OECD.

Ross, K. 2005. *Sample design. Quantitative research methods in educational planning. Module 3.* Paris: IIEP-UNESCO.

Ross, K. N.; Saito, M.; Dolata, S.; Ikeda, M.; Zuze, L.; Murimba, S.; Postlethwaite, T.N.; Griffin, P. (in press). *The conduct of the SACMEQ II Project.* Paris: IIEP-UNESCO.

Singh, M. (2004). *Understanding Life Skills.* Paper presented to the Interagency Working Group Meeting on Life Skills in EFA, Paris, 29-31 March 2004. Hamburg: UNESCO Institute for Education.

Sylla, K.; Saito, M.; Ross, K. 2005. SAMDEM: *Sample design manager software. User's guide.* Paris: IIEP-UNESCO.

UNESCO 2004. *Report of the Inter-Agency Working Group on Life Skills in EFA.* Paris: UNESCO.

UNICEF. 2005. *Life skills.* Retrieved on 10 November 2005 from http://www.unicef.org/lifeskills

Werquin, P. 2004. "Education and skills: a presentation on the OCED perspective on life skills". In: UNESCO (Ed.), *Report of the Inter-Agency Working Group on Life Skills in EFA*, p. 3. Paris: UNESCO.

World Health Organization (WHO). 1999. *Partners in life skills education: conclusions from a United Nations Inter-Agency Meeting:* Geneva: WHO.

Appendix
List of participants

Participants in the IIEP-InWEnt Policy Forum on 'Cross-national studies of the quality of education: planning their design and managing their impact'

Paris, 17-18 June 2004

Ahmed Al-Arashi
Monitoring and Evaluation Officer
Ministry of Education
Sanaa, Yemen

Ibrahim Al-Houthy
Senior Researcher
Ministry of Education
Sanaa, Yemen

Mohammed Al-Khateeb
Director General for the Office of the
Minister for Education
Ministry of Education
Sanaa, Yemen

Hamoud M.G. Al-Seyani
Technical Director of the Basic
Education Project
Ministry of Education
Sanaa, Yemen

Hamid Alawhadi
Permanent Delegate
Permanent Delegation of Yemen to
UNESCO
Paris, France

Ibrahima Bah-Lalya
Senior Programme Specialist
International Institute for Educational
Planning (UNESCO)
Paris, France

Herbert Bergmann
Technical Adviser
Gesellschaft für Technische
Zusammenarbeit (GTZ)
Sanaa, Yemen

Françoise Caillods
Deputy Director
International Institute for Educational
Planning (UNESCO)
Paris, France

Zangazanga Chikhosi
Principal Secretary
Ministry of Education Science and
Technology
Lilongwe, Malawi

Stephanie Dolata
Assistant Programme Specialist
International Institute for Educational
Planning (UNESCO)
Paris, France

Carola Donner-Reichle
Director for Social Development
Internationale Weiterbildung und
Entwicklung (InWEnt)
Bonn, Germany

Brahm Fleisch
Associate Professor
University of Witwatersrand
Witwatersrand, South Africa

Pierre Foy
Senior Researcher
IEA Data Processing Centre
Hamburg, Germany

Patrick Griffin
Professor of Education
University of Melbourne
Melbourne, Australia

Aletta Grisay
Independent Consultant
Paris, France

Miyako Ikeda
Policy Analyst
Organisation for Economic Co-
operation and Development (OECD)
Paris, France

Ingrid Jung
Head of the Education Division
Internationale Weiterbildung und
Entwicklung (InWEnt)
Bonn, Germany

Ilona Jürgens Genevois
Assistant Programme Specialist
International Institute for Educational
Planning (UNESCO)
Paris, France

Thomas Kellaghan
Director of the Education Research
Centre
St. Patrick's College
Dublin, Ireland

Carlos Lauchande
Statistical Technician
National Institute for Educational
Development
Maputo, Mozambique

Rainer Lehmann
Professor of Educational
Measurement and Research
Humboldt University
Berlin, Germany

Carl Lindberg
Deputy State Secretary
Swedish Ministry of Education and
Science
Stockholm, Sweden

Pirjo Linnakylä
Professor of Education
University of Jyväskylä
Jyväskylä, Finland

Douglas Lynd
Senior Programme Specialist
UNESCO Institute for Statistics
Montreal, Canada

Demus Makuwa
Senior Education Planner
Ministry of Education
Windhoek, Namibia

Carlos Malpica
Independent Consultant
Lima, Peru

Lomthandazo Mavimbela
Executive Director
Education Foundation
Johannesburg, South Africa

Katharina Michaelowa
Head of Programme
Hamburg Institute of International
Economics
Hamburg, Germany

Saul Murimba
Director of the Southern and Eastern
Africa Consortium for Monitoring
Educational Quality
Harare, Zimbabwe

John Mutorwa
Minister for Education
Ministry of Basic Education
Windhoek, Namibia

Kilemi Mwiria
Assistant Minister for Education
Ministry of Education
Nairobi, Kenya

Arnaldo V. Nhavoto
Co-ordinator of the Centre for
Educational Research
Universidade Pedagogica
Maputo, Mozambique

Juliana Nzomo
Regional Programme Officer
Aga Khan Foundation
Nairobi, Kenya

Daniel N. Odongo
Deputy Secretary
Uganda National Examinations
Board
Kampala, Uganda

Ana Passos
Head of the Teacher Training
Department
National Institute for Educational
Development
Maputo, Mozambique

Laura Paviot
Resident Fellow
International Institute for Educational
Planning (UNESCO)
Paris, France

Katharina Petri
Independent Consultant
Bernrieg, Germany

Mary Joy Pigozzi
Director of the Division for the
Promotion of Quality Education
United Nations Educational,
Scientific and Cultural Organization
(UNESCO)
Paris, France

T. Neville Postlethwaite
Professor (Emeritus)
University of Hamburg
Hamburg, Germany

Kenneth Ross
Co-ordinator, Technical Project
Management
International Institute for Educational
Planning (UNESCO)
Paris, France

Jeanne Rubner
Journalist
Süddeutsche Zeitung
Munich, Germany

Mioko Saito
Programme Specialist
International Institute for Educational
Planning (UNESCO)
Paris, France

Andreas Schleicher
Head of the Indicators and Analysis
Division
Organisation for Economic Co-
operation and Development (OECD)
Paris, France

Alette Schreiner
Deputy Director General
Ministry of Education and Research
Oslo, Norway

Khadim Sylla
Assistant Programme Specialist
International Institute for Educational
Planning (UNESCO)
Paris, France

Maria Teresa Siniscalco
Project Director
National Institute for the Evaluation
of Education
Rome, Italy

N.V. Varghese
Head of the Training Unit
International Institute for Educational
Planning (UNESCO)
Paris, France

Herald Voorneveld
Deputy Permanent Delegate
Permanent Delegation of the
Netherlands to UNESCO
Paris, France

Joachim Wagner
Education Specialist
Gesellschaft für Technische
Zusammenarbeit (GTZ)
Zomba, Malawi

Ulrike Wiegelmann
Senior Project Manager
Internationale Weiterbildung und
Entwicklung (InWEnt)
Bonn, Germany

Yanhong Zhang
Programme Specialist
UNESCO Institute for Statistics
Montreal, Canada

Linda Zuze
Resident Fellow
International Institute for Educational
Planning (UNESCO)
Paris, France

Index

IIEP publications and documents

More than 1,200 titles on all aspects of educational planning have been published by the International Institute for Educational Planning. A comprehensive catalogue is available in the following subject categories:

Educational planning and global issues
    General studies – global/developmental issues

Administration and management of education
    Decentralization – participation – distance education – school mapping
    –   teachers

Economics of education
    Costs and financing – employment – international co-operation

Quality of education
    Evaluation – innovation – supervision

Different levels of formal education
    Primary to higher education

Alternative strategies for education
    Lifelong education – non-formal education – disadvantaged groups
    – gender education

Copies of the Catalogue may be obtained on request from:
IIEP, Communication and Publications Unit
info@iiep.unesco.org
Titles of new publications and abstracts may be consulted at the
following web site: www.unesco.org/iiep

The International Institute for Educational Planning

The International Institute for Educational Planning (IIEP) is an international centre for advanced training and research in the field of educational planning. It was established by UNESCO in 1963 and is financed by UNESCO and by voluntary contributions from Member States. In recent years the following Member States have provided voluntary contributions to the Institute: Denmark, Finland, Germany, Iceland, India, Ireland, Norway, Sweden and Switzerland.

The Institute's aim is to contribute to the development of education throughout the world, by expanding both knowledge and the supply of competent professionals in the field of educational planning. In this endeavour the Institute co-operates with interested training and research organizations in Member States. The Governing Board of the IIEP, which approves the Institute's programme and budget, consists of a maximum of eight elected members and four members designated by the United Nations Organization and certain of its specialized agencies and institutes.

Inquiries about the Institute should be addressed to:
The Office of the Director, International Institute for Educational Planning,
7-9 rue Eugène Delacroix, 75116 Paris, France